Destinations 2
Writing for Academic Success

Nancy Herzfeld-Pipkin
GROSSMONT COLLEGE

HEINLE
CENGAGE Learning™

Australia • Brazil • Japan • Korea • Mexico • Singapore • Spain • United Kingdom • United States

Destinations 2:
Writing for Academic Success
Nancy Herzfeld-Pipkin

Publisher, Adult & Academic:
 James W. Brown
Senior Acquisitions Editor:
 Sherrise Roehr
Director of Product Development:
 Anita Raducanu
Director of Product Marketing:
 Amy Mabley
Product Marketing Manager:
 Laura Needham
Senior Field Marketing Manager:
 Donna Lee Kennedy
Development Editor: Sarah Barnicle
Editorial Assistant: Katherine Reilly
Production Editor: Chrystie Hopkins
Sr. Print Buyer: Mary Beth Hennebury
Compositor: Parkwood Composition
 Service
Cover Designer: Gina Petti/
 Rotunda Design House
Cover Image: © Getty Images/RubberBall
 Productions/RF

Credits appear on pages 245–246, which
constitutes a continuation of the
copyright page.

For product information and technology assistance, contact us at
Cengage Learning Academic Resource Center, 1-800-423-0563

For permission to use material from this text or product, submit all
requests online at **cengage.com/permissions**
Further permission questions can be emailed to
permissionrequest@cengage.com

ISBN 13: 978-1-4130-1936-0
ISBN 10: 1-4130-1936-6
ISE ISBN 13: 978-1-4130-2297-1
ISE ISBN 10: 1-4130-2297-9

Heinle
25 Thomson Place
Boston, Massachusetts 02210
USA

Cengage Learning is a leading provider of customized learning
solutions with office locations around the globe, including
Singapore, the United Kingdom, Australia, Mexico, Brazil and
Japan. Locate our local office at:
international.cengage.com/region

Cengage Learning products are represented in Canada by
Nelson Education, Ltd.

Visit Heinle online at **elt.heinle.com**
Visit our corporate website at **cengage.com**

Printed in Canada
7 8 9 10 —   13 12 11

Dedication

*T*o my students, who always provide new insight and understanding no matter how many years I have been teaching, and who continue to make my job a most rewarding one

Acknowledgments

As always I am extremely grateful to friends and family for their understanding and support. I especially want to thank my boys, Jack, Seth, and Scot for always "being there" for me and my friend Jean Riley for her insistence that I write another book.

Thanks to my colleagues at Grossmont College, Helen Liesberg, Bobbie Felix, Paula Emmert, and Donna Tooker, who helped me class test these materials. In addition, Virginia Berger, Chuck Passentino, and Dr. Janet Castanos have given me support and feedback during the process of writing these materials:

Several other people were helpful in brainstorming ideas and providing feedback and expertise on specific units.

Unit Two: Dr. Theresa "T" Ford and John Barnier (Grossmont College), Rev. Alfonso Wyatt
Unit Three: Dr. Shimon Camiel
Unit Four: Scot Pipkin
Unit Five: Seth Pipkin, Stephanie Mood (Grossmont College)
Unit Six: Seth Pipkin

Many thanks also go to the people at Heinle for helping make this book a reality. In particular, I thank Sherrise Roehr and Rosanne Flynn for encouraging me from the beginning, and Sarah Barnicle for working with me so closely and with such good humor and patience every step of the way.

Finally, I thank the following reviewers for their helpful comments and suggestions during the development of this text.

Myra Redman, *Miami Dade College,* Miami, Florida

Patricia Turner, *University of California (UCLA),* Los Angeles, California

Kathleen Flynn, *Glendale Community College,* Glendale, California

Sally Gearhart, *Santa Rosa Junior College,* Santa Rosa, California

Shawn Tran, *Independence Adult Center,* San Jose, California

Fred Allen, *San Jose City College,* San Jose, California

Contents

Unit Two   The African-American Experience   35

Unit Six   The Changing Face of Business   173

Preface

Destinations: Writing for Academic Success, Book 2 is designed to be used with high-intermediate level students of English. This text consists of six units, which have each been divided into four parts: preview, reading, sentence level writing, and paragraph or essay writing. The main focus of *Destinations* is writing of both paragraphs and essays through the writing process relating to specific academic themes. The text also covers vocabulary development, summary writing, some reading skills, and critical thinking through discussion and journal writing.

The bulk of each unit is made up of exercises and activities that afford students as much active involvement as possible. Many of the readings are authentic or have been adapted from other print sources. Samples of student essays are available on the teacher's Web site. The themes of the units are academic in nature and are intended to introduce students to some of the ideas and content they will find in other (non-ESL) classes.

Finally, studying in a college or university environment can be a daunting task, especially for those students studying in the United States whose first language is not English. In addition to dealing with more obvious language problems, students from other cultures or countries may have difficulty succeeding in native speaker environments due to differences in both background and cultural information. This book is intended to fill some of those gaps in order to help prepare non-native speakers for the academic writing they will be expected to produce in courses throughout their college careers.

To the Teacher

Destinations: Writing for Academic Success, Book 2 presents and provides practice with academic writing based on specific academic themes and content introduced through readings. The book is divided into six units, each of which focuses on writing at the sentence level, the paragraph level, and/or the essay level. Each unit also presents some practice with reading skills (such as comprehension and inference), vocabulary development, and critical thinking.

General Notes About Materials and Activities in This Book

In some sections, discussions or explanations are provided in the form of questions and answers. Teachers are encouraged to present this material in their own class discussions before reviewing these sections of a unit. Then these sections of the book can serve as review of the in-class discussions.

Each lesson includes a variety of activities and exercises. This will afford students many opportunities to participate, as well as offer students a chance to express themselves in varied ways using different language skills. Due to the variations in length and purpose of individual classes, it is not expected that every teacher will cover everything in each lesson. Teachers should feel free to choose those exercises and activities that best suit the needs and abilities of their particular students.

 Working in pairs and groups is encouraged throughout this book. Many of the exercises and activities are well-suited for this kind of work; those that lend themselves particularly well to group or pair work have an icon next to them.

Following are more detailed descriptions of all the parts and suggestions on how to present or follow up on them.

Unit Organization

Part 1: Preview

Part 1 of each unit introduces the topic or theme of the lesson through either discussion or a short activity, such as reading a map or answering a questionnaire. The preview is meant to activate schemata for the students and to give the teacher an idea of what the students might already know about the topic. If students know very little about the topic, Part 1 will serve as an introduction. A Quickwrite is also included here to give the students a chance to write freely on a subject that is related to the content of the unit.

Part 2: Reading and Vocabulary

In Part 2, the main reading of the unit is presented. This is the longest reading of each unit and presents both the theme and related vocabulary. Teachers may want to discuss the content of this material before students complete the exercises that follow. In addition, because of the length of these readings, it is strongly suggested that they be assigned as homework along with some of the exercises that follow (such as comprehension and vocabulary). Inference and vocabulary in context exercises might be better completed in class with students in pairs or groups so that they can work through the exercises together. The ideas and vocabulary items presented in this part are recycled in a number of ways:

- through discussion/writing topics that follow in the unit
- in exercises and activities in other parts of the unit
- in final writing assignments
- in the accompanying grammar workbook (*Destinations: Grammar for Academic Success, Book 2*)
- in word part and word form exercises on the student Web site

Part 3: Writing Sentences

In Part 3, writing is presented and practiced at the sentence level in a systematic way through various sentence-combining techniques and through work with sentence problems, such as fragments, run-ons, and comma splices.

- Different sentence-combining techniques

Each unit focuses on different ways to combine sentences, based on four major groups of connectors: coordinating conjunctions, subordinating conjunctions, transitions, and relative pronouns. A blank chart on the use of these groups is provided in the Appendix, and a completed chart is provided on the teacher's Web site. This blank chart is an excellent tool for students to understand the use of connectors in a logical and organized way. Teachers are encouraged to have students fill out each part of the blank chart as each different section is presented in a unit. When each group or part of a group on the sentence-combining chart is introduced in a unit, the relevant part of the chart is explained and highlighted in the explanation section of that unit. Students can check that the information on their charts is the same as the information in the explanation. For a full discussion of how to use this chart, please see the teacher's Web site.

In each unit, Part 3 begins with a short reading that includes examples of the sentence-combining technique to be discussed and practiced. Students are then asked to analyze parts of the reading by answering several questions. This section provides an inductive exercise for students to figure out (or state as review) the grammar and mechanics of the particular sentence-combining technique. An explanation section immediately follows in order to ensure that students understand the topic fully. Following these explanations are exercises and activities that provide sentence writing practice.

- Sentence problems (fragments, run-ons, and comma splices)

In the explanation section, a discussion of related sentence problems is provided. For example, in the units that present the use of subordinating conjunctions with dependent clauses, part of the explanation discusses problems of fragments and run-ons related to incorrect use of these clauses. Furthermore, each unit includes exercises that provide practice in identifying and/or editing these problems.

Part 4: Writing Paragraphs or Essays
* Part 4 covers various aspects of organizing and writing paragraphs and essays. Organizational patterns (process, opinion, compare/contrast, etc.) that students are likely to encounter in college classes are discussed in different units.
* At the end of each unit, students are given a choice of writing assignments related to the topic. These assignments will elicit as much of the information studied and practiced in the unit as possible regarding vocabulary, sentence combining, and organizational techniques.
* The writing process is explained in Unit One. After the final writing assignment in each unit is given, students are asked to follow the steps in the process. These steps are tailored to the particular assignments given. Also provided in Part 4 are:
  * some prewriting devices such as charts, outlines, and timelines for students to fill in before they write,
  * checklists that help students review their work before handing in their assignments.

Discussion/Writing Sections

Throughout each unit, questions for discussion and/or writing are provided. Teachers may utilize these questions in different ways:

* to stimulate thinking about and discussion of the information presented in the various parts of the unit.
* to provide students with an opportunity to write informally (journal writing, freewriting, etc.) before they are asked to write a more formal assignment at the end of the unit. Topics that are particularly suited for journal writing are indicated with this icon.
* to help students think about and prepare topics for the writing assignment at the end of the unit.

Summary Writing

Summary writing is explained and practiced in the Appendix. In addition, for those teachers who want their students to practice writing summaries on a regular basis, specific summary assignments are given in both the Instructor's Manual and in the Appendix.

Appendix

The appendix includes the following sections:

* Summary Writing—explanation and practice using part of the main reading found in Unit One.
* Journal Writing—a short explanation of how best to use this type of writing

- Timed Writing—a short explanation about in-class timed writing as well as tips on how to budget time
- Punctuation Review—a chart of punctuation marks and an indication of which units provide practice with specific ones. This review is followed by definitions and examples using each punctuation mark as well as rules of capitalization and proofreading marks.
- Feedback: Peer Review—a short explanation with two peer review sheets per unit for students to fill out: one for review of the organization chart and one for review of the first draft of the final writing assignment
- Sentence-Combining Chart—chart to be filled out as Part 3 of each unit is completed. Photocopiable charts for student use are provided on the Web site.
- Vocabulary Index—an alphabetized list of all vocabulary presented in the units with page numbers where the words first occur.
- Skills Index—an alphabetized list of all skills taught in the book including writing, reading, and critical thinking skills.

MATERIALS AND ACTIVITIES ON THE WEB: elt.thomson.com/destinations

Teacher site resources include:

- an answer key for each unit
- suggestions on how to use Web materials (including Internet assignments)
- additional unit writing prompts, which can be used for in-class timed writings
- the completed sentence-combining chart (all connectors and relevant information filled in)
- feedback sheets for teachers to use with student drafts of their writing (A complete explanation of these can be found on the Web site.)
- evaluation/grade sheets for final drafts (A complete explanation of these can be found on the Web site.)
- sample student writing—original student paragraphs and essays for each unit (Teachers can use these to highlight good writing points and to point out areas to revise.)

Student site resources include:

- word parts (stems, prefixes, suffixes) exercises
- word forms (different forms of words in the reading—i.e., nouns, verbs, and adjectives)
- vocabulary quizzes (one for each unit)
- links to Web sites related to the content and topics in the units (A complete explanation of these can be found on the teacher's Web site.)

Both teacher and student site resources include:

- learning objectives
- glossary
- flashcards with pronunciation
- crossword puzzles
- concentration game
- additional writing activities
- Internet exercises
- suggested Web site links

Content Area: Psychology

Reading: Learning Styles

Short Readings: Intelligence
IQ Tests
Multiple Intelligences

Sentence-Combining Focus: Coordinating Conjunctions

Editing Focus: Run-ons; Comma Splices

Writing Focus: Paragraphs (Topic Sentences, Supporting Sentences, and Concluding Sentences); The Writing Process

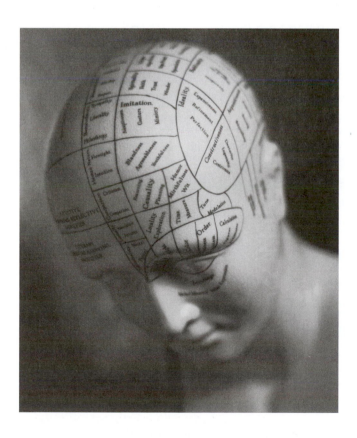

PART 1   UNIT PREVIEW

Preview Activity: Learning Styles Checklists

A. In each list, put a check mark (✓) next to the items that describe you.

LIST ONE

✓ I talk fast and often use my hands to communicate.

____ I like to take things apart and put them together.

✓ I prefer to stand while I am working.

____ I am good at sports.

✓ I learn through movement, and I like to explore the environment around me.

LIST TWO

✓ When someone gives me oral instructions, I often ask that person to repeat.

____ I usually watch a speaker's facial expressions and body language.

✓ I like to take notes when I am learning, and then I review these notes later.

✓ I can understand maps and follow directions.

____ I think the best way to remember something is to picture it in my head.

LIST THREE

✓ I follow oral directions better than written ones.

____ I understand better when I read aloud.

✓ I prefer listening to a lecture to reading the material in a textbook.

____ I dislike reading from a computer screen.

✓ I require explanations of diagrams, charts, and maps.

B. Share your lists with a partner and/or the class. In which list did you put the most checks? What do you think your responses might say about the way you learn?

Quickwrite

Each Unit Preview in this book includes a Quickwrite activity. This activity gives you a chance to put your ideas in writing without thinking about details such as organization, grammar, spelling, and punctuation.

The purpose of a Quickwrite is to let you simply start thinking about a topic and write down some ideas about it.

Write for five minutes about the following topic. Do not worry about grammar, spelling, or punctuation. Just write whatever comes into your mind about the topic.

- Topic: Write about one of your favorite or most successful classes. Why were you successful in this class? Why was it your favorite? (Try to think of some specific reasons.)

PART 2   READING AND VOCABULARY

Read about learning styles. Then complete the activities that follow the reading.

Reading
Learning Styles

Introduction

Are you having trouble learning new information in a class? You may want to find out more about your **unique** learning style. Your learning style is the way you prefer to learn. It is not related to how intelligent you are or what skills you have, but it is related to how your brain works most **efficiently** to learn new information. Your learning style has been a part of you since you were born.

There's no such thing as a "good" learning style or a "bad" learning style. Success comes with many different learning styles. There is no "right" approach to learning. We all have our own **particular** way of learning new information, and the important thing is to be aware of how you prefer to learn. If you are aware of how your brain learns best, you have a better chance of studying in a way that will have positive results on your schoolwork.

Three Styles of Learning

To start becoming aware of your learning style, think about the way you remember a phone number. Do you see in your mind how the numbers look on the phone, or can you see the number on a piece of paper, picturing it exactly as you wrote it down? Perhaps you can hear the number in the way someone said it to you. On the other hand, maybe you think about how your fingers move to dial the number. Each of these examples illustrates one of three different learning styles: **visual**, **auditory**, and **tactile/kinesthetic**.

This way of identifying learning styles uses different channels of **perception** (seeing, hearing, and touching or moving) as a model. This is a somewhat simplistic view of a very complicated subject (the activities of the human brain). However, looking at learning styles from a perceptual point of view is a useful place to begin.

Following is a short explanation of each of the three learning styles.

Visual Learning. Visual learners learn best when they can see information either in written language or in a picture or design. These learners also may need to see a teacher's nonverbal communication (body language and facial expressions) to fully understand the content of a lesson. In a classroom visual learners benefit from instructors who use a blackboard (or whiteboard) or an overhead projector to list important points of a lecture or use visual aids such as films, videos, maps, and charts. In addition, visual learners may learn best from class notes and outlines or pictures and diagrams in textbooks. They may also like to study by themselves in a quiet room and may visualize a picture of something or see information in their mind when trying to remember it.

Auditory Learning. Auditory learners learn best when they can hear information or when they are learning in an oral language **format**. In a classroom these learners benefit most from listening to lectures or participating in group discussions. Auditory learners may also read text aloud or use audio tapes or CDs to obtain information. When trying to remember something, these learners can often "hear" the information the way someone told it to them or the way they previously repeated it out loud. In general, these people learn best when interacting with others in a listening/speaking exchange.

Tactile/Kinesthetic Learning. Tactile/kinesthetic learners like to be physically engaged in "hands-on" activities or to actively explore the physical world around them. In the classroom they benefit from a lab setting, where they can **manipulate** materials to learn new information. These people learn best when they can be physically active in their learning environment. They may find it difficult to sit in one place for long periods of time, and they may also become **distracted** by their need to be exploring and active. Tactile/kinesthetic learners benefit most from instructors who encourage in-class demonstrations, hands-on learning experiences, and field work outside the classroom.

Adapting Your Learning Style to the Instructional Environment

While there is no "good" or "bad" learning style, there can be a good or bad match between the way you learn best and the way a particular course is taught. Suppose you are a visual learner enrolled in a traditional lecture class. It seems that the instructor talks on for hours, and you can't pay attention or stay interested. There's a mismatch between your learning style and the instructional environment of the class. As soon as you understand this mismatch, you can find ways to adapt your style to help make sure that you will be successful in the class. You might start tape-recording the lectures so that you don't have to worry about missing important information. You might decide to draw diagrams that illustrate the ideas presented in lectures. You might go to the media center and check out a video that provides some additional information on course material you're not sure about. What you're doing is developing learning **strategies** that work for you because they are based on your knowledge of your own learning style.

Comprehension Check

A. Circle the letter next to the best answer for each of the following sentences.

1. The main idea of the introduction for this reading is that
   a. everyone learns the same way, but some people have trouble learning in specific classes.
   b. there are different approaches to learning, and it is helpful to know your own style.
   c. there are different approaches to learning, and some ways are better than others.

2. A learning style is
   a. something you develop as you get older.
   b. related to what you have learned.
   c. each person's individual way of learning something.

3. The examples of ways of remembering a phone number
   a. illustrate three different ways of learning.
   b. show that learning a phone number is easy.
   c. prove that we all learn the same way.

4. The last part of the reading discusses why it is good to understand if your learning style matches the class environment. Which of the following is *not* a reason given?
   a. You can know if your style fits the way the teacher presents the class.
   b. You can learn how to ask the teacher to change the environment of the class to fit your style.
   c. You can try to find ways to help you learn in any class, even if the class doesn't fit your style.

5. According to the reading, if you are a visual learner in a traditional lecture class, your learning style is
   a. a good match for the class.
   b. not important for that type of class.
   c. a bad match for the class.

B. Below are a list of learner characteristics and a chart labeled with the three learning styles discussed in the reading. Write the numbers of the characteristics in the correct columns in the first row of the chart. One has been done as an example.

LEARNER CHARACTERISTICS

1. likes to listen to lectures
2. finds a teacher's body language helpful
3. likes to use audio tapes or participate in discussions
4. likes to be active and have "hands-on" learning experiences
5. learns well from maps, videos, and diagrams
6. learns well from field work, demonstrations, and lab work

Visual learner	Auditory learner	Tactile/kinesthetic learner
	1	4,6
✶ B, d	C, f	A,

Inference

An *inference* is a conclusion that a reader makes based on information that is given in a piece of text. Read the following sentences. What can you infer about the weather?

> Some people wearing warm jackets and gloves were standing on the street corner. As they were talking, we could see their breath in the air.

You can infer from these two sentences that it was cold outside or that it was winter. The sentences do not say anything about the weather, but they do mention warm jackets and gloves and seeing people's breath as they talk. These are all things we usually see in colder or winter weather.

Below is another list of learner characteristics that go with the three learning styles in the reading. These characteristics are not stated in the reading. Try to infer which learning style fits each characteristic. Write the letters of your answers in the correct columns in the second row of the chart in the Comprehension Check.

a. likes to do projects (such as artwork or crafts) in spare time
b. remembers things best by writing them down or drawing diagrams or pictures
c. would rather listen to a book on tape than read it
d. pictures things in his or her head (for example, "sees" answers to a test)
e. prefers to do something rather than read about it or watch someone else do it
f. prefers to listen to someone give directions rather than read them

Vocabulary Study

Choose a synonym from the following list for each of the underlined vocabulary words in the sentences. Write the letter of the synonym on the line next to the sentence. The first one has been done as an example.

a. relating to seeing
b. specific
c. control or influence
d. one of a kind
e. relating to movement
f. done well without wasting time
g. ~~plan~~
h. relating to hearing
i. take someone's attention away
j. relating to the sense of touch
k. observation, awareness of something through the senses
l. arrangement or organization

_g_ 1. A visual learner studying French in a listening lab might need to find a specific <u>strategy</u> to do well in that learning environment.

_b_ 2. John likes to use flash cards to study vocabulary—that's his <u>particular</u> way of studying new words.

_c_ 3. The students were able to <u>manipulate</u> the teacher, so he changed the test to an "open book" exam.

_d_ 4. If you are a <u>tactile</u> learner, you probably like to do lab experiments and enjoy working with your hands.

_i_ 5. I need to study in the library because the noise and music in our apartment <u>distract</u> me too much.

_l_ 6. The <u>format</u> of the lesson was very confusing, and I did not understand it well.

_d_ 7. Individuals all learn in different ways, and some people have a <u>unique</u> combination of learning styles.

_f_ 8. Sally will probably get an A in her science lab because she does all the experiments on time and completes all the assignments very <u>efficiently</u>.

_A_ 9. Sometimes it's easier to understand what you read in a textbook if you can look at something <u>visual</u> (such as a picture or a chart) in addition to the words.

_e_ 10. Dancers and athletes spend time doing <u>kinesthetic</u> activities.

_k_ 11. It was the teacher's <u>perception</u> that John was not a good student, but in reality he was having trouble in the large lecture class because he was a visual learner.

_h_ 12. I am not an <u>auditory</u> learner, so I prefer to look at a map rather than listen to directions.

Discussion/Writing

Answer these questions in writing or through discussion.

1. Look back at the Preview Activity for this unit. Which learning style do you think is represented by each list of characteristics? Why?
2. Which of the three learning styles do you feel is the strongest for you? Can you think of examples that show that this learning style affects how you learn?
3. Look again at your Quickwrite (from the Unit Preview) about a class you particularly enjoyed or did well in. Can you relate anything from that class to your learning style?
4. Do you think it is important for people to know their own learning style? How can knowledge of all three styles help people in school or on the job?

PART 3   WRITING SENTENCES WITH COORDINATING CONJUNCTIONS

Read the following about intelligence and answer the questions that follow it.

Intelligence

[1]Every culture has words for *smart* and *stupid,* and everyone has an opinion about what intelligence is. [2]People have been debating about intelligence for many years, asking questions about what it is, who has it, and how we can measure it.

[3]At the very least, we can define *intelligence* as the ability to do complex thinking and reasoning. [4]There is one thing that research clearly shows: much of the ability for complex reasoning depends on the situation. [5]For example, a person can be a genius at picking winning horses at the racetrack, yet this same person may not know anything about picking stocks on the stock market. [6]Both of these abilities require comparable mental activities, but the mind organizes the knowledge differently, so knowing about horse racing may not help a person choose stocks.

[7]Some people believe that the best way to measure intelligence in humans is to use IQ tests. [8]Other people are not so sure about these tests, for experts and researchers do not agree on their validity and fairness.

Questions

1. Look at sentences 1, 5, and 8 in the reading. Each sentence has two ideas, and each idea is presented in a smaller sentence. (Two small sentences are combined to make a larger one.) Put a line under each

smaller sentence. Then put a circle around the word between the two smaller sentences. Follow the example.

EXAMPLE: Every culture has words for *smart* and *stupid,* (and) everyone has an opinion about intelligence.

2. Write the three circled words below.

   _____   _____   _____

   What punctuation do you see with each of these words?

Explanation: Combining Clauses with Coordinating Conjunctions

1. *Simple sentences* are sentences with one subject-verb combination.

   EXAMPLES: Every culture has words for *smart* and *stupid.*
   subject   verb
   Everyone has an opinion about intelligence.
   subject   verb

   Simple sentences are also called *independent clauses.* A clause has a minimum of one subject-verb combination. Some clauses are independent and can stand alone as simple sentences, and some are not. You will study several different kinds of clauses in this book.

2. Speakers and writers don't always use simple sentences (independent clauses) when they communicate. They often put these sentences (clauses) together to make bigger sentences. There are several ways to put clauses together in English. In each case you add a "signal," an extra word or phrase to show you are combining more than one idea. Some people call these signals *connectors* because they connect clauses to make them into bigger sentences.

3. One group of connectors is called *coordinating conjunctions* (or *coordinators*). These words are used to connect independent clauses. There are seven words in this group, and their first letters spell FANBOYS:

   for   and   nor   but   or   yet   so

4. Conjunctions have specific meanings that establish the relationship between the connected clauses. For example, the conjunction *and* tells you that the second clause adds more information. The conjunction *but* tells you that the second clause provides contrast.

   EXAMPLES: Every culture has words for *smart* and *stupid,* **and** everyone has an opinion about what intelligence is.

   Some people believe in IQ tests, **but** others don't trust the results.

Sentence-Combining Focus

Coordinating Conjunctions

5. Sentences with coordinating conjunctions have a specific pattern, shown in the following chart.

Sentence Combining with Coordinating Conjunctions

Position in Sentence

S + V
Middle

| clause | conjunction | clause |

Punctuation: Comma

| clause , | conjunction | clause |

EXAMPLE: Some people believe in IQ tests, but others don't trust the results.

In short sentences, the comma may be left out.

ADDITION:	*and*
CONTRAST:	*but*
	yet
RESULT:	*so*
REASON:	*for*
CHOICE:	*or*
NEGATIVE:	*nor**

NOTE: Sometimes you will find these coordinators at the beginning of a sentence. This is acceptable in informal English and in some kinds of writing. When you are writing for school, try not to begin sentences with these conjunctions.

6. ***Using *nor*** The coordinating conjunction *nor* works differently than the others. When this connector joins two clauses that state negative ideas, the subject-verb order changes in the second clause.

   EXAMPLE: Some people do not learn through the auditory learning style, nor do they learn through visual methods.

This sentence means that some people do not learn through either of these two styles. Be sure to make the change in word order for the second clause.

7. Important Errors to Avoid
   a. Do not join independent clauses without a signal or connector such as a coordinating conjunction. Doing this will make a run-on sentence. A run-on sentence is not acceptable in written English.

b. Do not connect independent clauses with just a comma and no other signal. Doing this will make a comma splice. A comma splice is not acceptable in written English.

comma splice

INCORRECT: Every culture has words for *smart* and *stupid,* everyone
                subject   verb   subject
has an opinion about what intelligence is.
verb

run-on

INCORRECT: Every culture has words for *smart* and *stupid* everyone
                subject   verb   subject
has an opinion about what intelligence is.
verb

CORRECT: Every culture has words for *smart* and *stupid,* and everyone has an opinion about what intelligence is.

8. If a sentence has two independent clauses that have the same subject, it is not always necessary to repeat the subject or to use a comma. The sentence can be written with one subject and two verbs.

EXAMPLE: Some people are not sure about IQ tests and question
               subject   verb   verb
their fairness.

9. If a sentence has more than two independent clauses, put a comma after each clause and include a coordinator before the last clause.

EXAMPLE: Some people believe in IQ tests, others do not believe
                 independent clause   independent clause
in them, and some are undecided.
              independent clause

Practice: Coordinating Conjunctions

A. **Working with Clauses**   *Below are five numbered sentences followed by six independent clauses, each beginning with a coordinating conjunction. Add one of the independent clauses to each numbered sentence, using the correct punctuation. Use each lettered clause only one time.*

EXAMPLE: Some school districts use IQ tests.
Some school districts use IQ tests, and others choose not to use them. (e)

1. Every culture has its own words for *smart* and *stupid.*
   ___C nor do tret dive and kind of intelgent___

2. People may think that certain tests cannot measure intelligence.
   ___d&f___

3. A person may be very good at one kind of reasoning.
   ___a nor he or she ron not___

4. Some people do not agree about the validity of IQ tests.

_F & d_____

5. Some schools will not give IQ tests to students.

_b_____

a. yet she or he may not do very well at another kind.
b. nor do they give any other kind of intelligence tests.
c. but people continue to debate about what intelligence is.
d. so they continue to debate about using them.
e. and others choose not to use them.
f. or they may believe that some tests are not fair.

B. Writing Sentences   *Combine the first three pairs of sentences below using the coordinating conjunction given in parentheses. For the other four pairs of sentences, choose any coordinating conjunction, but use a different one in each case. Some of those sentence pairs can be combined with different conjunctions.*

EXAMPLE: (and) Some school districts use IQ tests. Others choose not to use them.

Some school districts use IQ tests, and others choose not to use them.

1. (but) Your learning style is not related to your intelligence. It is related to your personal way of learning efficiently.

   Your learning Style is not related to your intelligence, but it is related to your personal way of learning efficiently

2. (for) Your learning style has been with you a long time. You were born with it.

   _Your_____

   _____

3. (nor) Some people are not successful in traditional lecture classes. They are not successful in listening lab classes.

   _____

   _____

4. Success comes with many different learning styles. There is no correct approach to learning.

   _____

   _____

5. We all have a particular way of learning new information. We should be aware of our own style.

   _____

   _____

6. You may prefer to learn through pictures and diagrams. You may like to learn through listening to people and audio tapes.

   _____

   _____

7. You may find it easy to learn through pictures and other visuals. It may be much more difficult for you to learn through audio tapes or lectures.

   _____

   _____

C. **Finding Sentence Problems**   *The following paragraph about IQ tests has two run-on sentences and three comma splices. Fix these errors using different coordinating conjunctions.*

IQ Tests

There are two different kinds of popular IQ tests. One test is the Stanford-Binet Intelligence Scale, the other is the Wechsler Intelligence Scale. Generally these tests cost several hundred dollars, usually only psychologists give them. Sometimes you can find variations of them on the World Wide Web. The Stanford-Binet test measures things such as vocabulary, relationships between words, and comprehension, the Wechsler test measures similar kinds of skills. These standardized tests can assess what is necessary to succeed in school, they can predict school performance for many children. These IQ tests may not measure creativity or practical knowledge, many schools still use them today.

Discussion/Writing

Answer these questions in writing or through discussion. Try to use a variety of coordinating conjunctions in your sentences.

1. Have you ever taken a standardized intelligence test such as an IQ test? What is your opinion of this type of test? Do you think it can accurately measure intelligence?

2. Were IQ tests given in schools you attended as a child? If so, how were the results of those tests used?

3. Do you think there is a relationship between learning style and success on standardized tests? Do you think some people are more successful on certain types of tests because of their particular learning style?

PART 4   WRITING PARAGRAPHS

What is a paragraph? Look at examples A and B below. Which one looks like a paragraph? Why?

Example A

In the late 19th century, a man named Sir Francis Galton made the first attempt to scientifically measure human intelligence.
Galton tried to use a psychological approach to his testing, rather than the medical/anatomical approach of scientists and researchers before him.
From 1884 to 1890, Galton ran a service in a museum in London, where people could pay for a test of their intelligence.
However, the specific tests that Galton chose to use were not very good ones.
For example, in one test, Galton tried to find the highest-pitched sound a person could perceive, so he made a whistle for people to listen to.
In another test, he tried to measure people's sensitivity to the smell of roses.
Thus, Galton tried to show that intelligence could have a scientific measure, but he was not able to create a test that truly did this.

Example B

In the late 19th century, a man named Sir Francis Galton made the first attempt to scientifically measure human intelligence. Galton tried to use a psychological approach to his testing, rather than the medical/anatomical approach of scientists and researchers before him. From 1884 to 1890, Galton ran a service in a museum in London, where people could pay for a test of their intelligence. However, the specific tests that Galton chose to use were not very good ones. For example, in one test, Galton tried to find the highest-pitched sound a person could perceive, so he made a whistle for people to listen to. In another test, he tried to measure people's sensitivity to the smell of roses. Thus, Galton tried to show that intelligence could have a scientific measure, but he was not able to create a test that truly did this.

Paragraph Discussion

1. What is a paragraph?
   - A *paragraph* is a group of sentences about one main idea.

2. What should a paragraph look like?
   - When you write a paragraph, leave a space to the left of the beginning of the first sentence. This is called *indenting.* Indenting shows the reader that you are starting a new paragraph.
   - A paragraph also has *margins* on the left and right side of the paper. A *margin* is a space between the edge of the paper and the paragraph. The left margin should be the same for all lines. The right margin may not be exactly the same for every line. There will also be top and bottom margins for a single paragraph.
   - When you write a paragraph, the sentences follow one another. *Do not begin a new line with each sentence.* Your paragraph should not look like a list.

3. What are the parts of a paragraph?
   - The first sentence often tells the reader the main idea of the paragraph. This sentence is called the *topic sentence.*
   - The other sentences in the paragraph give more information about the main idea, such as examples, details, facts, and/or reasons. These sentences are called *supporting sentences.*
   - The last sentence in a paragraph is often a *concluding sentence.* This sentence is more general than the supporting sentences.

4. How long should a paragraph be?
   - There is no specific number of sentences in a good paragraph. If you have all three parts described in item 3, of course you will have at least three sentences. However, this is not usually enough when you are writing for college classes. To develop and explain the main idea for the reader, a good paragraph should have several supporting sentences.

Paragraph Organization

The house diagram on the next page shows the relationship of the three parts of a paragraph using the sentences from the example paragraph on Sir Francis Galton.

Writing Focus

Paragraphs: Topic Sentences, Supporting Sentences, and Concluding Sentences; The Writing Process

In the late 19th century, a man named Sir Francis Galton made the first attempt to scientifically measure human intelligence.

TOPIC SENTENCE

Support/Detail	Support/Detail
tried a psychological approach	1884–1890 ran a service for testing
Support/Detail specific tests not good	**Support/Detail** tested ability to hear high-pitched sounds
Support/Detail tested sensitivity to smell	

CONCLUDING SENTENCE

Thus, Galton tried to show that intelligence could have a scientific measure, but he was not able to create a test that truly did this.

A topic sentence is like the roof of a house; it covers everything below it. The walls and rooms under the roof support it in the same way sentences about facts, reasons, details, and examples support a topic sentence. The concluding sentence is like the floor.

Topic Sentences

A topic sentence is important because it tells the reader what the writer will discuss in the paragraph. A good topic sentence has two parts:

- The *topic* is the general subject of the paragraph.
- The *controlling idea* limits the topic so that the paragraph covers only a specific part or aspect of it.

This is the topic sentence from the example paragraph on page 14:

In the late 19th century, a man named Sir Francis Galton made the first attempt to scientifically measure human intelligence.

This topic sentence tells the reader that the topic of the paragraph is Sir Francis Galton. There are many different paragraphs that could be written about this person, but the example paragraph focuses on one aspect of his life. Which of the following is that controlling idea?

____ his family life   ____ his attempt to measure human intelligence

____ his education   ____ his childhood

Topics and Controlling Ideas

Think about your school as a topic. If someone asks you to write about this school, what might you choose to write about?

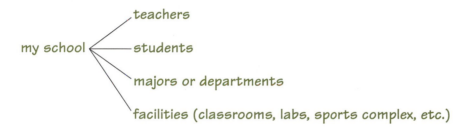

Do you think you could write one paragraph about all four of these aspects of your school? The answer is probably not, because there is too much information about these aspects to include in one paragraph. However, you could support each aspect with enough details or examples to write four good paragraphs, as follows:

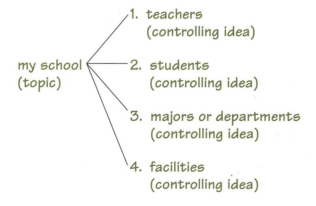

Following are some example topic sentences for paragraphs about these aspects of your school. Each of the topic sentences limits the topic to one aspect. What is the controlling idea for each sentence?

1. Teachers at my school must have several kinds of qualifications in order to teach there.

   Topic: teachers at my school   Controlling idea: _____

2. The students at my school come from many different backgrounds.

    Topic: students at my school   Controlling idea: _different backgrounds_

3. My school offers many different majors, including some unusual ones for a two-year school.

    Topic: majors at my school   Controlling idea: _different majors_

4. Some of the buildings at my school are quite new and modern.

    Topic: buildings at my school   Controlling idea: _new and incld._

Analyzing Topic Sentences   When you write a topic sentence, you need to be careful not to make the controlling idea too general or too specific. If the controlling idea is too general, there will be too much to say in one paragraph. If the controlling idea is too specific, there will not be enough to say.

   Look at the following three examples of topic sentences for a paragraph. Can you explain why one is too general and one is too specific? Why is the third example better than the others? (The answers are below the sentences.)

   EXAMPLES: 1. During the last two centuries, there have been many kinds of psychological tests.
                2. The name of one IQ test is the Stanford-Binet.
                3. There are two different kinds of popular IQ tests.

ANSWERS

1. This sentence is too general. It would be difficult to write one paragraph about the many kinds of psychological tests used in the last 200 years.
2. This sentence is too specific. The writer probably could not find enough information about the name of this one test to make a well-developed paragraph.
3. This is a possible topic sentence. The writer can briefly describe these two tests (as in the paragraph on page 13).

Practice: Topic Sentences
A. *Decide whether each of the following sentences could be a topic sentence for a paragraph. On the line before the sentence, write:* **TS** *if it is acceptable as a topic sentence,* **G** *if it is too general, or* **SP** *if it is too specific.*

_SP_ 1. Yesterday I took some notes during my Psychology 101 lecture.

_TS_ 2. The three learning styles use different senses.

_G_ 3. There are many different strategies people can use for each of the three learning styles.

_G_ 4. Some people do not believe that IQ tests are a good measure of intelligence for several reasons.

_SP_ 5. That student received a score of 125 on an IQ test.

_TS_ 6. Visual learners can use several strategies to succeed in a traditional lecture class.

_____ 7. Alfred Binet developed a test of intelligence that was published in 1905.

_G_ 8. Throughout history people have tried to define intelligence.

_____ 9. Learning styles can be divided into three main types.

_____ 10. Some IQ test scores can predict a student's school performance.

B. *Each of the following paragraphs needs a topic sentence. After reading each paragraph, choose one of the three sentences below as the best topic sentence. Write the letter on the line given.*

1. _b_   They think that these tests measure one general type of intelligence but do not test or measure enough of our capabilities. That is, IQ tests usually test in the areas of language and logic (math). However, there may be other types of intelligence, especially in more creative areas (such as music), that cannot be measured with paper-and-pencil tests. In other words, some people believe that testing and measuring intelligence is more complicated and not as exact as standardized tests make us believe.
   a. Some people do not believe that IQ tests can measure intelligence in any way.
   b. Some people do not believe that IQ tests can truly define or measure intelligence.
   c. Some people believe that only one kind of IQ test is an accurate measure of intelligence.

2. _c_   He suggests that human intelligence consists of several parts, and he has identified eight (possibly nine) different types of intelligence that people may have. These eight types are visual/spatial, verbal/linguistic, mathematical/logical, bodily/kinesthetic, musical/rhythmic, interpersonal, intrapersonal, and naturalist. (The ninth possible type of intelligence is existentialist.) Even though everyone has all of these intelligences, each person has a unique combination of them, depending on the individual's strengths and weaknesses. Just as each person has distinctive physical characteristics and a unique personality, Gardner believes that each person has a specific intelligence make-up.
   a. Howard Gardner, a Harvard psychologist, believes that everyone should try to have equal amounts of many kinds of intelligences.
   b. Harvard psychologist Howard Gardner has written eight new IQ tests in order to measure intelligence more accurately.
   c. Harvard psychologist Howard Gardner believes that not all of our skills and abilities can be measured with a simple number.

3. _A_   People strong in this type of intelligence may be very good speakers because they have high-level language skills. They think in words rather than pictures and are strong in the language arts in areas such as reading, writing, listening, and speaking. People with strong verbal/linguistic intelligence are often successful in a traditional classroom environment because this environment matches their abilities. These people are good at word games, storytelling,

and explaining things. Therefore, career interests for these people often include such professions as teacher, lawyer, politician, translator, writer, and journalist.

a. Verbal/linguistic intelligence includes the ability to use words well.

b. A traditional classroom is a good place for a student who is strong in verbal/linguistic intelligence.

c. Verbal/linguistic intelligence requires the learner to have strong tactile skills.

4. ___C___ Such people think in concepts and patterns and like to find relationships or make connections between things. They are curious about the world around them and like to experiment, ask questions, and solve puzzles. People with strong mathematical/logical intelligence may enjoy learning through logic games, investigations, and mysteries. In addition, these people usually do well in a traditional classroom environment because they are able to follow the logical, sequenced material that teachers often present. Because of these interests and characteristics, people with a high level of this type of intelligence may become scientists, engineers, computer programmers, accountants, and mathematicians.

a. Anyone who likes to solve puzzles has strong mathematical/logical intelligence.

b. People who are scientists and engineers do well in a traditional classroom environment.

c. The ability to reason, solve problems, and work with numbers is often evident in people with strong mathematical/logical intelligence.

C. For each of the following topics, underline one or more controlling ideas that might be acceptable for a paragraph on that topic. Then write a topic sentence for the paragraph, using one of the controlling ideas you underlined.

1. Topic: **learning styles**
   Possible controlling ideas:
   - definition or description of types of learning styles
   - how to use audio tapes with auditory learners
   - the best style for learning English
   - the importance of knowing one's own learning style

   Topic sentence: _____

   _____

2. Topic: **intelligence**
   Possible controlling ideas:
   - different definitions of intelligence
   - Albert Einstein's IQ score
   - the history of all intelligence tests
   - modern intelligence tests

   Topic sentence: _____

   _____

3. Topic: **IQ tests**

Possible controlling ideas:

- the highest score ever recorded on an IQ test
- the validity or fairness of IQ tests
- uses of IQ tests in the United States
- how many people take IQ tests every year
- types of IQ tests used in US schools

Topic sentence: _____

_____

Supporting Sentences

Irrelevant Sentences

A good paragraph has several supporting sentences. These sentences give details, such as facts, examples, or reasons, that relate to the topic sentence. A good writer does not include any sentences that are *irrelevant*, or not related to the topic sentence.

In the following paragraph about one of Gardner's nine intelligences, underline the topic sentence. Then find one sentence in the paragraph that is irrelevant. Cross out (put a line through) that sentence.

[1]People who are strong in visual/spatial intelligence perceive the world in terms of what they can see, and they are very aware of their environment. [2]These people learn best visually and tend to think in pictures or create images in their mind in order to remember things. [3]Since they like to see things as they learn, they enjoy looking at maps, charts, movies, illustrations, graphs, etc. [4]Such people may also like to draw, work on jigsaw puzzles, and daydream, and they may have a good sense of direction. [5]I don't understand how people can be good at these things. [6]As a result, people with a high level of this type of intelligence may be successful as architects, mechanics, engineers, sculptors, and sailors or navigators.

If you crossed out sentence 5, you are correct. That sentence is irrelevant because it does not give information about people with visual/spatial intelligence.

Practice: Finding Irrelevant Supporting Sentences

Each of the following paragraphs is about one of the intelligences described by Howard Gardner. Read each one and decide if there is an irrelevant sentence. If you find one, cross it out. One paragraph does not have an irrelevant sentence.

1.   People with a strong musical/rhythmic intelligence have an ability to produce and appreciate music, and they are sensitive to rhythms and sounds. This strength may relate not only to musical sounds but to sounds in the environment as well. My friend has strong musical/rhythmic intelligence, and she can sing and play the piano very well. Learners who excel in this area may enjoy using musical instruments, audio tapes, and CDs and may like to study with music playing in the background. Children especially may learn well with songs, patterns, rhythms, and any other kind of musical expression. Thus, teachers might want to include some kinds of musical or rhythmic activities in their classrooms for students who have strength in this intelligence.

2.   People who have a high level of bodily/kinesthetic intelligence have a strong awareness of body movements and can manipulate objects

with skill. They also can communicate well through body language. In addition, these people like to make and touch things, and they have a good sense of balance and hand-eye coordination. For example, they excel at playing soccer. People who are strong in this type of intelligence learn best through games, building things, hands-on activities, and acting or role-playing. It is not surprising that children with high bodily/kinesthetic intelligence may be viewed as "overly active" in a traditional classroom, and they are often told to sit still. In short, people who are active and skilled with their hands often have a high level of bodily/kinesthetic intelligence.

3.   Interpersonal intelligence involves understanding others and having an ability to relate to them. Therefore, people strong in this kind of intelligence enjoy interaction with others and often try to understand other people's views, thoughts, and feelings. They will use both verbal and nonverbal communication to interact with others, and they are very organized. Nonverbal communication is also known as *body language* and includes facial expressions and hand gestures. In general, people with a high level of interpersonal intelligence like to learn through seminars and group activities, and they enjoy using telephones, video conferencing, and e-mail. In a school setting, learners with strong interpersonal intelligence are clearly outgoing and enjoy cooperative learning through studying in pairs or groups. In a traditional classroom environment, these students may be considered too talkative or too social. In sum, we might call someone who is strong in interpersonal intelligence a "people person."

4.   Having strength in the naturalist type of intelligence means that a person has the ability to make distinctions among living things. For example, such people may be interested in plants and animals or other parts of the natural world, such as cloud and rock formations. This particular intelligence was especially important to our ancestors for thousands of years because they had to be able to understand

their environment in order to survive from day to day. It is important to learn about people from many years ago even if you don't like history. Today many people are part of a consumer society, so the ability to be aware of the cultural environment (such as types of cars on the road or clothes people wear) may now be part of this naturalist intelligence. That is, this intelligence may include knowledge of cultural objects as well as living things.

5.   The ninth possible type of intelligence is existentialist. It is the newest one to be added to the list although perhaps this type needs more study in order to say it is truly another intelligence. People who are strong in this intelligence learn in the context of where humankind stands in the "big picture" of existence. They often wonder about basic questions such as "Where do we come from?" "Why are we here?" and "What is our role in the world?" People who think too much may have problems in their lives and often cannot be successful. Therefore, it is not hard to understand why people with a high level of existentialist intelligence may become spiritual leaders or philosophical thinkers.

Concluding Sentences

The concluding sentence of a paragraph may restate the topic sentence (using different words), provide a summary of the paragraph, or give a result. Some typical words or expressions you might find at the beginning of a concluding sentence are *finally, in conclusion, therefore, thus, as a result, in summary* (or *in sum*), and *in short.* Make sure you choose the word or expression that has the meaning you want for your concluding sentence.

EXAMPLE:

Teaching students with different learning styles may seem like a difficult task, but a teacher can find ways to satisfy the various learning preferences found in a class. One effective way might be to use multimedia in the classroom as much as possible. For example, the use of visual aids will help in cases where words alone may not be effective. Realia, or tangible objects, may be useful for teaching new information as well as motor skills. Other helpful teaching techniques might utilize motion and performance so that students are actively involved in the learning process. Even testing, which most often is done through the printed word, can be handled through electronic media such as computers. In short, teachers may want to use various techniques in the classroom in order to help students with different learning styles.

Practice: Concluding Sentences

A.   *The following paragraphs do not have complete concluding sentences. Finish each concluding sentence to fit the paragraph.*

1. The ability to understand one's own inner feelings, interests, and values is characteristic of people with strong intrapersonal intelligence. These individuals are often shy around other people but are very good at recognizing their own strengths and weaknesses and relationships with others. They may appreciate their privacy. In addition, they are quite intuitive about what they learn and how they can relate it to themselves. They are often very independent learners and like to use books or diaries. Learning through independent study and introspection often works well for these students. People who are strong in this type of intelligence may have careers as researchers, theorists, and philosophers. In sum, people with strong intrapersonal intelligence _involves understanding others and having ability to relate to them._

2. For some students it may be quite important to identify their particular learning style and develop strategies to help them become successful even if they find themselves in a rather traditional learning environment. For example, a visual learner may want to make sure that she or he can see the teacher clearly (to watch body language), use color highlighting when reading texts, and use visual aids such as pictures and charts when studying or memorizing information. Auditory learners might use a tape recorder during a lecture or discuss ideas with others when learning or studying new material. On the other hand, tactile/kinesthetic learners will probably need to find a way to be as "hands-on" and as mobile as possible in order to learn. They may also need to take frequent breaks from studying. Thus, each learner _have their own way of studying the material arts._

B. *Look back at the example paragraph and the two practice paragraphs in this section. Which type of concluding sentence does each paragraph contain: a summary, a restatement, or a result? Write a different type of concluding sentence for each paragraph.*

Discussion/Writing

Answer these questions in writing or through discussion. Try to use a variety of coordinating conjunctions in your sentences.

1. a. Look at the following groups of careers. Name the type of intelligence (of the nine types discussed in this unit) that best fits each group. Explain your answers.

   • Athletes, physical education teachers, dancers, actors, firefighters
     _2_

   • Teachers, counselors, salespeople, politicians, businesspeople
     3   natural

   • Botanists, chefs, veterinarians _4_

   • Musicians, disc jockeys, singers, composers _1_

b. What kind of job do you have now or hope to have in the future? *paralegal*
   How might this job reflect your strength(s) in any of the nine types
   of intelligence?

2. a. Which type of intelligence (of the nine discussed in this unit) do you
      think is or was the strongest for each of the following people? Why?

   William Shakespeare ___3___   Dalai Lama ___4___

   Albert Einstein ___5___   Michael Jordan ___2___

   Charles Darwin ___4___   Mother Teresa ___2___

   John F. Kennedy ___5___   Ludwig von Beethoven ___1___

   Vincent van Gogh ___4___

   b. Think of two famous people you admire (either alive or dead).
      Which types of intelligence do you think are or were their strongest?

3. Which of the nine intelligences are your personal strengths, and which
   ones are your weaknesses? Explain your answers. *it help me keep my mide in peace.*

Summary Writing

For an explanation of summary writing and practice of this skill, read pages
212–217 in the Appendix. Follow the instructions given there. Be sure to
use coordinating conjunctions in your sentences in these summaries.

1. Summarize the reading about intelligence on page 8 by writing a
   one-sentence summary for each paragraph in the reading.
2. Summarize the paragraph about Sir Francis Galton on page 14. Your
   summary should be no longer than three sentences.
3. Summarize any one of the paragraphs on pages 22–23 that describes
   one of the types of intelligence proposed by Howard Gardner. Your
   summary should be no longer than three sentences.

The Writing Process

It is very difficult to write something perfectly on the first try. A good
writer usually follows several steps in order to create a well-written,
organized final product. In other words, writing is a process that
involves planning, writing, reviewing, and changing the work. This writing process includes the following steps.

Step One: Generating Ideas and Brainstorming

In the first step, the writer thinks about the topic and tries to generate
as many ideas as possible to answer the question.

When you do this step for the writing assignments in this book, you
should think about the information you learned from the readings and
the activities in the unit. If you wrote any journal entries, go back and
read those entries.

The next part of the first step is brainstorming. You make notes of everything that comes into your mind about the topic but don't worry about organization at this point. You do not need to write your ideas in complete sentences or think about spelling and grammar when you are brainstorming.

In addition, there are different ways you can write your ideas. For example, some people like to write lists of ideas, and other people like to use a technique called *clustering.* Clustering involves creating a kind of picture of your thoughts using circles or boxes and lines connecting them. The most general idea (the topic) goes in a circle or box in the middle, and the related ideas or details are in circles or boxes connected by lines to the middle one.

Look at the following examples of these two ways of brainstorming:

LIST

musical intelligence
playing an instrument
  piano since 5 years old
  guitar since 12 years old
playing in a band
singing in school chorus
CD collection
favorite singers
ability to play piano
  without music (by ear)
majoring in music and
  plan to teach it
dislike rap music

interpersonal intelligence
like to go to parties
have many friends

CLUSTERING

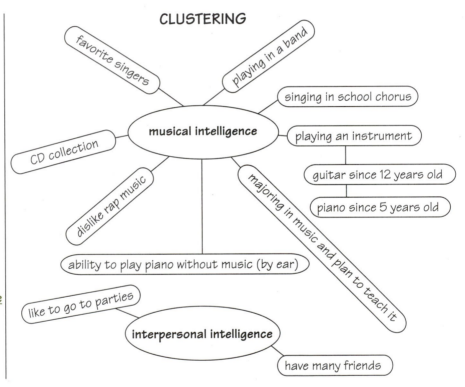

Notice that this writer tried to brainstorm about two topics: interpersonal intelligence and musical intelligence. She tried to write as many ideas as she could for each one.

Step Two: Organizing Ideas and Planning

In this step, the writer tries to organize the ideas from the first step. The writer may choose to keep some ideas from the brainstorming and leave out others. If brainstorming involved two or more topics, this is the time to decide which topic to focus on and write about. For example, the student who did the list and clustering examples above was considering writing about her musical intelligence or her interpersonal intelligence. She decided to write about her musical intelligence because she did not have enough ideas about her interpersonal intelligence. Next, she deleted some of the ideas about her musical intelligence because she realized they were not relevant to her paragraph.

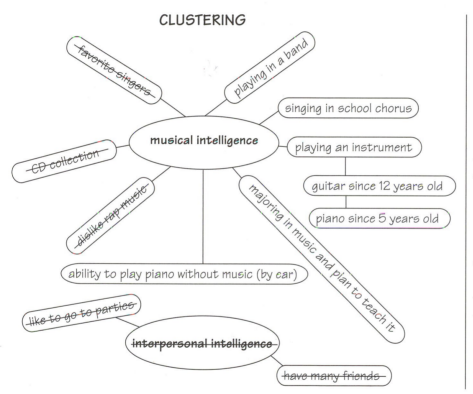

CLUSTERING

- ~~favorite singers~~
- playing in a band
- singing in school chorus
- musical intelligence
- playing an instrument
- guitar since 12 years old
- piano since 5 years old
- ~~CD collection~~
- ~~dislike rap music~~
- majoring in music and plan to teach it
- ability to play piano without music (by ear)
- ~~like to go to parties~~
- ~~interpersonal intelligence~~
- ~~have many friends~~

LIST

musical intelligence
playing an instrument
   piano since 5 years old
   guitar since 12 years old
playing in a band
singing in school chorus
~~CD collection~~
~~favorite singers~~
ability to play piano
   without music (by ear)
majoring in music and
   plan to teach it
~~dislike rap music~~
~~interpersonal intelligence~~
~~like to go to parties~~
~~have many friends~~

In addition, as part of the planning step, many people use a chart or an outline to help them organize the ideas from a list or clustering diagram. The following chart organizes the information from the student's list and clustering diagram about her musical intelligence. Notice that the student has not written the topic sentence or concluding sentence yet.

TOPIC   CONTROLLING IDEA
TOPIC SENTENCE

Support/Detail *playing an instrument* *piano since 5 years old* *guitar since 12 years old*	**Support/Detail** *playing in a band*
Support/Detail *singing in a school chorus*	**Support/Detail** *ability to play piano by ear*
Support/Detail *majoring in music and plan to teach it*	**Support/Detail**

SUPPORT   SUPPORT

CONCLUDING SENTENCE

Step Three: Getting Feedback

It is helpful to get another person's opinion (called *feedback*) about the ideas, organization, or other aspects of writing. This feedback might come from a teacher or from another student (a peer). Furthermore, this step can take place at several points in the process, such as after organizing ideas and after writing the first draft of the paper. Your teacher will decide when and how often you will get feedback during the writing process.

Step Four: Writing the First Draft (Rough Draft)

The first (or rough) draft is the writer's first attempt to write the complete paragraph or essay. A writer should try his or her best when writing this draft, but the work does not have to be perfect. The writer will have one or more chances to make changes to improve it.

Reminder: After finishing the first draft, the writer may get feedback.

Step Five: Revising

After the first draft the writer may want to change some ideas and/or their organization. The writer may want to improve the topic sentence or concluding sentence or change the organization of the supporting sentences. She or he may want to take out some sentences or possibly add some new ones. At this point the writer is making changes in ideas and organization before correcting any errors in grammar, punctuation, and spelling.

   Reminder: After this revision the writer may again get feedback.

Step Six: Editing

After the writer has received some feedback and revised some ideas and sentences, it is time to check grammar and mechanics. This step usually includes the correction of grammar, spelling, punctuation, capitalization, and any other details.

   Reminder: After the editing step the writer may again get feedback.

Step Seven: Preparing the Final Draft

The writer has made all of his or her changes, and the final draft is the finished product. It should be organized, neat, and as correct as the writer can make it. Usually a final draft of a writing assignment for school is typed and double spaced. It should follow correct format, including margins and indenting.

Writing Assignment

A. Picking the Topic

Choose one of the following questions, and write a paragraph that answers it. Be sure to include enough support (details, examples, facts, or reasons) in your paragraph.

1. What type of learner are you? Write about your learning style, choosing from one of the three described in the first reading of this unit.

2. Which one or two of Gardner's nine types of intelligence are you strongest in?

3. Think about the nine kinds of intelligences discussed in this unit. Which ones do you think are necessary for success?

B. Understanding the Assignment/Answering the Question

Before you start to write, make sure you understand the assignment. Your paragraph must answer the question you choose and should not discuss other things. Look at the following ideas for paragraphs that address each

of the questions. Decide which ideas will answer the question and which will not. Cross out the ideas that you think will not answer the question.

Topic 1: a paragraph about
• the three learning styles: auditory, visual, and kinesthetic/tactile
• your friend's ability to learn through auditory methods
• your visual style of learning
• how you use the auditory style but not the visual style
• how you learn through kinesthetic or tactile experiences

Topic 2: a paragraph about
• why you agree with Howard Gardner's theory of intelligences
• your strength in verbal/linguistic and interpersonal intelligences
• people who have strengths in several of the intelligences
• how you have high musical intelligence
• why you think IQ tests are a good measure of intelligence

Topic 3: a paragraph about
• the good and bad points of some of the nine intelligences
• the two or three types of intelligence you think people need in life
• why only one or two of the intelligences might be necessary for success
• how each type of intelligence might be helpful to people

Following the Steps in the Writing Process

Before You Write

■ ***Step One: Generating Ideas and Brainstorming***
First, think about the three possible writing assignments.

1. Circle the learning style that fits you best:
    auditory   visual   kinesthetic/tactile

2. Circle one or two types of intelligence you are strong in:
    visual/spatial   bodily/kinesthetic   musical
    intrapersonal   naturalist   interpersonal   verbal/linguistic
    mathematical/logical   existentialist

3. Circle the types of intelligence you think are necessary for success:
    visual/spatial   bodily/kinesthetic   musical
    intrapersonal   naturalist   interpersonal   verbal/linguistic
    mathematical/logical   existentialist

Now, think about the support you can provide for the items you circled for the three possible assignments.

d. Using a list or a clustering diagram, write your ideas in the spaces below. If you try to brainstorm more than one idea, make two separate lists or two separate clustering diagrams. Don't worry about organization at this time.

My Learning Style

My Strongest Type(s) of Intelligence

Intelligences Necessary for Success

e. Choose *one* of the lists or clustering diagrams you created to develop into a paragraph. Check your supporting details to make sure that there are enough and they are all relevant.

■ **Step Two: Organizing Ideas and Planning**
Think about the three parts of a paragraph. Answer the following questions regarding the paragraph you plan to write.

Topic Sentence
a. What is your topic? Are you writing about your learning style or kinds of intelligences?

Topic: _____

b. What is your controlling idea? Which aspect of the topic do you want to develop in your supporting sentences?

Controlling idea: _____

c. Write your topic sentence on the paragraph organization chart at the end of this unit.

Support
Make sure your paragraph has enough support to develop your controlling idea.

a. Why did you choose to write about a certain learning style or certain kinds of intelligence? Explain your reasons.
b. What are some examples of events in your life or personal characteristics that relate to your types of intelligence?
c. What are some examples showing how certain types of intelligence are needed for success?
d. Write your ideas for support on the chart at the end of this unit.

Concluding Sentence
Write your concluding sentence on the chart at the end of this unit.

■ **Step Three: Getting Feedback**
Your teacher may ask you to work with a partner and complete a peer review of your chart. Use the peer review sheet on page 228 in the Appendix for this step.

When You Write

■ **Step Four: Writing the First Draft (Rough Draft)**
Write the first draft of your paragraph using the ideas on your chart. Do the following when you write your paragraph:

a. Use at least three vocabulary words from this unit.
b. Use at least four of the coordinating conjunctions from this unit in your sentences.

After You Write

Check Your Work   After you finish writing the first draft and before you show it to anyone for feedback or revision, read your paragraph again. Check your work for the following.

☐ This paragraph discusses one of the following:
  • my learning style
  • my strongest types of intelligence
  • types of intelligence necessary for success

☐ This paragraph has a topic sentence.

☐ This paragraph has several supporting sentences (at least five or six).

☐ All of the supporting sentences relate to the topic sentence.

☐ This paragraph has a concluding sentence.

☐ I used at least three vocabulary words from this unit in the paragraph.

☐ I used at least four coordinating conjunctions in my sentences.

☐ I checked this paragraph for run-ons and comma splices.

☐ I indented the first line of this paragraph.

☐ I have correct margins on the left and right sides of the page.

☐ All of my sentences follow one another. (I did not go to the next line to begin each new sentence.)

Getting Feedback

Your teacher will decide the type of feedback you will receive on your first draft. It may be peer review, teacher review, or both. For peer review, use the sheet on page 229 of the Appendix.

Step Five: Revising

After you receive feedback, revise any sentences or their organization as necessary. For example, you may want to change your topic sentence or your concluding sentence. You may want to add, take out, or change the order of some of your supporting sentences.

   Reminder: Your teacher may want you to have more feedback after you revise.

Step Six: Editing

Make any necessary changes in grammar, spelling, punctuation, and capitalization.

   Reminder: Your teacher may again ask you to get feedback before you write your final draft.

Step Seven: Preparing the Final Draft

Prepare your final draft to be handed in to the teacher.

Organizing Your Ideas for Writing a Paragraph

TITLE: _____

TOPIC SENTENCE

SUPPORTING SENTENCES

Support/Detail	Support/Detail
Support/Detail	Support/Detail
Support/Detail	Support/Detail

SUPPORTING SENTENCES

CONCLUDING SENTENCE

The African-American Experience

Content Area: US History

Readings: Frederick Douglass—Years in Slavery
Frederick Douglass—Life after Slavery
Rosa Parks

Short Readings: Harriet Tubman
Mary McLeod Bethune
Jackie Robinson
Martin Luther King Jr.
Oseola McCarty
Thurgood Marshall
Oprah Winfrey
Maya Angelou

Sentence-Combining Focus: Subordinating Conjunctions of Time

Editing Focus: Fragments; Run-ons; Comma Splices

Writing Focus: Organization of an Essay (Narration); Introductions; Thesis Statements; Time Words; Quotations

PART 1   UNIT PREVIEW

Preview Activity: Timeline and Map

A. Below is a timeline with some dates in US history, followed by a list of events related to these dates. Can you match any of the events with the dates on the timeline? One date matches two events. The first one has been done as an example.

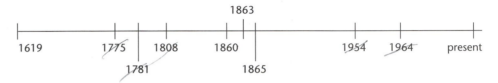

1863

| | | | | | | |
1619   1775   1808   1860   1954   1964   present
        1781   1865

___1619___ First Africans brought to Virginia as servants.

___1775___ US Civil War

___1808___ Revolutionary War (United States wins independence from Great Britain.)

___1860___ President Lincoln ends slavery in the United States with the Emancipation Proclamation.

___1963___ Slave trade outlawed (no more slave ships allowed into the United States).

___1964___ Martin Luther King's famous "I have a dream" speech

___1964___ Civil rights bills establishing desegregation and voting rights for African Americans passed.

___1964___ US Supreme Court declares that all states must integrate their schools.

desegregation   the ending by law of racial separation
integrate   to put different groups of people together, especially racial groups

B. Look at the following map of the United States at the beginning of the Civil War. Which states allowed slavery at that time? Mark those states.

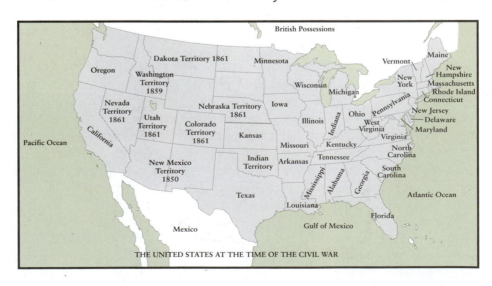

THE UNITED STATES AT THE TIME OF THE CIVIL WAR

Quickwrite

Write for five minutes about one of the following topics. Do not worry about grammar, spelling, or punctuation. Just write whatever comes into your mind about the topic.

1. Think of someone who was very important in history. (This person can be from any country.) Why was this person important? What did this person say and/or do to become important?
2. What do you know about any of the following times during the history of the United States?
   • Slavery in the United States (When did it begin? When did it end? What kind of life did slaves have?)
   • The Civil War (When was it? Who was fighting? Why was it fought?)
   • The civil rights movement (What was it? When did it happen? Why was it important?)

PART 2   READING AND VOCABULARY

Read the following about the life of Frederick Douglass before he escaped to freedom. Then complete the activities that follow the reading.

Reading
Frederick
Douglass—
Years in Slavery

Frederick Douglass was a slave who escaped to freedom when he was 20 years old. In the years that followed, he became a famous orator and abolitionist.

Frederick Bailey was born a slave around 1818 on Holmes Hill Farm near the town of Easton, Maryland. Frederick's mother, Harriet Bailey, worked in the cornfields surrounding Holmes Hill. He knew little about his father except that the man was white. He also heard rumors that his father was the master, Aaron Anthony, but he never knew if these stories were true. Because Harriet Bailey had to work long hours in fields far away, Frederick lived with his grandmother, Betsey Bailey. Frederick's mother visited him when she could, but he had very little memory of her. She died when he was about seven years old.

Frederick spent his childhood playing in the woods near his grandmother's cabin, so he did not realize he was a slave. Then, when he was six years old, his grandmother took him to a new plantation, where life for slaves was difficult. The children ate cornmeal mush from a wooden tray on the ground like animals and had to fight for every bite they could get. The only clothing they received was one linen shirt which covered them to their knees, and they had no beds or warm blankets. After watching his aunt receive a brutal whipping, Frederick learned that his master beat the slaves if they did not obey orders quickly enough.

On the plantation Frederick's chief friend and protector was Lucretia Auld, Aaron Anthony's daughter, who was married to Thomas Auld. One day in 1826 Lucretia told Frederick they were sending him to live in Baltimore with her brother-in-law, Hugh Auld. At the Auld house

Frederick's only duties were to run errands and take care of the Aulds' infant son. Hugh Auld's wife, Sophia, was a kind, religious woman. She taught Frederick to read the alphabet and a few simple words soon after he arrived there. However, when her husband found out, he became furious and angrily told his wife to stop the lessons. He told her it was unlawful to teach a slave to read, and such knowledge could make a slave rebellious. Frederick realized from Hugh Auld's strong reaction that learning how to read and write could be his route to freedom.

Frederick continued to learn to read on his own by making friends with poor white children he met on errands. He used them as teachers and paid for his lessons with pieces of bread. By the age of 13, he was reading newspapers and learning about abolitionists. In 1833 Frederick again became a field hand when he was sent to live at Thomas Auld's new farm. Auld starved his slaves, so they had to steal food from neighboring farms in order to live. Thomas Auld found Frederick especially difficult to control, so he sent Frederick to a well-known "slave breaker" named Thomas Covey. At first Frederick was happy with this change because Covey fed his slaves better than Auld did. However, soon Frederick learned that Covey's slaves worked from dawn until after nightfall, and if they tried to rest, they received a beating.

After only one week on Covey's farm, Frederick received a serious beating, and during the months to follow, he was continually whipped until he began to feel that he was "broken." Then, one hot day while working in the field, Frederick felt sick and collapsed to the ground. When Frederick could not get up, Covey kicked and beat him severely. Later Frederick walked seven miles to the Auld farm, where he begged his master to let him stay, but Auld sent him back to Covey. At that time Frederick was 16 and tall and strong. The next time Covey hit him, he fought back, and after two hours of fighting, Covey left him alone. Frederick was lucky because a slave could legally be killed for resisting his master.

Frederick worked for Covey for a year and then was sent to work for a farmer who was a kinder master, but all Frederick wanted was his freedom. He started an illegal school for blacks in the area, and with five other slaves he planned his escape to the North. However, someone exposed the plan, and the slaves were put in jail. Frederick was in jail for about a week, and he fully expected to be sold to a new master. To his surprise Thomas Auld came for him.

Then Thomas Auld sent Frederick back to Hugh Auld, who sent him to Baltimore to be a shipyard worker. After he worked in the shipyards for a while, he was allowed to collect his own pay, but at the end of each week, he gave all his earnings to Hugh Auld. During his free time he met with a group of educated free blacks and joined an educational association. There Frederick learned debating skills and met a free black woman named Anna Murray. Anna and Frederick were soon in love, and in 1838 they became engaged.

After Frederick's escape attempt Thomas Auld had promised to free him when he turned 25 if he worked hard. Frederick did not trust his master, and he decided that he had to escape even though it would be very difficult. Professional slave catchers watched the borders between slave states and free states, and free blacks traveling by train or steamboat had to carry official papers of identification. With money that he borrowed from Anna and a promise to bring her north after he got there, Frederick bought a train ticket. He also had a friend's papers of identification that said he was a free sea-man. Dressed in a sailor's red shirt and black tie, Frederick took the train.

Frederick arrived in Wilmington, Delaware, and from there he took a steamboat to Philadelphia. Even after stepping on Pennsylvania's free soil, he knew he was not safe from slave catchers, so he immediately took another train north. On September 4, 1838, Frederick arrived in New York City. He could not find the words to express his feelings about leaving behind his life of slavery. Later, he wrote, "A new world had opened upon me."

Adapted with permission from "Frederick Douglass: Abolitionist/Editor—The Slave Years" by Sandra Thomas (www.history.rochester.edu/class/douglass/home.html)

Comprehension Check

*Decide if the following statements about the life of Frederick Douglass are true or false based on the reading. Write **T** for "True" or **F** for "False" on the line next to the number of each sentence. The first one has been done for you as an example.*

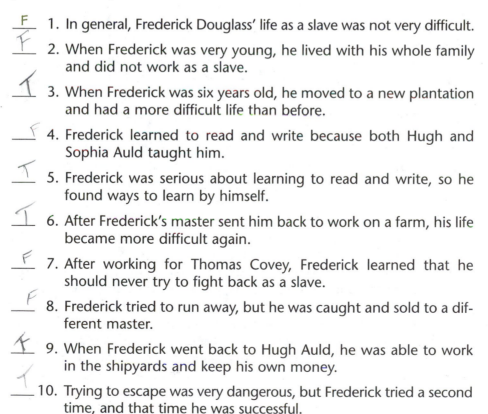

__F__ 1. In general, Frederick Douglass' life as a slave was not very difficult.

__F__ 2. When Frederick was very young, he lived with his whole family and did not work as a slave.

__T__ 3. When Frederick was six years old, he moved to a new plantation and had a more difficult life than before.

__F__ 4. Frederick learned to read and write because both Hugh and Sophia Auld taught him.

__T__ 5. Frederick was serious about learning to read and write, so he found ways to learn by himself.

__T__ 6. After Frederick's master sent him back to work on a farm, his life became more difficult again.

__F__ 7. After working for Thomas Covey, Frederick learned that he should never try to fight back as a slave.

__F__ 8. Frederick tried to run away, but he was caught and sold to a different master.

__T__ 9. When Frederick went back to Hugh Auld, he was able to work in the shipyards and keep his own money.

__T__ 10. Trying to escape was very dangerous, but Frederick tried a second time, and that time he was successful.

Inference

Answer the following questions based on what you learned in the reading. Do not try to find the answers directly in the reading. Use your ability to infer.

1. The reading says that Frederick Douglass was born around 1818. Why do you think no exact birth date is known for him?
2. Why do you think Frederick's master made his mother live and work far away from her child?
3. How did Thomas Auld show that he had no respect for slaves?
4. Why do you think Frederick worked so hard to learn to read? Why did he think this knowledge would help him become free?
5. When Frederick fought with Thomas Covey, he was lucky that Covey did not punish him. Why do you think Covey did not do anything to Frederick?
6. Why do you think Frederick wanted to meet with educated free blacks when he lived and worked in Baltimore?

Vocabulary Study

A. Vocabulary in Context

We often find unfamiliar words when we read. However, it is not always necessary to look for the meanings of these words in a dictionary. Sometimes we can try to guess the meaning of a word by looking at other parts of the sentence or by knowing other parts of the story. This skill is called understanding *vocabulary in context* (or context guessing). Examples: Try to guess the meanings of the words in **bold** type using other parts of the sentences.

1. Thomas Auld **starved** his slaves, so they had to steal food from neighboring farms in order to live.
2. Then, one hot day while working in the field, Frederick felt sick and **collapsed** to the ground. When Frederick could not get up, Covey kicked and beat him severely.

EXPLANATIONS

1. Auld's slaves had to steal food to live. This tells us that they did not get enough to eat, so *starving* someone probably means not giving the person enough food.
2. The sentences say that Frederick felt sick, was on the ground, and could not get up. Therefore, *collapsed* probably means that he fell down and could not move.

*Now try to guess the meanings of the words in **bold** in the following sentences from the reading.*

1. He also heard **rumors** that his father was the master, Aaron Anthony, but he never knew if these stories were true.
2. Then, when he was six years old, his grandmother took him to a new **plantation,** where life for slaves was difficult.
3. Frederick realized from Hugh Auld's strong reaction that learning how to read and write could be his **route** to freedom.
4. Later, Frederick walked seven miles to the Auld farm, where he **begged** his master to let him stay, but Auld sent him back to Covey.

B. Meanings

Choose a synonym from the following list for each underlined vocabulary word in the sentences. Write the letter of the synonym on the line next to the number of the sentence. The first one has been done as an example.

a. strong speakers
b. people who wanted to end slavery
c. small homes
d. beating
e. cruel, violent
f. try
g. ground

h. cornmeal boiled in water
i. very angry
j. showed or revealed
k. fought or went against
~~l.   short trips to take care of~~
~~business~~

__l__ 1. As a child Frederick had to run <u>errands</u> for people when he was not working in the fields.

__b__ 2/3. The <u>abolitionists</u> wrote newspaper articles and gave speeches
__a__   against slavery. Some of them were excellent <u>orators</u>.

__e__ 4. Many of the masters and supervisors on the plantations were <u>brutal</u> to the slaves.

__k__ 5. If a slave <u>resisted</u> a master, he or she could be killed.

__i__ 6/7. When a slave did something wrong, the master might
__d__   become <u>furious</u>. The master might give the slave a <u>whipping</u>.

__g__ 8. The slaves who were field hands had to work the <u>soil</u> because they were working on farms.

__c__ 9. The slaves lived in <u>cabins</u>, but the masters lived in large houses on the plantations.

__f__ 10. It was very dangerous for a slave to <u>attempt</u> to run away from his or her master.

__h__ 11. <u>Mush</u> was a typical food that slaves ate, but often they got very little of it.

__j__ 12. Because someone <u>exposed</u> Frederick's escape plan, he and his friends were put in jail.

Discussion/Writing

Answer these questions in writing or through discussion.

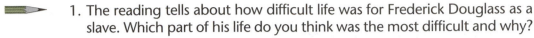

1. The reading tells about how difficult life was for Frederick Douglass as a slave. Which part of his life do you think was the most difficult and why?

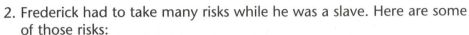

2. Frederick had to take many risks while he was a slave. Here are some of those risks:
   - learning to read and write after he was told not to
   - fighting back with the slave breaker Thomas Covey
   - trying to run away the first time
   - trying to run away a second time

   What do these actions tell us about Frederick's personality? Do you think you could act the same way in these situations? Why or why not?

3. Have you ever taken a risk in your life? If so, describe the situation, including what you did and why you did it. Were you glad you took the risk? Why or why not?

PART 3   WRITING SENTENCES WITH SUBORDINATING CONJUNCTIONS

Reading

Frederick Douglass—Life after Slavery

Read about Frederick Douglass' life after slavery. Then answer the questions that follow the reading.

[1]When Frederick Douglass arrived in New York City, he went to the home of an abolitionist named David Ruggles. [2]Ruggles took him in and helped him bring Anna Murray to New York. [3]As soon as Anna arrived, she and Frederick were married. [4]The next day, they took a boat to New Bedford, Massachusetts.

[5]In New Bedford Frederick changed his name from Bailey to Douglass in order to avoid slave catchers. [6]While he was living in New Bedford, he met a man named William Lloyd Garrison. [7]Garrison was the publisher of an antislavery newspaper called *The Liberator*. [8]Frederick also began speaking to audiences about his life as a slave and all its hardships.

[9]Soon the Massachusetts Antislavery Society asked Frederick to speak for them. [10]He spoke so well that many of his listeners could not believe that he had really been a slave. [11]To convince his audiences, he wrote *Narrative of the Life of Frederick Douglass, An American Slave*. [12]In this book he wrote about his life as a slave, including specific names of places, other slaves, and owners. [13]After he wrote the book, he traveled to

England. [14]He did this because he was afraid his old owner might try to find him. [15]He wanted to escape to another place <u>before</u> anyone could catch him as a runaway slave.

Questions

1. a. Look at sentence 15. How many clauses can you find? (Remember from page 9 in Unit One that a clause contains a subject-verb combination.)
   b. What punctuation can you find in this sentence? *one comma*
2. a. Look at sentences 1, 3, 6, and 13. Each of these sentences has two clauses. Put a line under each clause.
   b. In each of these sentences, put a circle around the word you think is joining the two clauses together.
3. Write all of the circled words below.
   <u>When , as soon as, while   after and before</u>
4. What punctuation do you see in sentences 1, 3, 6, and 13?

Explanation: Combining Clauses with Subordinating Conjunctions

1. In Unit One, you learned about combining independent clauses (simple sentences) with signals (connectors) called *coordinating conjunctions*. Another group of signals (connectors) that can join clauses together is called *subordinating conjunctions* (or *subordinators*).

2. A subordinator is a word that connects two different kinds of clauses: an independent clause and a dependent clause. A dependent clause always begins with a subordinator. NOTE: Sometimes these clauses have different names: an independent clause may be called a main clause, and a dependent clause may be called a subordinate clause.

   > EXAMPLE: He wanted to escape to another place before anyone
   >   independent (or main) clause   subordinator
   > could catch him as a runaway slave.
   >   dependent (or subordinate) clause

3. A subordinating conjunction can be in the middle of a sentence or at the beginning of a sentence. Note the two patterns:

   Pattern 1

   _____   _____   _____
   independent/main clause   subordinator   dependent/subordinate clause

   In this case you do not need a comma with the subordinating conjunction.

Sentence-Combining Focus

Subordinating Conjunctions of Time

EXAMPLE: He wanted to escape to another place **before** anyone could catch him as a runaway slave.

Pattern 2

| subordinator | dependent/subordinate clause | , | independent/main clause |

In this case you should put **a comma between the two clauses** in order to separate them. **The comma shows the reader exactly where the first clause ends and the second clause begins.**

EXAMPLE: **After** he wrote the **book**, he traveled to England.

4. Important Error to Avoid
   A dependent clause *cannot* stand alone because it is incomplete. It needs more information to make sense. You should always connect a dependent clause to an independent clause to make a correct sentence. A dependent clause by itself is not acceptable in written English and is called a *fragment.*

   INCORRECT: Before he escaped from slavery. (fragment)

5. English has many subordinating conjunctions. In this unit you will practice using some that have meanings related to time. Here are some subordinating conjunctions of time with examples showing how they are used:

   after = later than
   He traveled to England **after** he wrote his first book.
   _____independent clause_____   _____dependent clause_____

   before = earlier than
   Frederick escaped from slavery **before** he began speaking to audiences.

   when = at that time
   When Frederick Douglass arrived in New York City, he went to the home of an abolitionist named David Ruggles.

   until = up to that time
   Frederick lived as a slave in Maryland **until** he escaped to the North.

   since = from that time
   People have been reading Frederick's book about slavery **since** he wrote it in 1845.

   NOTE: The clause after the word *since* indicates the starting time of the activity mentioned in the independent clause.

   while = during that time
   While Frederick was living in New Bedford, he met a man named William Lloyd Garrison.

as = at the time that, when
As Frederick spoke, the people in the audience listened to him.

whenever = every time
People heard stories about slavery **whenever** Frederick Douglass gave a speech.

as soon as = immediately after
As soon as Anna arrived, she and Frederick were married.

6. Important Error to Avoid
   If you do not use a signal (connector) such as a subordinating conjunction when you put clauses together, you will make a run-on or a comma splice.

   INCORRECT: Frederick spoke the people in the audience listened to him.   run-on

   Frederick spoke, the people in the audience listened to him.   comma splice   It . not appropriate

   CORRECT: As (or When) Frederick spoke, the people in the audience listened to him.

7. Some subordinating conjunctions *(before, after, until,* and *since)* can also act as prepositions. Try to recognize when these words are prepositions and when they are conjunctions. They are subordinating conjunctions when they begin a dependent (subordinate) clause with a subject-verb combination following them.

   EXAMPLES:

   After Frederick wrote his first book, he traveled to England.
   subordinator   s   v   s   v
          dependent/subordinate clause   independent/main clause

   After his escape Frederick lived with David Ruggles.
   preposition   s   v

NOTE: Be careful when using the preposition *during,* which is not a conjunction and cannot join clauses together. Do not use *during* instead of *while* or *when.*

   INCORRECT: During Frederick was escaping, he took a train to New York.

   CORRECT: During his escape Frederick Douglass took a train to New York.
   When he escaped, Frederick took a train to New York.

8. Sentences with subordinating conjunctions of time have specific patterns. Look at the following chart.

Sentence Combining with Subordinating Conjunctions of Time

Position In Sentence

Middle

_____	_____	_____
clause	subordinator	clause

OR
Beginning

_____	_____	_____
subordinator	clause	clause

Punctuation: No comma

_____	*before*	_____
clause	subordinator	clause

EXAMPLE: He went to England after he wrote his first book.

Comma between clauses

_____	_____ ,	_____
subordinator	clause	clause

EXAMPLE: After he wrote his first book, he went to England.

TIME: after
as
as soon as
before
since
until
when
whenever
while

Practice: Subordinating Conjunctions of Time

A. Identifying Clauses
Look back at the example sentences in item 5 on pages 44–45. Each of these sentences has an independent clause and a dependent clause with a subordinating conjunction of time.

1. First label each clause in each of these sentences as independent or dependent.
2. Then circle the subordinating conjunction of time.

EXAMPLE: He traveled to England (after) he wrote his first book.
               independent clause   dependent clause

B. **Writing Sentences**

Below is a list of events in the life of Frederick Douglass from his escape from slavery to the end of the US Civil War. Use this information in this activity and the next one.

1838	Married Anna Murray
	Moved to New Bedford, Massachusetts
1841	Started to give his antislavery speeches
1845	May—published his first book (*Narrative of the Life of Frederick Douglass*)
	August—went to England
1846	December—became legally free
1847	Spring—returned to United States from England
	Fall—moved to Rochester, New York
	December—established his newspaper called *North Star*
1851	Changed the name of his newspaper from *North Star* to *Frederick Douglass' Paper*
1855	Wrote second book about his life *(My Bondage and My Freedom)*
1859	November—went to England again
1860	March—Abraham Lincoln became the president of the United States
	April—Start of US Civil War
	May—Returned to the United States
1863	Met with President Lincoln about discrimination against Blacks in the US Army
1865	End of US Civil War

Combine each pair of sentences below using the subordinating conjunction given in parentheses. Write your new sentence in two ways:

a. Use the conjunction between the two clauses.
b. Use the conjunction at the beginning of the sentence.

Be sure to use correct punctuation in each sentence you write.

EXAMPLE: (as soon as) He married Anna Murray. He moved to New Bedford, Massachusetts.

a. He moved to New Bedford, Massachusetts as soon as he married Anna Murray.

b. As soon as he married Anna Murray, he moved to New Bedford, Massachusetts.

1. (after) He moved to New Bedford, Massachusetts. He started to give antislavery speeches, *after* ~~After~~

   a. *After he moved to give antislavery speeches,*
   b. *After he moved to new bedford, massachusetts*

2. (while) He was living in England. He continued to give antislavery speeches.

   a. *While he was living in england, he continued to give speeches*
   b. *while he continued to give antislavery speeches.*

3. (until) He stayed in England. He became legally free. *until*

   a. *Until he stayed stayed in england.*
   b. _____

4. (before) A group of his supporters bought his freedom from Hugh Auld for $710.96. He returned to the United States.

   a. _____
   b. _____

5. (when) He returned to the United States from England. He settled in Rochester, New York.

   a. _____
   b. _____

C. **Sentence Completion**   *Complete each sentence below by adding a complete clause that uses some information about Frederick Douglass from the list on page 47. Be sure to include any necessary punctuation in each sentence.*

   EXAMPLE: He moved to New Bedford, Massachusetts as soon as **he married Anna Murray.**

1. The name of Frederick Douglass' newspaper was *North Star* until
   1851

2. While Lincoln was president of the United States _____
   1860 civil war began

3. After Frederick Douglass wrote his second book *in*
   1859 or he went to english

4. The Civil War in the United States began before *he meet*
   with president

5. When Frederick Douglass moved to Rochester, New York, *he started to glares 'ndi'slcw*

6. Before the Civil War ended *A lot of People Died*

7. As the Civil War was taking place, *he return do the united stocte*

D. *Finding Sentence Problems*

Read the following about another runaway slave and abolitionist named Harriet Tubman. This story has some sentence problems. There are six frag-ments with subordinating conjunctions of time as well as one run-on sentence and one comma splice. Find all these mistakes and show how to correct them.

Editing Focus
Fragments, Run-ons,
Comma Splices

Harriet Tubman

Harriet Tubman was born a slave in Maryland around 1821. Because she was a slave, she could not learn to read or write, she spent her days working as a field hand. When Harriet was about 15 or 16 years old, her master threw a rock at her. As she tried to help another slave. For the rest of her life, she had seizures and blackouts from this injury. After this hap-pened, She also had visions and heard voices telling her to escape.

Harriet lived the life of a slave until she was 28 years old. At that time she decided to escape to the North. She used the North Star in the sky to help her find her way. While she was escaping, She went to Philadelphia she joined a group of people operating a secret escape system for slaves called the Underground Railroad. She worked as a "conductor" on the Underground Railroad and made dangerous trips back to the South. Whenever she made a trip to help more slaves, She planned the escapes for Saturday nights. This plan gave the people at least 36 hours to run. Before the angry owners could send out wanted posters for their slaves on Monday.

(continued on next page)

Harriet Tubman made approximately 19 dangerous trips back to the South in order to bring more than 300 slaves to freedom. She lived to be 92 years old. When she died, She was buried in Ohio. Many people remembered her as "the general" or the "Moses" of her people.

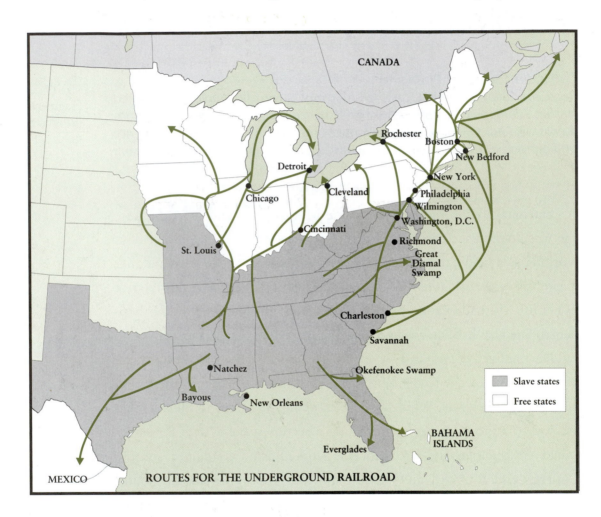

ROUTES FOR THE UNDERGROUND RAILROAD

Discussion/Writing

Answer these questions in writing or through discussion. Try to use a variety of subordinating conjunctions of time in your sentences.

1. Frederick Douglass became an abolitionist and gave speeches against slavery after he escaped. Why was it dangerous for him to do this? What things did he do to protect himself from slave catchers?

2. Why do you think Frederick Douglass' audiences could not believe that he had been a slave? What do you think was their view of a slave, and why didn't he fit that view? Do you think his decision to write the story of his life was a good one? Why or why not?

3. Each time Harriet Tubman helped more slaves to escape, she risked her life. Why do you think she returned to the South so many times? Why do you think people called her "the general" or the "Moses" of her people?

PART 4   WRITING ESSAYS (NARRATION)

The following background information will help you better understand the essay about Rosa Parks: After the Civil War many states passed laws known as "Jim Crow" laws. These laws segregated people in everyday life based on their skin color. One such law was about seating on public buses. In Montgomery, Alabama, Blacks had to pay their money to the driver, get off the bus, and then reboard through the back door to sit in the back. Sometimes the bus would drive away before Blacks who had paid got to the back entrance. If the white section was full and another white customer entered, Blacks had to give up their seats and move farther to the back. A black person was not even allowed to sit across the aisle from a white person.

Now read about Rosa Parks and then answer the questions after the essay.

Rosa Parks

Do you think one person's actions can make a difference? Some people say that each person must do what she or he thinks is right, and perhaps in the end each person *can* make a difference. One example of this can be found in the story of a woman named Rosa Parks. She was a black woman who grew up in Alabama and lived under many Jim Crow laws. On December 1, 1955, Rosa Parks became the "mother" of the civil rights movement when she was arrested because she would not give up her seat on a city bus to a white person.

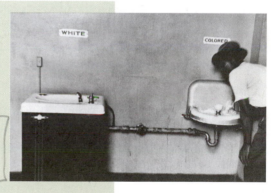

On that day Rosa was planning to take the bus home from work as usual, but this bus ride did not turn out to be typical. She had just finished working as a seamstress at a department store and then walked to the bus stop. As she first boarded the bus, she noticed that the driver was the same man who had sent her off his bus years earlier because she would not go around to the back door after she was already on the bus. She decided to get on anyway and sit down, but she did not sit at the very front of the bus. She took a seat next to a black man in the first row that "colored" people were allowed to sit in. At the next stop some white people got on the bus. After they filled up the white seats, one man was left standing. When the driver noticed him standing, he told Rosa and the others in her row to let the man have a seat. Three people stood up, but the driver saw that Rosa

was still sitting there. He asked if she would stand up, and she refused. Then he told her he would have her arrested, and Rosa told him he could do that. At that point the driver refused to move the bus any further, and several black people left the bus.

A few minutes later, two policemen got on the bus to take care of the situation. When the driver told them that Rosa would not stand up, the policemen walked over to her and asked her why she wouldn't get up. Rosa said she didn't think she should stand up and asked, "Why do you push us around?" One policeman answered, "I don't know, but the law is the law, and you are under arrest." As soon as he said that, Rosa stood up. Then one of the policemen picked up her purse while the other picked up her shopping bag, and the three of them left the bus together. The policemen had their squad car waiting near the bus. Finally, they took Rosa to the police station in the car.

Rosa's actions that day started a citywide boycott of the bus system by Blacks that lasted more than a year. This later resulted in the US Supreme Court decision against segregation on city buses. Sometimes when people tell this story, they say that Rosa did not give up her seat because she was tired, but she says, "No, the only tired I was, was tired of giving in."

Essay Discussion

Look back at the essay about Rosa Parks and answer these questions.

1. How many paragraphs are in the essay?   4

2. What do you think is the purpose of the first paragraph? Is there one sentence in the first paragraph that seems most important or that gives the main idea of the story? Where is that sentence in the paragraph? Put a line under that sentence.

3. What is the purpose of the two middle paragraphs? What information do those paragraphs give? Support each paragraph

4. What kind of information is in the last paragraph? How is that information different from the information in the two middle paragraphs?
  What she did to help segregation end how she was tired of it all.

Essay Organization

Look at the following diagrams of the organization of a paragraph and an essay. Do you see similarities and differences? What are they?

Organization of an
Essay (Narration),
Introductions,
Thesis Statements,
Time Words,
Quotations

PARAGRAPH

ESSAY

Topic Sentence

Support/Details
1.

2.

3.

Concluding
Sentence

Introductory Paragraph
(four or five sentences)
with Thesis Statement

Topic Sentence

Support/Details
1.
2.
3.

Body
Paragraphs

Topic Sentence

Support/Details
1.
2.
3.

Concluding Paragraph
(two or three sentences)

1. What is an essay?
   • An essay is a piece of writing that has at least three paragraphs.
     All of the paragraphs in an essay are related to the same topic.

2. What are the parts of an essay? What should an essay look like?
   An essay usually has a specific organization. It has three main parts:
   an introduction (or introductory paragraph), at least one body para-
   graph, and a conclusion (or concluding paragraph).
   • *Introduction:* The introductory paragraph has several sentences
     and gives the reader general information about the topic of the
     essay. The main idea is in one sentence called the *thesis statement.*
   • *Body Paragraph(s):* A body paragraph follows the paragraph
     organization discussed in Unit One. That is, a body paragraph
     begins with a topic sentence that has a topic and controlling idea.
     A body paragraph also has details to support the topic sentence.

However, a body paragraph in an essay may or may not have a concluding sentence.

- *Conclusion:* The concluding paragraph is more general than the body paragraphs. It may summarize the body paragraphs or may discuss results. It should be more than one sentence.

3. How is a paragraph similar to an essay?
   - Both paragraphs and essays have three main parts.
   - In both paragraphs and essays, the writer starts out with more general information in the first part, then gives specific information in the next part, and ends with more general information.
   - In a paragraph the writer provides the main idea in a sentence: the topic sentence. In an essay the writer provides the main idea in a sentence: the thesis statement.
   - In both a paragraph and an essay, the middle part contains facts, details, reasons, or examples as support. For a paragraph this support is provided in several sentences. For an essay, it is given in one or more paragraphs.

4. How is a paragraph different from an essay?
   - A paragraph is shorter than an essay. Since an essay is longer (and includes more information), the topic of an essay is usually more general than the topic of a paragraph.
   - A paragraph has one indentation at the beginning, and all of the sentences follow one another. An essay has several indentations, one for each paragraph.

Introductory Paragraphs

As you learned in Unit One, the topic sentence gives the reader the general idea of a paragraph. An essay should also begin with general information, but in the form of a small paragraph instead of just one sentence. This paragraph is called the *introductory paragraph* or *introduction.* The purpose of the introduction of an essay is to give the reader general or background information and to catch the reader's interest.

A very important sentence in the introduction of an essay is called the *thesis statement.* This sentence tells the reader more specifically what the essay will be about. The thesis statement provides the main idea of the essay, so the reader understands what to expect. Just like a topic sentence of a paragraph, a thesis statement should not be too general or too specific. The thesis statement should be the last sentence in the introductory paragraph.

Organization of the Introductory Paragraph

Introductory paragraphs usually begin with general information, become more specific in the middle, and end with a thesis statement. Look at the sentences from the introduction of the essay about Rosa Parks:

Do you think one person's actions can make a difference?

Some people say that each person must do what she or he thinks is right, and perhaps in the end each person *can* make a difference.

One example of this can be found in the story of Rosa Parks.

She was a black woman who grew up in Alabama and lived under many Jim Crow laws.

On December 1, 1955, Rosa Parks became the "mother" of the civil rights movement when she was arrested because she would not give up her seat on a city bus to a white person.

Practice: Introductions and Thesis Statements

A. *Each of the following introductions needs a thesis statement for an essay about a person's life. Read each introduction. Then choose the best thesis statement for the essay from the three sentences that follow the introduction. Circle the letter of your answer.*

1. After the Civil War life was difficult for many former slaves. They often worked hard on other people's farms but lived under harsh rules, in poverty, and without education. Former slaves Patsy and Samuel McLeod struggled to buy and run a farm as well as raise 17 children. Their 15th child, Mary, was able to go to school, and she saw education as a way for African Americans to improve their lives.

   a. Mary McLeod Bethune was born and raised in poverty, yet she succeeded in becoming an important educator and political activist.

   b. Mary McLeod Bethune was an important educator and political activist because she went to school at an early age.

   c. Mary McLeod Bethune loved school, so she studied hard.

2. People know baseball as one of the most popular sports in the United States, and children dream of becoming famous major league baseball stars. However, for years African-American children could only dream of playing in the separate Negro League because the major league was open to white ballplayers exclusively. In 1947 one African-American baseball player, Jackie Robinson, broke this color barrier and opened the way for other African-American baseball players to enter the major league.

a. Jackie Robinson became a Brooklyn Dodger in 1947, when he was 28 years old.

b. In 1962 Jackie Robinson became one of the first baseball players to enter the Baseball Hall of Fame.

c. From 1947 until 1962, when he retired from baseball, Jackie Robinson was a top baseball player and a symbol of hope to many African Americans.

3. During the second half of the 20th century, the struggle to change segregated conditions in the United States became known as the civil rights movement. This movement began in the mid-1950s with the Supreme Court's ban on segregation in public schools in 1954 and the bus boycott in Montgomery, Alabama after Rosa Park's arrest in 1955. One of the leaders of the Montgomery bus boycott was a young minister named Martin Luther King Jr., and through the 1950s and 1960s, he emerged as a peaceful leader of the civil rights movement.

a. Martin Luther King Jr. led the civil rights movement but died in 1968.

b. For over 20 years Martin Luther King Jr. promoted nonviolence as a way to make changes in a society.

c. Martin Luther King Jr. helped Rosa Parks become famous through the bus boycott in Montgomery, Alabama.

4. Sometimes an ordinary or unknown person can surprise people through his or her extraordinary actions. Before 1995 most people knew Oseola McCarty as an elderly African-American woman who had spent 75 years washing and ironing other people's clothes for a living. However, at age 87, Ms. McCarty surprised even her friends and family with an incredible gift of $150,000 in scholarship money to the University of Southern Mississippi. This donation was the largest gift that this university had ever received from an African American.

a. Oseola McCarty gave the money to the university because she was a very unselfish person.

b. The story of how Oseola McCarty saved so much money to share with others spans almost her entire lifetime of 91 years.

c. Oseola McCarty retired from her job in 1996 and lived to be 91 years old.

B. *The following are introductions for essays about the lives of some successful African Americans. The introductions are missing the first (most general) sentence and the thesis statement (the last sentence). Choose one of the two sentences below each paragraph to complete each blank line.*

EXAMPLE:
(b) **Do you think one person's actions can make a difference?**

Some people say that each person must do what s/he thinks is right, and perhaps in the end each person can make a difference. One example of this can be found in the story of a woman named Rosa Parks. Rosa was a black woman who had grown up in Alabama and lived under the rule of many Jim Crow laws. *(a) On December 1, 1955, Rosa Parks became the "mother of the civil rights movement" when she was arrested because she would not give up her seat on a city bus to a white person.*

    a. On December 1, 1955, Rosa Parks became the "mother of the civil rights movement" when she was arrested because she would not give up her seat on a city bus to a white person.

    b. Do you think one person's actions can make a difference?

1. __________

He spent much of his life fighting ignorance, hate, and viciousness and was especially successful through his work in the US legal system. As a young lawyer, he worked for poor, forgotten African Americans in Baltimore, Maryland. Later, he became chief counsel for an organization known as the NAACP (National Association for the Advancement of Colored People).

    a✓ _____

    a. In 1954 his work on a case called Brown v. Board of Education changed American education when he successfully challenged segregation in schools.

    b. Many people consider Thurgood Marshall a valiant warrior because he was one of the greatest fighters for justice this country has ever seen.

2. _*a✓*_____

In addition to all of these achievements, Oprah Winfrey has influenced millions of viewers in the United States and over 100 countries worldwide with her entertaining and thought-provoking shows and programs to help the less fortunate. Where does such ability and talent for success come from?

     _____

    a. Few people have achieved the kind of success that includes hosting an award winning talk show, owning a film and television production company, and demonstrating abilities as an accomplished actress.

    b. The foundation for Oprah Winfrey's success probably began during the first six years of her life when she lived with her grandmother on a farm in Mississippi.

3. _____

However, very few of therse girls have grown up to become women who can both tell their stories and help others as Maya Angelou has. Born in St. Louis, raised in rural segregated Arkansas, and then moving between those cities and San Francisco, Maya Angelou experienced tragic and difficult circumstances that shaped her outlook on life.

    a✓ _____

    a. The story of how Maya Angelou has become internationally known as a writer and poet for her works of pain and hope is linked to those experiences.

    b. There are many stories of young Black girls who have lived difficult lives and grown up with much pain.

Narration and Organization of Narrative Essays

Narration is telling a story about events or actions. The first reading in this unit is a narrative about the life of Frederick Douglass during his years as a slave. The second reading is a shorter narrative about the first few years after he escaped from slavery. The first book Frederick Douglass wrote was about his life as a slave and was called *Narrative of the Life of Frederick Douglass, An American Slave*. The story of Rosa Parks is an example of a narrative essay, and it tells the events of one important day in her life. It also follows the organization of an essay described earlier on page 53.

   Look at the following blank organization chart for an essay. Fill in the parts that are labeled. Use information from the narrative essay on Rosa Parks (pages 51–52). You do not have to write whole sentences for the support. Follow the example on the chart.

INTRODUCTION

Thesis statement: Do you think one person auctine can make dessrences

---

BODY PARAGRAPH 1

Topic sentence: On that Day ... be typical

Details/Support

finished work and walked to the bus stop

BODY PARAGRAPH 2

Topic sentence: A few minute later ... of the sutction

Details/Support

when the driver told them ---- You are under arrest

CONCLUSION

this leader resulted ---- was tired of giving in

Practice: Narrative Essays

Below are the thesis statements from the introductions about successful African Americans on pages 55–57. The narrative essay developed from each thesis statement will describe or discuss some part of the life of one of these people. Read each thesis statement. Then state what story or part of the life of this person you expect to read about in the body paragraphs of the narrative essay.

EXAMPLE: **Rosa Parks** Thesis statement: On December 1, 1955, Rosa Parks became the "mother" of the civil rights movement when she was arrested because she would not give up her seat on a city bus to a white person.

From this thesis statement, I expect to read about how or why she became the "mother" of the civil rights movement. I expect to find the story about what happened on the bus in this essay. I will learn what happened on that particular day in Rosa Parks' life.

Mary McLeod Bethune Thesis statement: Mary McLeod Bethune was born and raised in poverty, yet she succeeded in becoming an important educator and political activist.

From the thesis statement, We

_____

Jackie Robinson Thesis statement: From 1947 until 1962, when he retired from baseball, Jackie Robinson was a top baseball player and a symbol of hope to many African Americans.

_____

_____

Martin Luther King Jr. Thesis statement: For over 20 years Martin Luther King Jr. promoted nonviolence as a way to make changes in a society.

_____

_____

Oseola McCarty Thesis statement: The story of how Oseola McCarty saved so much money to share with others spans almost her entire lifetime of 91 years.

_____

_____

Thurgood Marshall Thesis statement: In 1954 his work on a legal case called *Brown v. Board of Education* changed American education when he successfully challenged segregation in schools.

_____

_____

Oprah Winfrey Thesis statement: The foundation for Oprah Winfrey's success probably began during the first six years of her life, when she lived with her grandmother on a farm in Mississippi.

_____

_____

Maya Angelou Thesis statement: The story of how Maya Angelou has become internationally known as a writer and a poet for her works on pain and hope is linked to those experiences.

_____

_____

Time Words

Often a narrative essay tells a story in _chronological order_ by describing the events in order of time. In Part 3 of this unit, you learned how to use subordinating conjunctions of time (_when, while, as, after, before,_ etc.). In a narrative essay you may use other time words. These words help the reader understand the _chronology_ (time sequence) of the story.

Here are some examples of words of chronology:

first	_second_	_then_	_finally_
at first	_later_	_next_	_at last_

These words are often found at the beginning of a sentence although sometimes you might see them in other parts of a sentence.

Practice: Time Words
Look back at the essay about Rosa Parks (pages 51–52) and do two things:

1. _Find the subordinating conjunctions of time and put a line under each one._

2. _Find other time words (words of chronology) and circle each one._

Quotations

Sometimes when you write a narrative essay, you may want to use quotations. _Quotations_ are the exact words that a speaker uses. When you write sentences that contain quotations, you must use specific punctuation: Quotation marks (" ") are placed just before the first word in the quotation and just after the last word of the quotation. The first word of the quotation should begin with a capital letter. Before the quotation begins, include a comma.

EXAMPLE: One policeman answered, "I don't know, but the law is the law, and you are under arrest."

If a quotation is at the beginning of a sentence, you add a comma at the end of the quotation.

EXAMPLE: "I am getting off the bus," said one passenger.

The end punctuation of the quotation (for example, a comma, period, or question mark) is placed just before (to the left of) the end quotation mark.

As a general rule, punctuation such as commas, periods, and quotation marks are found to the left of a quotation mark.

Practice: Quotations
Put the correct punctuation, including quotation marks, commas, periods, and question marks in each of the following sentences. Also, add capital letters where necessary.

EXAMPLE: Rosa Parks said, "I did not get on the bus to get arrested."

1. Frederick Douglass' master said you must go back to Thomas Covey

2. Someone in Frederick Douglass' audience asked you are such a good speaker so how can we believe you were a slave

3. I have come to take you north to freedom said Harriet Tubman to her parents

Discussion/Writing

Answer these questions in writing or through discussion. Try to use a variety of subordinating conjunctions of time in your sentences.

1. Do you think Rosa Parks was brave when she refused to give up her seat? Why or why not? Did she take a risk in doing this? (Explain your answer.)

2. What do you think other people on the bus with Rosa Parks were thinking? Why did some black people get off the bus? Do you think their decision to get off the bus was a good one? What might you do in the same situation?

3. What do you think Rosa meant by the following statement? "No, the only tired I was, was tired of giving in."

4. The introductions on pages 55–57 introduced you to several successful or well-known African Americans. Use the information you learned in several of those introductions to answer the following questions.
   a. When Thurgood Marshall became a lawyer, he decided to help poor people with legal matters. Why do you think he made that decision?
   b. What kind of life do you think Oseola McCarty had? How do you think she was able to save all that money? Why do you think she decided to save the money and give it away?
   c. What kind of childhood do you think Mary McLeod Bethune had? Why do you think she decided that education was so important?

d. Do you think Jackie Robinson took a risk joining an all-white team? How do you think he felt as the only nonwhite person in a large group such as a baseball league? How do you think you might feel in that situation?

Summary Writing

For an explanation of summary writing and practice of this skill, read pages 212–217 in the Appendix. Follow the instructions. Be sure to use subordinating conjunctions of time in your sentences in these summaries.

1. Summarize the first two paragraphs of the reading about the early life of Frederick Douglass on pages 37–39. Your summary should be one paragraph of no more than five sentences.

2. Summarize the short reading about Harriet Tubman on page 49 in four or five sentences.

3. Summarize the entire essay about Rose Parks on pages 51–52 by writing one or two sentences about each paragraph.

Writing Assignment

A. Picking the Topic

You are going to write a three- or four-paragraph narrative essay for your final writing assignment for this unit. Choose one of the following topics:

1. Have you ever had to overcome a problem or difficult situation at some time in your life? What was the problem? What did you do to overcome it or take care of it? Write the story of this situation or time in your life.

2. Everyone makes decisions at one time or another. What was one important decision you had to make? What did you do to make this decision? Write the story of a time you had to make an important or difficult decision.

3. Was there a time when you had to do something dangerous or take a risk? What was the situation, and what was the danger or risk? What did you do in this situation? Write the story of this time you did something dangerous or took a risk.

B. Understanding the Assignment/Answering the Question

Before you start to write, make sure that you understand the assignment. Your essay must answer the question and should not discuss other things. You should also make sure that your essay is in the form of a story (narrative) about something that happened in your life. This story must be about

solving a problem, making an important decision, or taking a risk. Look at the following ideas for essays on the three possible topics. Decide which ones fit the assignment and which ones do not. Cross out the ideas that you think will not answer the questions.

Topic 1: an essay that
- tells the story of how you solved a problem you had in school or on a job
- tells a story about how a problem developed in your life
- gives reasons why you had a specific problem
- tells the story of two problems you had

Topic 2: an essay that
- explains the reasons you decided to go to college
- tells the story of how you made the decision to study at this school
- tells what your parents and friends thought of your decision to go to college
- tells the story of how you decided to go to college

Topic 3: an essay that
- tells the story of how you took a risk when you moved to a new place
- explains the reasons why you took the risk of moving to a new place
- tells the story of a time you risked your safety to do something important to you
- tells the story of something you did that was interesting but not very dangerous

Following the Steps in the Writing Process

Before You Write

- **Step One: Generating Ideas and Brainstorming**
  a. Use the timeline below to help you remember some important times in your life.
     - When did you solve a difficult problem?
     - When did you make an important decision?
     - When did you take a risk?
     - When did you do something dangerous?

     Put those dates on this timeline and label each date.

     ┤───├

     date of birth   present

  b. What kind of support can you provide for a narrative essay about each date on your timeline? Using a list or a clustering diagram, write your ideas in one or more of the spaces below. Don't worry about the organization of your ideas.

Solved a Difficult Problem
Yes, I have, the Problem was that I once plagerized a hole essay by an accident. me and my Parents had to deal with it and went throw a hole proccess to finish it

Made an Important Decision

Took a Risk or Did Something Dangerous

c. Choose *one* of your lists or clustering diagrams for your essay. Then check the details to make sure that there are enough and they are all relevant.

■ *Step Two: Organizing Ideas and Planning*
To begin organizing your ideas, think about the three parts of an essay.

INTRODUCTION WITH THESIS STATEMENT
a. What is the problem, decision, or risk you are going to write about? Write a thesis statement about it.

____when I ploygorized it Almost got my____

____self kicked out by an accident____

b. Write your thesis statement on the organization chart for a narrative essay on page 68 at the end of this unit.

BODY PARAGRAPHS
Topic Sentences
Do you need one body paragraph or two body paragraphs to tell your story?

a. If you are going to write one body paragraph, think of a topic sentence for this paragraph. What is the topic? What is the controlling idea?

    Topic: _____

    Controlling idea: _____

    Write your topic sentence on the chart on page 68.

b. If you are going to write two body paragraphs, what are the two parts of your story?

    1. _____

    2. _____

    Think of a topic sentence for the first body paragraph. What is the topic? What is the controlling idea?

    Topic: _____

    Controlling idea: _____

    Write your topic sentence on the chart on page 68.
    Think of a topic sentence for the second paragraph. What is the topic? What is the controlling idea?

    Topic: _____

    Controlling idea: _____

    Write your topic sentence on the chart on page 68.

Support

a. Think about exactly what happened during the time you are going to talk about, including the time order.

b. Describe how this story happened using notes. Write these notes about the details of the story on the chart on page 68. Be sure that all of the details are related to your topic sentence(s) and thesis statement and that you have enough support for each body paragraph.

CONCLUDING PARAGRAPH
Write some ideas for a concluding paragraph on the chart on page 68. Think about giving a short summary of what happened or telling about some results of the decision you made or the risk you took.

■ ***Step Three: Getting Feedback***
Your teacher may ask you to work with a partner and complete a peer review of your chart. Use the peer review sheet on page 230 in the Appendix for this feedback.

When You Write

■ ***Step Four: Writing the First Draft (Rough Draft)***
Write the first draft of your narrative essay. Be sure to write your essay as a story and tell this story as it happened. Do the following when you write the essay:

- Use some words of chronology (for example, *first, then, next, finally*).
- Include both coordinating conjunctions and subordinating conjunctions of time in some of your sentences. Use at least three of each kind of conjunction.
- Use at least one quotation in your story.
- Use at least two or three of the new vocabulary words you learned in this unit.

After You Write

Check Your Work
After you finish writing the first draft and before you show it to anyone for feedback or revision, read your paragraph again. Check your work for the following:

☐ This essay tells the story of a time I made an important decision, solved a problem, or took a risk.

☐ This essay has three main parts: introduction, body, and conclusion.

☐ The introductory paragraph is general and has several sentences. It ends with a thesis statement.

☐ This essay has one or two body paragraphs that tell the story as it happened.

☐ Each body paragraph has a topic sentence.

☐ The body paragraphs are related to the thesis statement.

☐ I have several supporting sentences with enough details or examples in my body paragraphs.

☐ In each of my body paragraphs, my supporting sentences relate to the topic sentence.

☐ Some sentences in this essay include coordinating or subordinating conjunctions.

☐ I looked for run-ons, comma splices, or fragments and corrected them.

☐ I checked the punctuation of any quotations I included in the essay.

☐ I used some of the vocabulary from this unit in the essay.

Getting Feedback

Your teacher will decide the type of feedback you will receive for the first draft. It may be peer review, teacher review, or both. For peer review, use the sheet on page 231 in the Appendix.

Step Five: Revising

After you receive feedback, revise the organization of your essay or any sentences in it, if necessary. You may want to change your thesis statement, your topic sentences, or parts of your introduction or concluding paragraph. You may want to add, take out, or change the order of some supporting sentences. Your teacher may want you to get feedback again after you revise.

Step Six: Editing

Make any necessary changes in grammar, spelling, punctuation, and capitalization. Your teacher may want you to have feedback after editing as well.

Step Seven: Preparing the Final Draft

Prepare your final draft to be handed in to the teacher.

Organizing Your Ideas for Writing a Narrative Essay

TITLE: _____

INTRODUCTION

Thesis statement: _____

_____

BODY PARAGRAPH 1

Topic sentence: _____

_____

Details/Support

_____

_____

_____

_____

_____

_____

_____

BODY PARAGRAPH 2

Topic sentence: _____

_____

Details/Support

_____

_____

_____

_____

_____

_____

_____

CONCLUSION

_____

_____

_____

Content Area: Health

Readings: Health and Wellness
Folk Medicine
Stress and Stress Management

Short Readings: Nature's Pharmacy
Herbal Medicines

Sentence-Combining Focus: Transitions

Editing Focus: Fragments; Run-ons; Comma Splices

Writing Focus: Essay Writing (Process); Thesis Statements;
Concluding Paragraphs

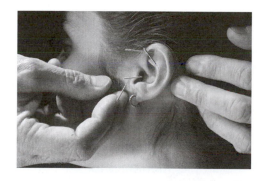

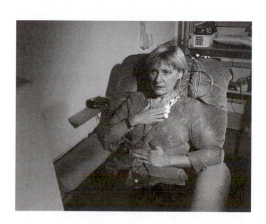

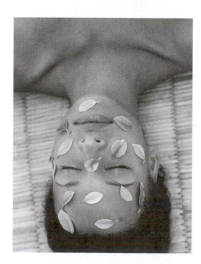

PART 1   UNIT PREVIEW

Preview Activity: Self-Inventory— Healthful Lifestyle

There are five sections to this inventory.

- *Circle the number next to the answer that best describes your behavior.*
- *Add the numbers you circled in each section to get your score. The highest score for each section is 10.*

A. Cigarette Smoking

If you never smoke cigarettes, write a score of 10 for this section.

1. I avoid smoking cigarettes.

   almost always (2)   sometimes (1)   almost never (0)

2. I smoke only cigarettes low in tar and nicotine.

   almost always (2)   sometimes (1)   almost never (0)

Cigarette Smoking Score: ___2___

B. Alcohol and Drugs

1. I avoid drinking alcoholic beverages, or I have no more than one or two drinks a day.

   almost always (4)   sometimes (1)   almost never (0)

2. I avoid using alcohol or other drugs (especially illegal drugs) as a way of handling stress or problems in my life.

   almost always (2)   sometimes (1)   almost never (0)

3. I am careful not to drink alcohol when taking certain medicines (for example, medicines for pain or allergy).

   almost always (2)   sometimes (1)   almost never (0)

4. I read and follow the label directions when I use prescribed and over-the-counter drugs.

   almost always (2)   sometimes (1)   almost never (0)

Alcohol and Drugs Score: ___10___

C. Eating Habits

1. I eat a variety of foods every day, such as fruits, vegetables, breads, cereals, lean meats, and dairy products.

   almost always (4)   sometimes (1)   almost never (0)

2. I limit the amount of fat I eat (for example, fat in meat, eggs, and butter).

   almost always (2)   sometimes (1)   almost never (0)

3. I limit the amount of salt I eat.

almost always (2)   sometimes (1)   almost never (0)

4. I avoid eating too much sugar.

almost always (2)   sometimes (1)   almost never (0)

Eating Habits Score: _____

D. Exercise/Fitness

1. I stay at a desired weight and avoid becoming overweight or under-weight.

almost always (3)   sometimes (1)   almost never (0)

2. I do vigorous exercises for 15 to 30 minutes at least three times a week.

almost always (3)   sometimes (1)   almost never (0)

3. I do exercises that help my muscle tone for at least 15 to 30 minutes at least three times a week.

almost always (2)   sometimes (1)   almost never (0)

4. I use part of my leisure time participating in activities that increase my level of fitness.

almost always (2)   sometimes (1)   almost never (0)

Exercise/Fitness Score: _____

E. Stress Management

1. I have a job (including school) or do other work that I enjoy.

almost always (2)   sometimes (1)   almost never (0)

2. I find it easy to relax and express my feelings freely.

almost always (2)   sometimes (1)   almost never (0)

3. I recognize and prepare for events and situations that will probably be stressful for me.

almost always (2)   sometimes (1)   almost never (0)

4. I have people I can talk to about personal things. I can call these people for help if I need it.

almost always (2)   sometimes (1)   almost never (0)

5. I participate in group activities or hobbies that I enjoy.

almost always (2)   sometimes (1)   almost never (0)

Stress Management Score: ___6___

To find out what your scores mean, turn the page.

What your scores mean to YOU. (Be sure to score each section separately.)

Scores of 9–10: Excellent! You are practicing healthful habits. Keep up the good work.

Scores of 6–8: Your health practices are good, but there is room for improvement. Even small changes can improve your health.

Scores of 3–5: Your health risks are higher than they should be. You should try to change some of your behavior.

Scores of 0–2: You are taking serious and unnecessary risks with your health.

Quickwrite

Write for five minutes about the following topic. Do not worry about grammar, spelling, or punctuation. Just write whatever comes into your mind about the topic.

- When you are sick, do you usually go to a doctor, or do you try to get better by yourself? Why?

PART 2   READING AND VOCABULARY

Reading

Health and Wellness

Read the following on health and wellness. Then answer the questions that follow the reading.

Defining Health and Wellness

Health is the **achievement** of physical, mental, social, and spiritual fitness that allows someone to live life to the fullest. The World Health Organization (WHO) of the United Nations defines *health* as "a state of complete mental, physical, and social well-being and not merely the absence of disease or **infirmity.**" Wellness is the best functioning that an individual can achieve at the present time within **genetic** limits and environmental conditions.

Areas of Health and Wellness

Physical Well-Being When you think of a physically fit person, what do you **envision**? Physical well-being involves having the energy to complete necessary daily tasks as well as enough extra for physically active play and for emergencies if necessary.

Mental Well-Being We can all agree that health is more than being physically fit. A healthy mind (including the emotions and intellect) is also **vital** for high-level functioning. Mental well-being involves the entire person and includes a positive body self-image, a constructive personal philosophy of living, and supportive social relationships. In addition, it involves satisfying work, enjoyable and worthwhile leisure activities, a happy family life, good personal relationships, and love.

Social Well-Being   Human beings are social animals. We live together, and we depend on each other for meeting our basic needs. People who have strong social support systems are more likely to be in good health. A socially healthy person has a connected group of family members, friends, and others who can help in times of need and who are continually available to learn from. Social support is a two-way street because we must give similar support to those around us.

Spiritual Well-Being   The spiritual area is that part of ourselves that looks for personal meaning in life. It is not **synonymous** with religion, but for many people this meaning is found through religion. Our spiritual aspect helps us define what the good life is and concerns the establishment of future **goals**. Spiritual well-being is a basic and unifying part of wellness.

Holistic Health

Continued growth and development are **crucial** to the achievement of high-level wellness and so is the integration of the four areas of health. The integrated functioning of the total self is called *holistic health*. *Holistic* means considering the whole person in his or her environment, not just the separate parts, each operating by itself. Each person is a total functioning unit, with the whole greater than its parts.

Instead of concentrating only on disease processes and treatment, holistic medicine gives importance to prevention of disease and promotion of good health. The philosophy of holistic **practitioners** is not to treat diseases that happen to exist in people but to treat people who happen to have a disease. Doctors practicing holistic medicine consider the social and physical environments in which their patients live as factors affecting the disease process and the **prescribed** treatment method.

Factors Affecting Health and Wellness

What affects the level of health and wellness you will achieve? We can put the important factors of health into categories of elements that interact. Four of these categories are human biology, environment, lifestyle, and healthcare organizations.

Human Biology   This category has to do with an individual's **inherited** abilities, the aging process, and the **organic** systems of the body. People possess a genetically-based range of abilities that present the possibility of illness as well as high-level wellness.

Environment   The environment's effect on our health is much more global and less local today than it was in the past. For example, the **radiation** given off from the 1986 nuclear energy plant disaster at Chernobyl in the Ukraine affected the health of people in countries thousands of miles away. Keeping a safe and secure **ecosystem** involves controlling environmental factors to **ensure** clean air, water and food supplies, safe and **sanitary** waste systems, avoidance of noise pollution, and safe public transportation and social surroundings.

Lifestyle Every minute of every day, we make decisions to act or not act in ways that influence our well-being. The combination of these behaviors makes up what we call our lifestyle. Personal health habits have become more important to **longevity** and quality of life as we have overcome many **communicable** diseases and are increasingly **threatened** with **chronic** diseases.

Health Care Organizations The provision of health care by doctors, nurses, clinics, and hospitals is taken for granted by some people in the United States, Canada, and other countries (especially in the developed world). However, even in those countries, unemployed and poor people often find medical care to be unavailable or unaffordable. A healthcare system that answers the needs of all the people is necessary for achieving good health. In addition, economic and political factors play an important part in health care systems because they determine how much money will be provided for health care and where it will go.

Public Health

People in public health work toward supporting and improving the health of communities and populations. People in this field respond to community problems using basic ideas about prevention of disease and promotion of well-being. Public health workers are involved in many areas such as delivery of healthcare services, study of communicable diseases, and improvement of the environment and nutrition. The field of public health is also concerned with other community-wide issues, such as children's health, women's health, and housing (poor housing conditions, homelessness, etc.).

The ideas of public health can be applied to both the national and international levels. The health of nations and the health of the world are not separate concerns. Both are directly and indirectly influenced by world economies, politics, cultural factors, biological forces, ethical and moral decisions, geographical considerations, and historical **perspectives.** In addition, the health of the people of the world is dependent on both the availability of money and resources and the equal distribution of these resources.

Comprehension Check

*Decide if the following statements are true or false based on the reading. Write **T** for "True" or **F** for "False" next to the number of each sentence. The first one has been done as an example*

___F___ 1. Physical and mental factors are the only things we should think about when we think about our health.

F _____ 2. In general, this reading is about the World Health Organization and public health.

T _____ 3. Wellness exists when someone is functioning at a high level at the present time even though there may be some negative factors in the environment or in the person's family history.

F _____ 4. If a person has social well-being in addition to physical and mental well-being, the person will surely have good health.

T _____ 5. The combination of physical, mental, social, and spiritual areas of wellness is known as holistic health.

F _____ 6. People who treat health problems holistically believe that you should solve each problem separately when it happens.

F _____ 7. Only two things affect a person's health: lifestyle and environment.

F _____ 8. A good health care system is not really necessary for people to have good health.

T _____ 9. Public health workers try to work toward the good health of communities and populations in general.

_____ 10. Both nationally and internationally, public health is dependent on many things, including economics, politics, and culture.

Vocabulary Study

A. Meanings

Choose a synonym from the following list for each of the underlined vocabulary words in the sentences. Write the letter of the synonym on the line next to the number of the sentence. The first one has been done as an example.

a. necessary, essential
b. ordered, advised, suggested
c. view, understanding of
d. illness, weakness
e. aims, objectives
f. very important, critical
g. biological, related to life
h. length of life, great age
i. long-lasting, persistent
j. ~~accomplishments, successful conclusions~~
k. hereditary, inherited, related to genes
l. get from one's parents, receive through heredity
m. clean, germ-free
n. transmittable, able to spread from person to person
o. living things and their environment
p. gave warning, indicated something unpleasant was coming

___j___ 1. We have made many <u>achievements</u> in medicine to cure diseases, but we still cannot cure some, such as cancer and AIDS.

___a___ 2. Some people continue to lead very active and productive lives even though they have an <u>infirmity</u>.

___j___ 3. The colors of our eyes and hair are <u>genetic</u>.

___o___ 4. When I went to the emergency room last night, the nurse checked my <u>vital</u> signs, such as my temperature and blood pressure.

___f___ 5. Scientists are busy working toward many <u>goals</u> in medicine, such as finding cures for some deadly diseases.

___e___ 6. Everyone says it is <u>crucial</u> to exercise as well as diet when you are trying to lose weight.

___n___ 7. The doctor <u>prescribed</u> a new kind of medicine for my problem.

___d___ 8. Doctors believe that we <u>inherit</u> many things from our parents and grandparents, even the tendency to get certain diseases.

___g___ 9. Sometimes people suffer from mental problems that are <u>organic</u>.

___c___ 10. Today we must be very careful about pollution and other environmental problems because they hurt our <u>ecosystem</u>.

___j___ 11. When you cook, you should make sure you keep the kitchen <u>sanitary</u>, so you do not spread germs or illness.

___h___ 12. Some people live to be older than 100 years, but nobody knows why they have such <u>longevity</u>.

___d___ 13. Colds and the flu are <u>communicable</u> illnesses, so you should be careful to stay away from people who have them.

___m___ 14. When the health department found that the hospital was not always clean, they <u>threatened</u> to close it.

___k___ 15. Some people have <u>chronic</u> health problems, such as back pain, but they live with these problems as best they can.

___l___ 16. Sometimes it may be important to know a person's <u>perspective</u> on a topic before you start a serious discussion about it.

B. Vocabulary in Context

Using your knowledge of vocabulary in context, try to guess the meanings of the words in bold type in these sentences from the reading.

1. When you think of a physically fit person, what do you **envision**?
2. It is not **synonymous** with religion, but for many people this meaning is found through religion.
3. The philosophy of holistic **practitioners** is not to treat diseases that happen to exist in people but to treat people who happen to have a disease.

4. For example, the **radiation** given off from the 1986 nuclear energy plant disaster at Chernobyl in the Ukraine affected the health of people in countries thousands of miles away.
5. Keeping a safe and secure ecosystem involves controlling environmental factors to **ensure** clean air, water and food supplies, safe and sanitary waste systems, avoidance of noise pollution, and safe public transportation and social surroundings.

Discussion/Writing

Answer these questions in writing or through discussion.

1. Do you agree with the definitions of *health* given in the first paragraph of the reading? Why or why not?

2. The reading talks about four different types of well-being: physical, mental, social, and spiritual. Do you feel they are equally important? If not, which is more important to you? Why?

3. Is holistic medicine popular in your culture? Have you ever gone to a holistic practitioner for a health problem? If so, what were the results?

4. The reading discusses four general factors affecting health: human biology, environment, lifestyle, and health care organization. What effect do these factors have on (a) your personal health and (b) the health of people in the area where you live?

PART 3   [WRITING SENTENCES WITH TRANSITIONS]

Read the following about traditional healers and folk medicine. Answer the questions that follow.

Reading
Folk Medicine

[1]More than ever before, people in the United States are showing an interest in using herbs and other plant preparations for treating illnesses and injuries. [2]Some people consider this "folk medicine" to be a healing method used mostly by the poor and/or uneducated. [3]The truth is that all of us have used some form of folk medicine at one time or another. [4]This kind of medicine is often called a "home remedy" or a "mother's (or grandmother's) cure," and many people have tried it; for example, many people use teas, soups, or herbal remedies when they are sick. [5]In addition, these remedies may help with a wide variety of illnesses and conditions, ranging from cures for the common cold to cures for exhaustion.

[6]Personal beliefs, often related to social and ethnic backgrounds, form the basis for folk medicine. [7]These folk remedies are usually passed along from generation to generation by word of mouth. [8]The reasons for the use of these remedies vary. [9]For example, for some people it is not necessary to consult a doctor for treatment of a minor illness or injury. [10]Other people

find the costs of medical care and prescription drugs too expensive, or they may not have access to medical care at all for economic or other reasons. [11]Still others like to feel that they are in control of their lives, so they try to take care of themselves. [12]Some people are concerned about the side effects of many medications; in addition, they may have a distrust of the traditional (conventional) healthcare system.

[13]There are many different forms of folk medicine. [14]The very strong ties to nationalities, backgrounds, and heritage create forms of folk medicine that are very clearly identified from area to area. [15]Furthermore, many of these remedies have been in existence for thousands of years and may well have physical benefits.

Questions

1. a. Look at sentences 5 and 12. Where do you find the words *in addition* in these two sentences? What punctuation do you find with the words *in addition* in each sentence?
   b. Look at sentence 12 again. How many clauses do you see? What is the signal putting these clauses together?
2. a. Look at sentences 4 and 9. Where do you find the words *for example* in these two sentences? What punctuation do you find with these words?
   b. Look at sentence 4 again. How many clauses do you see? Think about the signals (connectors) discussed in Unit One (coordinating conjunctions) and in Unit Two (subordinating conjunctions of time).

Explanation: Linking Transitions

Sentence-Combining Focus

Transitions

1. You have already learned about two kinds of signals/connectors that join clauses together. In this unit, you will learn about another kind of connector called *linking transitions*. (NOTE: In some books you may see these words called *conjunctive adverbs*.)
2. Linking transitions are words or expressions that connect independent (main) clauses. They are another kind of coordinator. (You learned about coordinating conjunctions in Unit One.)
3. When you use a linking transition to put independent clauses together, you must include a semicolon and a comma.

   EXAMPLE:
   Some people are concerned about the side effects of many
         independent clause
   medications; **in addition**, they may have a distrust of the
         linking transition   *independent clause*
   traditional healthcare system.

4. The following chart shows how to use linking transitions and gives examples of some that signal additional information, time, result, example, and summary.

Sentence Combining with Linking Transitions

Position in Sentence			

Middle

clause	transition	clause

Punctuation: Semicolon and comma

clause ;	transition ,	clause

EXAMPLE: Some people use herbal medicines; for example, they drink special teas.

MORE INFORMATION:	in addition
	also
	furthermore
	moreover
TIME:	then
RESULT:	therefore
	thus
	as a result
	consequently
EXAMPLE:	for example
	for instance
SUMMARY:	in other words

5. When you use any of these words or expressions to link clauses, be sure you have a complete clause (subject-verb combination) before *and* after the linking transition.

CORRECT: Many people use a mother's or grandmother's cure for
                 s   v
a cold; for example, they might eat chicken soup.
    linking transition   s   v

Do *not* use a semicolon if you do not have a complete clause after the linking transition.

INCORRECT: Many people use a mother's or grandmother's cure
                       s   v
for a cold; for example, chicken soup.

In this case, *chicken soup* is not a complete clause, so a comma before the words *for example* is all that is necessary. A semicolon is not necessary.

CORRECT: Many people use a mother's or grandmother's cure for a cold, **for example**, chicken soup.

Practice: Linking Transitions

Combine each pair of sentences below into one sentence, using the linking transition given in parentheses. Be sure to include the correct punctuation.

EXAMPLE: (also) Some people worry about the side effects of medicine. They have a distrust of traditional healthcare.

Some people worry about the side effects of medicine; also, they have a distrust of traditional healthcare.

1. (in addition) Many people have an interest in using folk remedies. The number of people using such cures is increasing.

_____

_____

2. (for example) Some people use special teas to help them sleep. They may drink herbal teas before they go to bed.

_____

_____

3. (furthermore) There are many kinds of folk medicine. These different kinds usually vary from culture to culture.

_____

_____

4. (for instance) People often learn folk remedies from someone in their family. Mothers and grandmothers may pass along this information.

_____

_____

5. (then) Children learn about folk remedies from their parents and grandparents. They teach their own children these same remedies.

_____

_____

Explanation: Introductory Transitions

1. Sometimes you will find a *transition* at the beginning of a sentence. This kind of transition does not link clauses. It is an *introductory transition*.

EXAMPLE: **In addition**, these remedies may help with a wide variety of illnesses and conditions.

2. You have seen examples of introductory transitions in both Unit One and Unit Two. In Unit One some (*in short, finally, therefore,* etc.) were used in concluding sentences, and in Unit Two some (*first, next, then,* etc.) were used to show time order. Introductory transitions are found at the beginning of a sentence and are usually followed by a comma.

3. The following chart shows the two kinds of transitions. Notice that the same words and expressions can sometimes be used as either introductory transitions or linking transitions. Other words or expressions are usually used only as introductory transitions. Which words on the chart are usually used only as introductory transitions?

Introductory Transitions	Linking Transitions (sentence combining)
These words or expressions often appear at the beginning of a sentence with a comma.	These words or expressions join two clauses and appear in the middle of a sentence. They require a semicolon and a comma.
EXAMPLES: **First**, you might try herbal medicine. **Next**, you should go to the doctor. **In addition**, you should rest.	EXAMPLES: You might try herbal medicine; **then**, you should call the doctor. You should take some medicine; **in addition**, you should rest.
MORE INFORMATION: in addition also furthermore moreover	MORE INFORMATION: in addition also furthermore moreover
TIME: first, second, third (etc.) later finally last next then	TIME: then
CONCLUSION: in conclusion finally	
EXAMPLE: for example for instance	EXAMPLE: for example for instance
RESULT: therefore thus as a result consequently	RESULT: therefore thus as a result consequently
SUMMARY: in sum in short in summary in other words	SUMMARY: in other words

4. Linking and introductory transitions are important in writing because they make a clear connection or provide a smooth jump from one idea to another (or sometimes from one paragraph to another). You should try to use both kinds of transitions in your writing to make these smooth connections.

Practice: Transitions

Rewrite each pair of sentences using the transition given in parentheses. Write the sentences in two ways:

a. *Rewrite the sentences as two separate sentences using the word or expression in parentheses as an introductory transition at the beginning of the second sentence.*

b. *Combine the two sentences into one longer sentence using the expression given in parentheses as a linking transition.*

Be sure to use the correct punctuation in all of the sentences you write.

EXAMPLE: (in addition) A healthy person has more than just physical health. The person has mental, social, and spiritual well-being.
   a. A healthy person has more than just physical health. In addition, this person has mental, social, and spiritual well-being.
   b. A healthy person has more than just physical health; in addition, this person has mental, social, and spiritual well-being.

1. (therefore) Some aspects of your health can depend on inherited problems. It is a good idea to know about your family's health history. *therefore* *; therefore,*

   a. _____

   b. _____

2. (for instance) A disaster to the environment can cause a problem for an ecosystem. An oil spill in the ocean will affect the health of many living things in the area.

   a. _____

   b. _____

3. (also) Holistic health practitioners consider a patient's medical problem. They consider other things such as the patient's social and physical environment.

   a. _____

   b. _____

4. (then) People in public health study the situation of homeless people. They might make recommendations about improving the health of those people.

   a. _____

   b. _____

5. (moreover) The health of people all over the world depends on economics. The equal distribution of money and other resources is important for ensuring good health for more people.

a. _____

b. _____

Explanation: Problems Using Transitions

1. **Fragments** Be careful not to write fragments when you use transitions. Remember, a fragment is an incomplete sentence. When you use a transition at the beginning of a sentence, you must have a complete sentence. When you use a transition to put clauses together, you must have two complete clauses.

   CORRECT: Many people use a mother's or grandmother's cure for a cold. For example, they might eat chicken soup. (two separate complete sentences)

   Many people use a mother's or grandmother's cure for a cold; for example, they might eat chicken soup. (two clauses connected by a transition)

   INCORRECT: Many people use a mother's or grandmother's cure for a cold, For example, chicken soup. (The second "sentence" is a fragment. It is not a complete sentence because it does not have a subject-verb combination.)

2. **Run-ons and comma splices**
   a. Do not connect independent clauses without a signal. Do not connect independent clauses with only a transition and no punctuation. These mistakes will create a run-on sentence.

   INCORRECT: Many people use a mother's or grandmother's cure for a cold for example they might eat chicken soup.
                                    run-on

   b. Do not connect independent clauses with just a comma and no other signal. Do not connect independent clauses with a transition and one or two commas. These mistakes result in comma splices.

   INCORRECT: Many people use a mother's or grandmother's cure for a cold, for example they might eat chicken soup.
                                comma splice

3. **Punctuation at the end of the line** Most punctuation should not appear at the beginning of a line. (See the punctuation review in the Appendix on page 222.) Do not put a comma or a semicolon at the beginning of a line.

   CORRECT: You should try herbal medicine;
              in addition, you should call the doctor.

   INCORRECT: You should try herbal medicine
                ; **in addition**, you should call the doctor.

> CORRECT: First, you should try herbal medicine. Then, you should go to the doctor.
>
> INCORRECT: First, you should try herbal medicine. Then , you should go to the doctor.

4. **Using *such as*** *Such as* is not a linking transition and cannot connect clauses. Also, *such as* will not begin a sentence. When you use *such as* to give an example, use a comma before it.

> INCORRECT: Many people use home remedies; **such as**, they use chicken soup.
>
> INCORRECT: Many people use home remedies. **Such as** chicken soup.
>
> CORRECT: Many people use home remedies, **such as** chicken soup.

Practice: Finding Sentence Problems

Editing Focus

Fragments, Run-ons, Comma Splices

A. *All of the following sentences have problems. Find the problems and correct them. Be sure to look carefully at the punctuation in each sentence.*

> EXAMPLE: I do not like to take prescribed medicine too **often, furthermore,** I try to take only natural remedies as much as possible.
>
> <u>I do not like to take prescribed medicine too often; furthermore, I try to take only natural remedies as much as possible.</u>

1. People drink certain liquids to cure illnesses; for instance, teas and soups.

_____

_____

2. Sometimes parents or grandparents teach their families remedies for sickness, Such as eating garlic or other strong plants.

_____

_____

3. A person may have many reasons not to go to a doctor for an illness; for example, the cost of the medical care may be too expensive.

_____

_____

4. Some people take a piece of a plant called *aloe* as a natural remedy for a cut; then they squeeze the liquid from the plant directly on the cut.

_____

_____

5. Many societies have their own kinds of folk medicine, in addition, this medicine is often related to the culture or background of the group.

_____

_____

6. Scientists hope to find cures for diseases in undiscovered plants. For example, some plants in the rain forest.

_____

_____

 B. The following is a short reading about folk medicine. This reading has three fragments, one run-on, and two comma splices. Find these mistakes and show how to correct them.

Nature's Pharmacy

Across the United States and throughout the world, many people still rely on nature's pharmacy to remedy their aches and illnesses. The use of natural products is probably almost as old as humankind; for example people have been using leaves, barks, roots, blossoms, and other parts of herbs and trees for ages. In fact, plants were often the main source of all drugs before people began using synthetic medicines during the past century.

In some places people may not go to doctors at all. Instead, they use the herbs that grow around them to stay healthy. Sometimes they give these remedies to crying babies. For example, a little warm catnip tea. Other times they may use honey and vinegar to make a cough medicine, in addition for some people a mixture of honey and vinegar will cure problems ranging from coughs and burns to shingles, food poisoning, and varicose veins.

Of course, there can be real dangers in self-medication with herbal remedies, Some herbalists caution people about experimenting with wild plants because you must know what you are doing when using them. Many plants can cause unpleasant side effects furthermore some are even deadly poisonous. For example, if the tea you make to help you sleep is too strong, a side effect can be nightmares.

Today natural medicines continue to help fight age-old illnesses and diseases. For instance, malaria, smallpox, and leprosy. In addition, they offer hope for developing cures for other illnesses, Such as cancer, heart disease, and mental health problems. Some people hope that in the future marine scientists will be able to find even more natural drugs through undersea research. Perhaps nature will be able to speak to those people who are listening and give them clues to more long-hidden mysteries found in plants.

Discussion/Writing

Answer these questions in writing or through discussion. Try to use a variety of both linking and introductory transitions in your sentences.

1. Are folk remedies popular in the place where you grew up or the place where you are living now? Which ones are most popular?

2. Have you had any experience with folk medicine or home remedies? If so, describe one such experience.

3. What do you think is best or most helpful—home remedies or cures from a doctor, or a combination of both? Why do you feel this way?

PART 4   WRITING ESSAYS (PROCESS)

Read this essay about stress management and then answer the questions that follow.

Stress and Stress Management

Stress is a reaction to something that we all feel at one time or another, sometimes even on a daily basis. It can be caused by something positive or negative. Furthermore, it is not always bad; in fact, sometimes it can actually be necessary or helpful. However, most people do not enjoy feeling stress, and many people try to find ways to cope with it and relax. For some people, trying to relieve stress by relaxing through meditation is very helpful. When a person wants to relax or reduce stress using a meditative technique, she or he can follow a procedure of two main steps involving comfort and mental attitude.

First, finding a comfortable place and getting into a comfortable position are important steps to this technique. A comfortable environment may be different for each person. In other words, whether this place is inside a home or outside on a beach or in a park will depend on the person. In any case, finding a place that will provide maximum comfort and minimum disturbance for each person as an individual is essential. Also, while you are trying to relax through meditation, the environment should be free from noise. For example, there should be no interruptions or distractions in the area. In addition, getting into a comfortable position is equally important. For some people the most comfortable position might be sitting, but for others it might be lying down. Clothing should not be tight but should be comfortable. This step is important because without a comfortable environment and position, you may not be able to truly relax.

Next, if someone wants a positive relaxation response, he or she should have a passive attitude and a mental focus. In this step, most people try to clear their minds as much as possible. This can be done through deep breathing; for example, the person can inhale deeply and then empty his or her mind as he or she slowly exhales. Someone who does some of this deep breathing every hour or two during the day can easily reduce his or her stress on a regular basis. It is also a good idea to have something to think about. Closing your eyes will help you concentrate on a relaxing thought or mental image. For instance, you can think about your last relaxing vacation or your favorite place to relax. Thus, after your mind is clear and focused on positive thoughts, you can more fully relax.

In short, many people find themselves trying to cope with stressful situations that occur in everyday life. Although everyone is different and may try a unique way to relieve stress, many people find meditation to be an excellent technique. When you are "stressed out" and looking for a way to relax, try finding a comfortable place, clearing your mind with deep breathing, and concentrating on pleasant thoughts. It just might work.

Essay Discussion

1. How many paragraphs in the essay are about how to relax and deal with stress?

2. Does this essay have the organization pattern discussed in Unit Two? Does it have all of the following parts?

   ____ an introduction

   ____ a thesis statement

   ____ one or two body paragraphs

   ____ a topic sentence for each body paragraph

   ____ supporting sentences that relate to the topic sentences

   ____ good organization of each body paragraph

   ____ a concluding paragraph

3. What kind of information does the author give in the conclusion?

Organization of a Process Essay

Writing Focus
Essay Writing
(Process),
Thesis Statements,
Concluding
Paragraphs

The essay on stress and stress management tells the reader how to reduce or relieve stress. This kind of writing is called a *process essay* because it describes a procedure. Sometimes this kind of essay gives the reader a series of steps that instruct or explain how to do something. Other times this kind of essay may inform the reader how something happens or how it works.

A process essay has three main parts as described in Unit Two:

Introduction

The first paragraph of an essay should introduce the topic and give background information. In a process essay, the introductory paragraph might explain when, why, or in what situation a procedure is used. The thesis statement will be the last sentence in the introductory paragraph, and it narrows down the main idea of the process. In a process essay, the thesis statement identifies the process or procedure and might include the main steps as well. (You will learn more about this kind of thesis statement later in the unit.)

Body Paragraphs

Each body paragraph of a process essay should contain information about a main step in the process or procedure. When you write the details in the body paragraphs, you should be sure to think about your audience (the reader of the essay). If your audience does not know much about your subject, be sure to explain the details, define specific terms, or describe steps that might be unfamiliar to the reader. If you do not give enough explanation or information, the reader may not be able to follow or understand the process.

Conclusion

The concluding paragraph of a process essay may summarize the essay by restating the main steps, or it may describe the results of the procedure.

Review of Time Words

Process essays often use time words (words of chronology) because steps in a procedure usually are done in a certain order. In Unit Two you learned about subordinating conjunctions of time and other time words.

Find any subordinating conjunctions of time in the process essay about stress and write them below.

_____

_____

Find other words that indicate chronology in the essay about stress and write them below.

_____

_____

Thesis Statements in Process Essays

The thesis statement of a process essay may include the specific main steps of the procedure that will be described in the body paragraphs. Usually each step will be the main idea of one of the body paragraphs. Thus, the reader knows specifically what to expect in the body paragraphs. For example, look at the thesis statement from the essay about stress:

> When a person wants to relax or reduce stress using a meditative technique, she or he can follow a procedure of two main steps involving comfort and mental attitude.

- What process does this essay describe?

  _____

- How many body paragraphs can the reader expect in this essay?

  _____

- What information should the reader expect in each of the body paragraphs that follows this thesis statement?

  _____

Practice: Thesis Statements

For each introductory paragraph below, do three things:

a. *Find the thesis statement. Put a line under this sentence.*
b. *What process or procedure do you think each essay will describe? Write your answer on the line provided.*
c. *State what kind of information you expect to find in the body paragraphs that will follow the introduction. (In other words, what will be the main idea of each body paragraph?)*

EXAMPLE:
   Sometimes when people find themselves in a negative situation and under much stress, they become upset. This may cause their bodies to react in certain ways. For example, being tense and upset can cause tight muscles and an increase in heart rate as well as some difficulty in breathing. It is a good idea to try to increase breathing capacity so that when stress occurs, a person can avoid these negative physical reactions. **This increase in breathing capacity can be achieved by following a few specific steps that focus on breathing slowly and deeply.**

(one body paragraph)

Process: how to increase breathing capacity (to relieve stress)

Body paragraph: the steps to breathing slowly and deeply

1. Some medicinal herbs work best when they are used outside the body on a person's skin. There are several ways to use herbs on the skin. One popular method is called a *poultice,* which is often used when someone has an infection or muscle pain. Traditionally, a poultice is made with some of the "cooler" herbs, such as burdock, comfrey, and flaxseed, so that the preparation does not burn the skin. It is easy to use this type of remedy as it requires only two steps: preparing the herb and then applying the preparation to the skin.

(two body paragraphs)

Process: _____

Body paragraph 1: _____

Body paragraph 2: _____

2. People use different types of herbs and other plants for healing, and often it is the oil of those plants that is most important. This is because the oil in some herbs contains the active ingredients that are effective for treating various problems. Moreover, some people like to grow their own herbs and then prepare the oil on their own. The preparation of herbal oil for medicinal use can be done in steps that include mashing the herbs, heating them, and adding beeswax or lard to the herbs.

(three body paragraphs)

Process: _____

Body paragraph 1: _____

Body paragraph 2: _____

Body paragraph 3: _____

3. It is easy to find many kinds of herbal medicine in natural food stores or other places that sell health foods and vitamins. It is also possible to make your own herbal remedies from plants in your own backyard. In fact, this method of getting herbal remedies may be cheaper and much more satisfying than buying them from a store or someone else. Making your own natural, herbal remedies often involves only a few simple steps that include planting and picking the herbs or medicinal plants, drying them, and storing or bottling them for future use.

(three body paragraphs)

Process: _____

Body paragraph 1: _____

Body paragraph 2: _____

Body paragraph 3: _____

4. Since most people experience stress on a daily basis, it is advisable to try to take relaxation breaks every day. For example, some people make sure to set aside time for one long relaxation break of 15 to 20 minutes each day. Other people try to take a shorter relaxation break several times a day to help deal with stressful situations as they occur. Even if a person can only take one or two such breaks in a day, this may help relieve the stress. Each of these short relaxation breaks consists of a series of steps involving taking deep breaths, relaxing tight muscles, and concentrating on feeling calm.

(three body paragraphs)

Process: _____

Body paragraph 1: _____

Body paragraph 2: _____

Body paragraph 3: _____

Writing Concluding Paragraphs

The last part of your essay should be a concluding paragraph. In general, this paragraph completes the essay by telling the reader it is the end and ensuring that you get your point across. There are several ways that you can write this paragraph:

- Summarize or briefly restate the main points of the essay.
- Restate the thesis in order to emphasize the main idea.
- Add some final comments in any of the following ways:
  — make a prediction about the future regarding your essay topic
  — give advice or make suggestions about the situation or topic
  — show results of the situation or topic

There are also some things you should *not* do in a concluding paragraph:

- Do not add any new information.
- Do not review only some of the information in your essay. If you want to summarize or restate the main points, include all of them.

Practice: Concluding Paragraphs

Below you will find several of the introductions to process essays from the thesis statement activity. A conclusion is given for each introduction.

a. *Decide whether each concluding paragraph fits well with its introduction or has problems that could be improved.*

b. *If you think a conclusion might be improved, make suggestions about how to do this. Look for the following kinds of problems:*

- *The conclusion adds new information.*
- *The conclusion does not fully summarize the main points or restate the thesis.*

1. **Introduction:** Sometimes when people find themselves in a negative situation and under much stress, they become upset. This may cause their bodies to react in certain ways. For example, being tense and upset can cause tight muscles and an increase in heart rate as well as some difficulty in breathing. It is a good idea to try to increase breathing capacity so that when stress occurs, a person can avoid these negative physical reactions. This increase in breathing capacity can be achieved by following a few specific steps that focus on breathing slowly and deeply.

   Conclusion: In sum, we live in a stressful world, and sometimes our bodies feel the negative effects of everyday stress. This does not mean that we must just live with these situations. Following a few simple steps that involve breathing deeply and slowly can help us manage some of the problems. Of course, there are other ways, and it is also possible to try some form of meditation instead.

2. **Introduction:** Some medicinal herbs work best when they are used outside the body on a person's skin. There are several ways to use herbs on the skin. One popular method is called a *poultice,* which is often used when someone has an infection or muscle pain. Traditionally, a poultice is made with some of the "cooler" herbs such as burdock, comfrey, and flaxseed so that the preparation does not burn the skin. It is easy to use this type of remedy as it requires only two steps: preparing the herb and then applying the preparation to the skin.

   Conclusion: Thus, one of the many ways to use medicinal herbs and plants is to make a poultice. This kind of remedy is not difficult to make. If you follow the simple steps of preparing and applying a poultice, it might help your problem.

3. **Introduction:** It is easy to find many kinds of herbal medicine in natural food stores or other places that sell health foods and vitamins. It is also possible to make your own herbal remedies from plants in your own backyard. In fact, this method of getting herbal remedies may be cheaper and much more satisfying than buying them from a store or someone else. Making your own natural, herbal remedies often involves only a few simple steps that include planting and pick-

ing the herbs or medicinal plants, drying them, and storing or bottling them for future use.

Conclusion: In conclusion, it is not hard to buy herbal medicines these days, but for a variety of reasons, some people prefer to make their own. One reason might be how easy it is to do this with plants from the garden. Simply following the steps for storing and bottling will enable the average person to have his or her own home remedies.

 Now try to write your own conclusions using the other introductions from the activity about thesis statements.

1. **Introduction:** People use different types of herbs and other plants for healing, and often it is the oil of those plants that is most important. This is because the oil in some herbs contains the active ingredients that are effective for treating various problems. Moreover, some people like to grow their own herbs and then prepare the oil on their own. The preparation of herbal oil for medicinal use can be done in steps that include mashing the herbs, heating them, and adding beeswax or lard to the herbs.

   Conclusion: _____

   _____

   _____

2. **Introduction:** Since most people experience stress on a daily basis, it is advisable to try to take relaxation breaks every day. For example, some people make sure to set aside time for one long relaxation break of 15 to 20 minutes each day. Other people try to take a shorter relaxation break several times a day to help deal with stressful situations as they occur. Even if a person can only take one or two such breaks in a day, this may help relieve the stress. Each of these short relaxation breaks consists of a series of steps involving taking deep breaths, relaxing tight muscles, and concentrating on feeling calm.

   Conclusion: _____

   _____

   _____

Discussion/Writing

Answer these questions in writing or through discussion. Try to use a variety of both introductory and linking transitions in your sentences.

1. What are some things that cause stress in many people's lives? Can you think of positive things that cause stress as well as negative things?

2. When you feel too much stress, what do you do? Have you found ways to relax and reduce stress?

3. Are there ways to avoid feeling too much stress in the first place? What are some of these ways?

Summary Writing

For an explanation of summary writing, read pages 212–217 in the Appendix and follow the directions. Be sure to use both linking and introductory transitions in your sentences in these summaries.

1. *Summarize the two paragraphs that follow the subheading "Holistic Health" on page 73. Your summary should be one paragraph.*

2. *Summarize each paragraph in the short reading titled "Nature's Pharmacy" (on pages 85–86) in one sentence.*

3. *Summarize both body paragraphs in the process essay about stress and stress management on pages 86–87. Your summary should be one paragraph.*

Writing Assignment

A. Picking the Topic

You are going to write a process essay of four or five paragraphs for your final writing assignment for this unit. Choose one of the following topics:

1. Do you (or family members) usually or often use a home remedy when you are sick? Be sure to describe the steps that are involved in making or using this remedy.

2. Do you have an effective way of dealing with stress that involves steps? Describe your process for relieving stress.

3. Do you follow any particular exercise or fitness routine to stay in good health physically and/or mentally? Describe the steps in your routine.

Important: Your essay should be about a step-by-step plan that follows a specific order and should not be general advice about staying healthy.

B. Understanding the Assignment/Answering the Question

Before you start to write, make sure that you understand the assignment. Your essay must answer the question and should not discuss other things. You should also make sure that your essay describes a process or procedure. That is, your essay should explain how to do something, and each body paragraph should describe a different main step in the process. Look at the following ideas for essays on the three possible topics. Decide which ones fit the assignment and which ones do not. Cross out the ideas that you think will not answer the questions.

Topic 1: an essay that
- describes two or three home remedies you learned from your mother or grandmother

- describes how to prepare a special kind of tea your mother or grand-mother uses for treating an illness
- describes step by step how to use a special cure you have for headaches
- discusses why you like to use your mother's or grandmother's remedies

Topic 2: an essay that
- describes step by step how you relax at the end of a difficult day
- describes the reasons you feel stressed
- describes step-by-step how you become stressed at work or school
- gives a step-by-step description of a special way you get rid of stress
- gives step-by-step instructions for two or three ways to relieve stress

Topic 3: an essay that
- discusses why eating well and getting exercise are both good for your health
- describes your diet (what you eat and what you do not eat)
- discusses the specific steps you use in your workout every day
- gives steps for preparing one healthy meal
- describes a step-by-step exercise routine you follow every day or several times a week

Giving Instructions

This activity will help you prepare for writing about a step-by-step process. Your instructor will assign you a partner. You will each need two pieces of paper.

1. On one piece of paper, make a *simple* drawing of something you see in your classroom. Do not show this drawing to your partner.

2. Give your partner instructions about how to make the same drawing. Be sure you do not tell your partner what you have drawn. Just explain how to draw it. Try to use the words of chronology that you practiced in this unit (*first, second, next, then, finally,* etc.). While you explain, your partner will try to draw the object.

3. After your partner makes a drawing from your explanation, you should do the same. That is, your partner will tell you how to make a drawing like his or hers, and you try to draw that object following his or her instructions.

4. After you and your partner make drawings following each other's instructions, look at the drawings. How closely do the drawings you and your partner made from each other's instructions match the original ones you drew? Do you think you gave your partner good instructions? Why or why not?

Follow Up: Was your partner able to follow your instructions well because you gave them in clear, detailed steps? Did your partner have a problem following your directions because you left out some details or skipped a step? When you give instructions, you must be sure to include all the steps. Make sure you provide enough details in your process essay so that the reader can follow your instructions.

Following the Steps in the Writing Process

Before You Write

■ **Step One: Generating Ideas and Brainstorming**
a. Think about the three topics for the writing assignment.

1. What home remedy will you talk about? What are the steps involved in making or using it? Are these steps in a specific order?

   _____

   _____

2. How do you relieve stress? What are the steps involved? Are these steps in a specific order?

   _____

   _____

3. What plan of fitness or staying healthy will you talk about? What are the steps involved in your exercise or fitness routine? Are these steps in a specific order?

   _____

   _____

b. What kind of support can you provide for a process essay about the steps you wrote above? Using lists or clustering diagrams, write your ideas in one or more of the spaces on the next page. If you wrote something for two of the assignment questions above, write notes to support each one. Don't worry about the organization of your ideas.

Steps for a Home Remedy

Steps for Relieving Stress

Steps in an Exercise or Fitness Routine

c. Choose <u>one</u> of your lists or clustering diagrams for your essay. Then check the details to make sure that there are enough and they are all relevant.

■ ***Step Two: Organizing Ideas and Planning***
To begin organizing your ideas, think about the three parts of an essay.

INTRODUCTION WITH THESIS STATEMENT

a. Write a thesis statement for your essay. Be sure to include the following information in this sentence: the remedy, plan, or routine you are going to write about and the main steps involved in this remedy or procedure.

_____

_____

b. Write your thesis statement on the organization chart for a process essay at the end of this unit.

BODY PARAGRAPHS
Topic Sentences

How many main steps does your process have? Will you explain the process with two body paragraphs or three body paragraphs? _____

a. What is the first main step, or what will your first paragraph be about? What are the topic and the controlling idea for your topic sentence?

Topic: _____

Controlling idea: _____

Write your topic sentence on the chart on page 101 at the end of this unit.

b. What is the second main step, or what will your second paragraph be about? What are the topic and the controlling idea for your topic sentence?

Topic: _____

Controlling idea: _____

Write your topic sentence on the chart from page 101.

c. If you are going to have a third body paragraph, what will it be about? That is, what is the third main step? What are the topic and the controlling idea of the topic sentence?

Topic: _____

Controlling idea: _____

Write your topic sentence on the chart on page 101.

Support

Think about the details that support each of the main steps you will write about. Write notes about these details on the chart on page 101.

Make sure that all of your support relates to your topic sentence(s) and thesis statement and that you have enough support for each body paragraph.

CONCLUDING PARAGRAPH

Write some ideas for a concluding paragraph on the chart on page 101. Will you summarize the main points of the essay, restate your thesis, or add final comments?

■ ### Step Three: Getting Feedback

Your teacher may ask you to work with a partner and complete a peer review of your organization chart. Use the peer review sheet on page 232 in the Appendix for this feedback.

When You Write

■ ### Step Four: Writing the First Draft (Rough Draft)

Write the first draft of your process essay. Be sure that your essay describes a step-by-step process with body paragraphs and supporting sentences in chronological order. Do the following when you write the essay:

- Use some words of chronology (for example, *first, then, next,* and *finally*).
- Include coordinating conjunctions and subordinating conjunctions of time in some of your sentences.
- Include some of the transitions (both introductory and linking) discussed in this unit.
- Try to use at least two or three of the new vocabulary words you learned in this unit.

After You Write

Check Your Work

After you finish writing the first draft and before you show it to anyone for feedback or revision, read your paragraph again. Check your work for the following:

☐ This essay explains a process about using a home remedy, about relieving stress, or about an exercise or fitness routine.

☐ This essay has three main parts: introduction, body, and conclusion.

☐ The introductory paragraph is general and has several sentences. It ends with a thesis statement.

☐ The thesis statement names the process and two or three main steps.

☐ This essay has two or three body paragraphs that describe the steps of the process in chronological order.

☐ Each body paragraph has a topic sentence.

☐ The body paragraphs relate to the thesis statement.

☐ Some sentences in this essay include coordinating or subordinating conjunctions.

☐ Some sentences in this essay include transitions (introductory and linking).

☐ I looked for run-ons, comma splices, and fragments and corrected them.

☐ I used some of the vocabulary from this unit in the essay.

Getting Feedback

Your teacher will decide the type of feedback you will receive for the first draft. It may be peer review, teacher review, or both. For peer review, use the sheet on page 233 of the Appendix.

■ **Step Five: Revising**

After you receive feedback, revise the organization of your essay or any sentences in it, if necessary. You may want to change your thesis statement, your topic sentences, or parts of your introductory or concluding paragraph. You may want to add, take out, or change the order of some supporting sentences.

Reminder: Your teacher may want you to get feedback again after you revise.

■ **Step Six: Editing**

Make any necessary changes in grammar, spelling, punctuation, and capitalization.

Reminder: Your teacher may want you to have feedback after editing as well.

■ **Step Seven: Preparing the Final Draft**

Prepare your final draft to be handed in to the teacher.

Organizing Your Ideas for Writing a Process Essay

TITLE: _____

INTRODUCTION

Thesis statement: _____

_____

BODY PARAGRAPH 1 (STEP 1)

Topic sentence: _____

_____

Details/Support

_____

_____

_____

BODY PARAGRAPH 2 (STEP 2)

Topic sentence: _____

_____

Details/Support

_____

_____

_____

BODY PARAGRAPH 3 (STEP 3)

Topic sentence: _____

_____

Details/Support

_____

_____

_____

CONCLUSION

_____

_____

_____

Our Earth, Our Resources, Our Environment

UNIT FOUR

Content Area: Environmental Studies/Geography

Readings: Human Use of the Earth's Resources
Earth Summits
Causes of Deforestation
Effects of Deforestation

Short Readings: Signs of Environmental Progress
London's Air Pollution
Some Environmental Setbacks

Sentence-Combining Focus: Connectors to Show Reasons,
Results, or Conditions

Editing Focus: Fragments, Run-ons, and Comma Splices;
Punctuation

Writing Focus: Organization of Cause Essay
Organization of Effect Essay

PART 1   UNIT PREVIEW

Preview Activity: Environmental Questionnaire

How much do you know about the earth's population, its natural resources, and their energy uses? Try to answer the following questions. (If you are not sure, just make a guess.) Circle the letter of your answer.

1. What is the approximate population of the world today?

   a. almost 10 billion   b. less than 5 billion   c. about 6 billion

2. What do scientists expect the world's population to be by the year 2040?

   a. less than 10 billion   b. 20 billion   c. 12 billion

3. What percent of the world's population lives in the United States?

   a. about 50%   b. about 6%   c. about 10%

4. According to scientists, how many more years will the world's supply of oil last at the current rate of use?

   a. 50 to 100 years   b. 100 to 150 years

   c. several hundred years

5. In what year was the first oil well started?

   a. 1859   b. 1902   c. 1925

6. How old are the world's known petroleum sources?

   a. less than 1 million years   b. at least 1 to 2 million years

   c. thousands of years

7. In 1900 how much of the energy needs of the United States did coal supply?

   a. 50%   b. 100%   c. 90%

8. How much of the energy needs of the United States does coal supply today?

   a. 25% to 55%   b. 90%   c. 100%

9. How much of Canada's electricity comes from hydroelectric power?

   a. 15%   b. 75%   c. 50%

10. About how many nuclear power plants are there in the world today?

    a. 575   b. 150   c. 1,000

11. How much of France's electricity comes from nuclear reactors?

    a. 100%   b. 75%   c. 65%

12. What percent of the people who live in developing countries depend on firewood as their primary source of fuel?

    a. one-third   b. one-half   c. three-quarters

Quickwrite

Write for five minutes about the following topics. Do not worry about grammar, spelling, or punctuation. Just write whatever comes into your mind about the topics.

- How much electricity, gas, water, and/or firewood do you use in your everyday life? Do you think it would be easy for you to use less of any of these things? Why or why not?
- Do you try to reuse or recycle things such as newspapers, paper, aluminum cans, and glass bottles? Why or why not?

PART 2   READING AND VOCABULARY

Read the following about use of the earth's resources. Then answer the questions that follow.

Reading
Human Use of the Earth's Resources

Until recently the Earth's resources were believed to be unlimited. However, today we face serious **shortages** of many essential materials. For example, scientists believe that the world's obtainable supply of high-quality **crude** oil, from which we get gasoline, may last only another 50 to 100 years at the current rate of use. How have we managed to **exhaust** our supplies so quickly? What can we do to make up for these losses?

To find the answers to these questions, we must understand the growth rate of the world's population, the amount of natural resources used by each individual, and the search for alternative resources. The United States, which possesses only 6% of the world's population, uses almost 30% of its minerals, metals, and energy. One person in the United States uses as many as 30 times as much material and energy as a person in a developing nation. In addition, resource use worldwide is rising at an increasing rate as world population grows and people everywhere try to achieve the benefits of technological development. If we do not identify new supplies of **depleted** resources or if we do not find substitutes for them, we will be faced with shortages. We must also manage industrial development in ways that will limit the wasting of resources. If we do not do these things, future shortages will force people everywhere to change their lifestyles.

Resources and Reserves

Resources are deposits that we know or believe to exist but cannot **exploit** today. There are many reasons we may not be able to use them today, including technological, economic, and political reasons. However, we can estimate resources beneath the Earth's surface in several ways, such as through exploration or by guessing from already known reserves.

Reserves are natural resources that have been discovered and can be exploited. We know the locations of most reserves, and we have the ability to **extract** them. More

importantly, their economic value in the marketplace is higher than the cost of their extraction.

To illustrate the difference between resources and reserves, consider world oil supplies. World oil resources are thought to total 2 trillion barrels (a barrel equals 159 liters or 42 US gallons); however, world oil reserves have been estimated at 700 billion barrels.

Some natural resources are *renewable*. This means they are naturally **replenished** over short periods of time (such as trees), or they are available continuously (such as sunlight). *Nonrenewable* natural resources form so slowly that they are typically used much more quickly than nature can replenish them. Some examples are **fossil fuels** (such as coal, oil, and natural gas) and metals (such as iron, aluminum, gold, silver, and copper). Some resources, such as copper and aluminum, can be recycled for reuse. Others may be renewable or nonrenewable, depending on how we use them. For example, soil is a renewable resource if farmers use good agricultural practices. It is nonrenewable when its nutrients are removed through overplanting or when it **erodes** because of **overgrazing**, overplanting, or **deforestation**.

To maintain our standard of living and at the same time protect the global environment, we must all become more knowledgeable about the Earth's energy and mineral resources. To use **dwindling** resources wisely, we need to understand how they formed, how their use will affect the environment, and how long the known supplies are likely to last.

Alternative Energy Sources

As fossil fuel reserves dwindle and environmental damage related to their use increases, governments and industries are seeking alternative ways to meet their populations' growing energy needs. Most existing alternative energy sources, such as solar and wind power, are renewable. One major alternative, nuclear energy, depends on uranium, a nonrenewable natural resource.

Renewable Alternative Energy Resources

Renewable alternative energy resources are those resources that can be used **virtually** without depletion or that are replenished over a relatively short period of time. They include geothermal, hydroelectric, tidal, solar, and wind energy and the energy produced by burning such renewable organic materials as trees and agricultural **waste**.

Geothermal Energy

Reykjavik, the capital of Iceland, is relatively pollution-free because it has a clean, inexpensive source of energy. Heat from hot rocks and **magma** beneath the surface comes to the surface in an area known as a "hot spot." In such an area the heat is used to change groundwater to hot water and steam. The hot water is circulated through pipes and radiators to heat homes and other buildings and the steam drives electric generators.

Since people started using geothermal heat as an energy source in 1904, only about 20 countries have used it. Only a few countries can use this relatively inexpensive, nonpolluting energy because there are only a few dozen hot spots in the world. Furthermore, unlike oil, coal, and natural gas, geothermal energy cannot be transported from one place to another and must be used close to its source. Therefore, every nation using geothermal energy is located near an area that is "hot," or has magmatic activity.

Hydroelectric Energy

For many centuries humans have used falling water as an energy source to power machines. Today, hydroelectric facilities use falling water to produce electricity. To generate this kind of power, a dam must be built on a river so that the water can power **turbines.**

Hydroelectric power is widely available; however, only 6% of the world's hydroelectric potential is being used. It has been estimated that if every fairly large river in the United States could be used to produce this kind of power, 50% of the country's electrical needs would be met. Hydroelectric power is nonpolluting, but it still may create some environmental problems. Dams can disrupt local ecosystems by destroying wildlife **habitats,** and they can also change natural erosion processes. For these reasons the decision to build dams for creating hydroelectric energy must be carefully made.

Tidal Power

In coastal areas where there is a big difference between high and low tides, energy can be obtained from the rising and falling water levels by building a dam. The dam's gates are opened during rising tides and then closed to keep the water at its maximum height. During low tide the elevated water is sent through turbines connected to electrical generators that produce renewable pollution-free energy.

Tidal power production requires a large tidal range (8 meters or 26 feet), and it disturbs the ecology of the surrounding coastal areas. So far, only a few tidal-power facilities have been constructed.

Solar Energy

The sun, which is expected to shine for another 5 billion years or so, is a totally renewable and easily obtainable energy source. Solar power can be used to heat buildings and living spaces and to generate electricity. These energy needs together account for two-thirds of North America's energy consumption. Solar heating is most productive in mild, sunny climates, but it is possible to have solar heating in cooler areas as well. Solar energy can also be used to generate electricity, although this is done more efficiently in some regions than in others. Unfortunately, the technology to maximize its effectiveness at low cost is not yet widely available. Therefore, wide use of solar energy to produce electricity is probably decades away.

Wind Power

Like falling water, the tidal motion, and sunlight, wind power is a clean, renewable, nonpolluting energy source that has long been used by humans. For example, the picturesque windmills of the Netherlands have pumped groundwater and provided power for centuries. However, wind power is rarely cost-effective on a large scale. There are few places where winds blow constantly, forcefully, and from a **consistent** direction, and these are all requirements for the practical application of wind power.

Biomass Fuels

Fuels taken from plants and animals are known as *biomass fuels*. In developing countries as much as 35% of the energy used for cooking and heating comes from two common biomass fuels: wood and animal dung. The most widely used biomass fuel is wood, which today heats about 10% of North America's homes, more than are heated by electricity from nuclear power plants.

Biomass fuel is a renewable source. Although trees grow slowly, continuous planting and harvesting of these plants can produce a steady supply. Unlike most other renewable resources, biomass fuels can create air pollution and **desertification** problems when used on a wide scale or **implemented** poorly.

Comprehension Check

*Decide if the following statements are true or false based on the reading. Write **T** for "True" or **F** for "False" next to the number of each sentence.*

___ 1. The first two paragraphs discuss wise use of resources such as oil through the years.

___ 2. Reserves are natural resources that people can find, use, and make money from.

___ 3. Resources can be taken from the Earth and used today.

___ 4. Renewable resources are things that will grow again or will be available for a long time.

___ 5. Finding alternative energy resources is necessary because of a growing world population and a decrease in available energy sources.

___ 6. Only about 20 countries use geothermal energy because it is expensive.

___ 7. Hydroelectric energy uses steam made from groundwater to power machines known as turbines.

___ 8. Hydroelectric power is clean and never causes any environmental problems.

_F_ 9. Tidal power is not widely used because it is not good for the environment, and it is difficult to find a place that has a large enough tidal range.

_T_ 10. Solar energy is available and renewable, but it is not widely used today because the technology is expensive.

_F_ 11. Wind power can be easily used in many places because wind is so available everywhere.

_T_ 12. The use of biomass fuels can cause problems such as pollution and desertification.

Inference

Answer the following questions based on what you learned in the reading. Do not try to find the answers directly in the reading. Use your ability to infer.

1. The second paragraph of the reading discusses the rate at which natural resources are used by people in the United States and worldwide. What can you infer about the use of natural resources by people in developing nations? What do you think is the reason for this?
2. The first two paragraphs in the section called "Resources and Reserves" mention that economics plays an important role in the use of these two kinds of resources. What can you infer about how the economy is related to both resources and reserves?
3. After reading about the six renewable alternative energy resources, what can you infer about why they are not all used on a large scale at the present time?

Vocabulary Study

A. Vocabulary in Context

Using your knowledge of vocabulary in context, try to guess the meanings of the words in bold in the following sentences from the reading.

1. Until recently, the earth's resources were believed to be unlimited. However, today we face serious **shortages** of many essential materials.
2. How have we managed to **exhaust** our supplies so quickly? What can we do to make up for these losses?
3. We know the locations of most reserves, and we have the ability to **extract** them.
4. Some examples are **fossil fuels** (such as coal, oil, and natural gas) and metals (such as iron, aluminum, gold, silver, and copper).

B. Meanings

Choose synonyms from the following list for the underlined vocabulary words in the sentences. Write the letter of the answer you choose on the line before the sentence.

a. eat too much of the grass
b. used up, emptied
c. practically, almost entirely
d. unused, useless material
e. a rotary engine
f. natural, unprocessed
g. uniform, regular
h. making into a desert

i. replace, resupply
j. use for their own profit
k. grow less, decrease
l. carry out, enact
m. native, natural environment
n. eat away, wear away
o. clearing, destroying forest land
p. melted rock inside the earth

__f__ 1. When we take resources from the earth, they are often in <u>crude</u> form, and we have to refine them in order to make them usable for our purposes.

__b__ 2. In some areas mines have been <u>depleted</u> of their supplies of gold or silver, so nobody works in those mines anymore.

__j__ 3. People <u>exploit</u> various natural resources, but sometimes they forget that doing this can damage the environment.

__i__ 4. If we use up all of the available oil supplies, we will not be able to <u>replenish</u> them because oil takes millions of years to create.

__n__ 5. Wind and water <u>erode</u> rocks into very interesting shapes and sometimes make big canyons.

__a__ 6. If there are too many cows in one field, they may <u>overgraze</u>, and then there will be nothing left for them to eat.

__o__ 7. <u>Deforestation</u> of some of the earth's biggest rain forests could cause some serious problems for the environment.

__k__ 8. As supplies of a material <u>dwindle</u>, it can become expensive because many people want to buy it, but there is not enough of it available.

__c__ 9. <u>Virtually</u> all of the highest mountains on earth have been climbed by people.

__d__ 10. Usually when people make things in a factory, some <u>waste</u> is produced along with the product they are making. They often throw away that <u>waste</u>.

__p__ 11. When you see a volcano erupting, you may see some <u>magma</u> coming out from beneath the surface of the earth.

__e__ 12. If you want to produce the amount of power needed to generate electricity from water or wind, you may need a large <u>turbine</u>.

__m__ 13. When a forest is destroyed by fire, many animal <u>habitats</u> are destroyed as well.

14. We need a <u>consistent</u> policy regarding rules that all countries will follow if we really want to help the environment.

15. If too many trees are cut down or if farmland is ruined, this could lead to <u>desertification</u> of an area.

16. Governments of various countries should <u>implement</u> strict rules about the environment in order to help stop the problems we are having.

Discussion/Writing

Answer these questions in writing or through discussion.

1. Do you use more renewable or nonrenewable energy resources in your present lifestyle? Which specific resources do you think you use the most?

2. Are any of the alternative energy resources discussed in the reading used in the area you live now or an area you lived before? Why do you think they are or are not used in these places?

3. Which of the alternative energy sources discussed in the reading do you think will most likely be more widely used in the near future? Explain your answer.

PART 3   WRITING SENTENCES WITH CONNECTORS SHOWING REASONS, RESULTS, OR CONDITIONS

Read the following about environmental issues. Then answer the questions that follow.

Reading

Earth Summits

¹In 1992 representatives from more than 178 countries gathered in Rio de Janeiro to plan how to protect the world's resources. ²Because of this Earth Summit, some countries made promises to protect ecosystems and reduce global-warming gases. ³They also promised to promote human welfare through sustainable development. ⁴Ten years later, world leaders and activists wanted to talk again, so they met in Johannesburg for another Earth Summit, the so-called Rio + 10. ⁵At this meeting delegates tried to determine what (if any) progress had been made since the first summit in Rio de Janeiro. ⁶The following are some signs of progress they found.

Green Thinking

⁷People gained a new sensitivity to humanity's impact on the environment because they became more aware of the problems at the summit in Rio de Janeiro. ⁸As a result, some corrective actions have been taken. ⁹For example, in 1997 there was a conference in Kyoto, Japan, and most

industrialized nations agreed to reduce global emissions. [10]However, the US government has withdrawn its support of this agreement. [11]According to the United States, if it supports this agreement, it can cause potential harm to the economy.

Alternative Transportation

[12]Some companies are producing hybrid cars. [13]These vehicles do not release as many harmful emissions into the environment since they do not run solely on gas. [14]Several companies are making these hybrids as well as cars that run on hydrogen fuel cells; therefore, emissions of gases harmful to the atmosphere (such as carbon dioxide) are being reduced.

Ban on the Dirty Dozen

[15]The United Nations held a conference in Stockholm in 2001. [16]At this conference a treaty was adopted to control the use of 12 carbon-based chlorinated chemicals, for they have been polluting both our air and our water. [17]Chemicals such as chlordane, DDT, and PCBs pollute and destroy the Earth's Ozone layer. [18]If we continue to use these chemicals, pollution and damage to the Ozone layer will increase. [19]Consequently, the Convention on Persistent Organic Pollutants asked for a ban on these chemicals.

Ecotourism

[20]Ecotourism is considered responsible travel because it both conserves the environment and respects the well-being of the local people. [21]This industry has had a growth rate of 30%; as a result, some governments have tried to protect their countries' natural areas as well as traditional cultures.

Questions

1. Look at sentence 16 in the reading. Underline the clauses and circle the conjunction. Is this word a coordinating conjunction or a subordinating conjunction? What is the meaning of this conjunction?
2. Look at sentence 7. How many clauses are in this sentence? Underline the clauses. Circle the word that connects those clauses. Is this word a coordinating conjunction or a subordinating conjunction? What is the meaning of this conjunction?
3. Look at sentence 21. How many clauses are in this sentence? Underline the clauses and circle the expression that connects them.

Explanation: Sentence Combining to Show Reasons, Results, or Conditions

1. You have already learned about using different kinds of conjunctions and transitions as signals/connectors to put clauses together. In this unit you will practice using conjunctions and transitions to show reasons, results, and conditions.

2. The following examples for connectors showing reasons, results, or conditions use information from the reading about Earth Summits.

   a. Connectors showing reasons

   Coordinating conjunction: *for*

   EXAMPLE: A treaty was adopted to control chemicals, **for** they have been polluting our air and our water.

   Subordinating conjunctions: *because/since*

   EXAMPLES: People gained a sensitivity to the environment **because** they became more aware of the problems. **Since** some vehicles do not run solely on gas, they do not pollute the environment as much.

   b. Connectors showing results

   Coordinating conjunction: *so*

   EXAMPLE: World leaders and activists wanted to talk again, **so** they met in Johannesburg for another Earth Summit.

   Transitions: *thus/therefore/as a result/consequently*

   EXAMPLE: Certain chemicals destroy the ozone layer; **consequently,** some people want to ban these chemicals.

   c. Connector showing factual condition with a result

   Subordinating conjunction: *if*

   EXAMPLES: **If** we continue to use these chemicals, damage to the
                condition   result
                Ozone layer will increase.

                Damage to the Ozone layer will increase **if** we continue
                result   condition
                to use these chemicals.

The *if* clause states the condition, and the independent clause states what will happen as a result of this condition.

Sentence-Combining
Focus

Connectors
Showing Reasons,
Results, or
Conditions

3. The following chart reviews words and expressions that show reasons, results, and conditions.

Sentence Combining to Show Reasons, Results, and Conditions

Coordinating Conjunctions	Subordinating Conjunctions	Transitions
Position in Sentence Middle ____ ____ ____ clause conjunction clause	**Position in Sentence** Middle ____ ____ ____ clause subordinator clause OR Beginning ____ ____ ____ subordinator clause clause	**Position in Sentence** Middle ____ ____ ____ clause transition clause
Punctuation: Comma ____, ____ ____ clause conjunction clause EXAMPLE: A treaty was adopted to control chemicals, for they have been polluting our air and our water.	**Punctuation:** No comma ____ ____ ____ clause subordinator clause EXAMPLE: People gained a sensitivity to the environment **because** they became more aware of the problems. Comma between clauses ____ ____, ____ subordinator clause clause Example: **Since** some vehicles do not run solely on gas, they do not pollute the environment as much.	**Punctuation:** Semicolon and comma ____; ____, ____ clause transition clause EXAMPLE: Chemicals destroy the Ozone layer; **consequently,** some people want to ban these chemicals.
REASON: *for*	REASON: *because* *since*	
RESULT: *so*		RESULT: *thus* *therefore* *as a result* *consequently*
	CONDITION: *if*	

4. Using the conjunction *because* and the expression *because of*
Because is a subordinating conjunction that is used for putting clauses together.

EXAMPLE: People gained a new sensitivity to humanity's impact on the environment **because** they became more aware of the problems at the Earth Summit.

Because of is followed by a noun. It does not join clauses together.

EXAMPLE: **Because of** this Earth Summit, some countries made promises to protect their ecosystems.

5. Important Errors to Avoid
   a. Do not use a coordinating conjunction at the beginning of a sentence.

INCORRECT: Ten years later, world leaders and activists wanted to talk again. **So** they met in Johannesburg for another Earth Summit.

CORRECT: Ten years later, world leaders and activists wanted to talk again, **so** they met in Johannesburg for another Earth Summit.

   b. Fragments
   Do not write a dependent/subordinate clause by itself. This is a fragment. When you use a subordinating conjunction, you must have both a dependent/subordinate clause and an independent/main clause.

INCORRECT: **Because** ecotourism involves conserving the
                      dependent/subordinate clause only
             environment.   **fragment**

CORRECT: **Because** ecotourism involves conserving the
                    dependent/subordinate clause
           environment, it is considered responsible travel.
                         independent/main clause

   c. Run-ons and comma splices
   Do not connect clauses without a signal such as a coordinating conjunction, a subordinating conjunction, or a transition. If you connect clauses without one of these, you will make a run-on sentence. Do not connect clauses with just a comma and no other signal. If you do this, you will make a comma splice.

INCORRECT: More companies are making hybrid cars emissions
                                                  run-on
             harmful to the atmosphere are being reduced.

             More companies are making hybrid cars, emissions
                                                 comma splice
             harmful to the atmosphere are being reduced.

CORRECT: More companies are making hybrid cars, so emissions harmful to the atmosphere are being reduced.
           More companies are making hybrid cars; therefore, emissions harmful to the atmosphere are being reduced.
           If more companies make hybrid cars, emissions harmful to the atmosphere can (might/will) be reduced.

Practice: Connectors Showing Reasons, Results, or Conditions

A. *Identifying Conjunctions and Transitions*
The following short reading describes three more signs of progress that were identified during the Rio + 10 Summit. Find all the conjunctions and transitions that show reason, result, or condition. Underline the words that show reason and condition and circle the words that show result.

Signs of Environmental Progress

Corporations Clean Up

Big business is realizing that conservation may help it. For example, because Xerox instituted its Waste Free program, the company recycled 80% of the nonhazardous solid waste that came from its factories. In addition, it had a program of remanufacturing, so the company kept 158 million pounds of electronic waste out of landfills.

Healthier Buildings

In some places builders are creating environmentally sensitive structures; as a result, energy use is being reduced. For example, the Chesapeake Bay Foundation headquarters in Annapolis, Maryland has composting toilets, cisterns that collect rainwater, and solar panels to generate electricity. Since this building has all of these features, it uses one-third the electricity and one-tenth the water of buildings of a similar size.

Acid Rain Reduction

The United States and Europe have lowered emissions of sulfur dioxide and nitrogen oxides. Consequently, the acidity of rain in those areas has been reduced. If coal is burned in electrical power plants, sulfur dioxide is released. Some nations switched to natural gas and cleaner coal to generate their electricity; therefore, the release of these bad chemicals was reduced.

B. *Choosing the Correct Word or Expression*
Circle the one or two words or expressions that fit best in each sentence in the following short reading about air pollution in London. Be sure to check each sentence carefully for punctuation.

London's Air Pollution

Pollution is any atypical contribution to the environment that results from human activity. For example, (if / thus / since) humans use machines that use combustion and rely on industrial processes, they produce waste products. These waste products are then released into the atmosphere, (therefore / because / so) they create air pollution.

As far back as 700 years ago, people burned coal in England, producing smoke and soot; (therefore / as a result / so), London recorded air pollution problems even in the late 1200s. (Because / Because of / Since) pollution problems increased from using very smoky types of coal, there was a tax placed on their use. (If / As a result / Since) the air pollution did not improve by the 1600s, King Charles asked a famous scholar to study the situation in London. In his report, the scholar described the bad air in that city and the breathing problems some people had (for / because / because of) it. However, the Industrial Revolution was about to begin. (So / Therefore / If), people ignored this report.

Through the years London has experienced several disasters from air pollution; (consequently / since / for), many people have died there. People with heart and lung problems can be at risk in London, (since / for / because) that city can have a deadly combination of smoke and fog (called smog).

C. **Sentence Writing**   The sentences in this activity are about El Niño. El Niño is an occasional disruption of the atmospheric system in the tropical Pacific Ocean. It can affect the weather in many parts of the world.

Combine each pair of sentences into one sentence, using the conjunction or transition given in parentheses. Follow any other instructions appearing in the parentheses as well. Be sure to have the clauses in correct order in each sentence you write and be sure to use the correct punctuation.

EXAMPLE: Unusually warm water spreads during an El Niño.
It creates much more rain than usual in some areas.

(so) Unusually warm water spreads during an El Niño, so it creates much more rain than usual in some areas.

(therefore) Unusually warm water spreads during an El Niño; therefore, it creates much more rain than usual in some areas.

1. El Niño can make a change in the precipitation patterns in the areas
   of land on both sides of the Pacific Ocean. Indonesia and Australia can experience drought.
   (since—in middle of sentence) _____

   _____

   (since—at beginning of sentence) _____

   _____

   (as a result) _____

   _____

   (so) _____

   _____

2. This change in precipitation happens.
   Both Ecuador and Peru can experience heavier than normal rains.
   (if—in middle of sentence) _____

   _____

   (if—at beginning of sentence) _____

   _____

3. The 1982–1983 El Niño was one of the worst since 1910.
   It was responsible for the loss of as many as 2,000 lives.
   (because—in middle of sentence) _____

   _____

   (because—at beginning of sentence) _____

   _____

   (for) _____

   _____

4. That El Niño caused droughts and bush fires in Indonesia and
   Australia as well as very heavy rainfall in Peru.
   Thousands of people were displaced from their homes.
   (consequently) _____

   _____

   (so) _____

   _____

   (therefore) _____

   _____

Editing Focus

Fragments, Run-ons,
and Comma Splices;
Punctuation

D. **Finding Sentence Problems**   You have already read about some signs
   of progress in solving environmental problems during the years
   between the two Earth Summits. In this activity you will read about
   some environmental setbacks that also occurred during those years.

Each paragraph of the short reading contains at least one mistake, some paragraphs contain two mistakes, and one has three. There are several kinds of mistakes, including fragments, run-ons, comma splices, and incorrect or missing punctuation. Find the mistakes and show how to correct them. Be sure to check punctuation carefully.

Some Environmental Setbacks

Global Warming

Many scientists predict higher sea levels and violent weather, because of the greenhouse effect from the burning of fossil fuels. Average temperatures have been warmer than ever recorded. So many scientists are worried that this warming trend is a problem.

An Appetite for Oil

Because oil consumption grew 14% during the 1990s carbon dioxide continued to be added to the atmosphere. In fact, the burning of oil accounts for about 40% of the tons of the carbon dioxide produced annually. If we continue to use this oil in large quantities. This percentage will probably not decrease.

Disappearing Wetlands

Freshwater and saltwater wetlands remove pollutants and provide habitat for fish and other wildlife therefore it is important for countries to try to keep their wetlands from disappearing. However, scientists estimate that 50% of wetlands have been destroyed in the past century.

Rise of Megadams

In some places people build large dams, as a result, the flow of rivers may change. In addition, these dams interfere with fish migration and flood cultural sites. In 1850 there were 5,000 large dams worldwide. By the year 2000 that number had grown to 45,000.

Coral Reefs

One-fourth of all marine species live in coral in the oceans, but oceans have lost 27% of their coral in the last 50 years. Some of the coral has been dying because increased solar radiation and warmer water. In addition, fishermen have been using explosives and cyanide (a poison) to kill and collect fish around delicate reefs; Thus, they are contributing to the loss of these areas.

Overfishing

Because of technology, people are able to catch more fish than the oceans can replace fish populations are decreasing. Since this has become such a problem; scientists want to designate large areas of the oceans as marine reserves and close them to fishing.

Nuclear Waste

Many nations use nuclear reactors for making electricity, these create radioactive spent fuel. This waste is a risk. For there could be accidental leakage or this fuel could be a terrorist target. In the United States many people live within 75 miles of an aboveground waste storage facility, thus; in the future much of the waste may be put under a mountain in Nevada.

Discussion/Writing

Answer these questions in writing or through discussion. Try to use words and expressions showing reason, result, and condition in your sentences.

1. After reading about the progress and the setbacks regarding environmental problems, do you feel the world is moving in a positive or negative direction? Explain your answer.

2. Have you ever thought about using alternative transportation? Why or why not?

3. Which of the problems mentioned in the short reading on environmental setbacks have you seen in the area where you are now living or in an area where you lived before?

PART 4   WRITING ESSAYS (CAUSE OR EFFECT)

Read this essay about the causes of deforestation. Then answer the questions that follow it.

Causes of Deforestation

There are many different forests in the world, including woodlands and tropical rain forests, and people have been clearing these areas for centuries. More recently, the permanent destruction of forests and woodlands, known as *deforestation*, has been recognized as a global problem. Today, more than half the Earth's original rain forests are gone, and at the current rate of destruction, rain forests could disappear completely within 100 years. Deforestation now occurs in areas that previously remained untouched because modern transportation and equipment allow people to exploit those areas more easily. While there are several reasons for deforestation, two important causes are related to this exploitation: clearing the land for agricultural purposes and commercial logging.

People often destroy trees in order to open up land for agricultural use. They clear forest areas for agriculture because they need to feed themselves or because they want to produce cash crops. Some people, such as poorer farmers, chop down trees in small areas so that they can plant crops to sustain themselves and their families. Other people clear forest areas on a larger scale, for they want to earn money. In some cases the cleared forest areas become cattle ranches. In other cases people might grow rubber or coffee plants on these deforested areas. In all of these larger-scale cases, the forest is cleared because of a need or desire to earn money through the sale of products such as beef, rubber, coffee, and other crops that are produced on the land. However, the soil is often too poor to support the crops that are planted in these cleared humid tropical areas. Since these farmers and ranchers are seeking land to satisfy their agricultural needs, they move to new areas and clear more forests. Because of this movement, the deforestation may increase rapidly.

Another important cause of deforestation is commercial logging. Because of the large international demand for timber and the international trade that has developed from this demand, commercial logging has become a big business. Since both the demand for wood and its products and the wood-processing industry have grown, the rate of forest loss has increased as well. Trees are cut for sale as timber, or the wood may be used to make paper or other products such as furniture. Growing populations and urbanization have made demands on the logging industry to supply timber for houses and other kinds of buildings. Sometimes commercial logging is done selectively. That is, certain kinds of trees are cut because their wood is more valuable than others. On the other hand, a practice known as *clear cutting* is often used. In this case all trees in a certain area are cut down at once.

Deforestation is a serious problem facing the world today. Two important causes of this problem are controlled by people through the ways they choose to destroy forests and woodlands. Clearing these areas for agricultural use or commercial logging is common, but these practices could be changed in order to try to save these important forested areas before they are gone forever.

Essay Discussion

1. How many paragraphs are in this essay about deforestation?

2. Does this essay have the organization pattern discussed in Unit Two? Does it have all of the following parts?
   ____ an introduction
   ____ a thesis statement
   ____ two or three body paragraphs
   ____ a topic sentence for each body paragraph
   ____ supporting sentences that relate to the topic sentences
   ____ a concluding paragraph

3. What is the purpose of this essay? What kind of information is the writer trying to give to the reader?

Organization of a Cause or Effect Essay

Sometimes a writer wants to discuss the reasons for or the results of a situation. For example, in an environmental studies class, a student may be asked to write about the reasons for or the results of an environmental problem. An essay that discusses reasons for a situation, problem, etc., is a *cause essay*. An *effect essay* discusses results of a situation, problem, etc. Some essays may discuss both cause and effect, but you will write an essay dealing with one or the other.

Look back at the sample essay you just read about the causes of deforestation. What two causes are discussed in the essay on deforestation on page 120?

```
┌─────────────────────┐
│                     │
│                     │
└─────────────────────┘
                            ─────────────────────▶  Deforestation
┌─────────────────────┐
│                     │
│                     │
└─────────────────────┘
```

Practice: Essay Organization

Answer the following questions about the organization of the cause essay about deforestation on page 120.

1. What is the thesis statement of this essay? Write that sentence below.

   _____

   _____

Does this thesis statement name the situation and its causes (reasons for it)?

_____

2. What is the topic sentence of the first body paragraph? Write that sentence below.

_____

_____

Does this sentence tell you one cause of deforestation? _____

Is everything in this body paragraph about that cause? _____

3. What is the topic sentence of the second body paragraph? Write that sentence below.

_____

_____

Does this sentence tell you one cause of deforestation? _____

Is everything in this body paragraph about that cause? _____

Now read this essay about the effects of deforestation. Then answer the questions that follow it.

Effects of Deforestation

There are many different forests in the world, including woodlands and tropical rain forests, and people have been clearing these areas for centuries. More recently, the permanent destruction of forests and woodlands, known as *deforestation*, has been recognized as a global problem. Today, more than half the Earth's original rain forests are gone, and at the current rate of destruction, rain forests could disappear completely within 100 years. Deforestation has already had negative effects on the environment, including a loss of biodiversity, more erosion of the land, and a change in the water cycle.

Deforestation causes a loss of biodiversity and can lead to a breakdown of the ecosystem of an area. For example, rain forests are home to millions of species of animals, insects, and plants. That number is dwindling every day as rain forests are destroyed. Animals, some found in certain forested areas and nowhere else, lose their habitat and may begin to die out when an area is deforested. In addition to animal species, we lose innumerable plant species as rain forests are cut down. Many modern medicines come from plants found in rain forests, and the vast majority of tropical plants haven't even been tested yet for their curative powers. Thus, we may lose the next medical breakthrough or nutritional supplement if many plants are destroyed by deforestation before we can find out more about them.

Erosion of the land is another serious effect of deforestation. When commercial logging takes place, workers bring in trucks, bulldozers, and road graders, so the soil in that area becomes eroded from the use of that heavy equipment. In addition, logging makes new roads in areas that previously had no or few roads, and these worsen erosion in those areas. Furthermore, when an area is cleared of trees, there are no roots to hold the soil, and there is little or no vegetation on the land to decrease the effects of rain that may fall there. Therefore, rain will wash topsoil away from that area, and this erosion increases silt in lakes, rivers, or marine coastal areas. Thus, deforestation not only causes erosion in the immediate area, but may also change the composition of waterways far away as a secondary result of this erosion.

Finally, deforestation affects the water cycle by causing a drier climate. Trees take in water through their roots and then release some of that water into the atmosphere through a process known as *transpiration*. This process cools the air and keeps clouds in the area low so that some rain can fall. This is especially helpful if an area has a dry season. However, when trees are cut down in an area, the process of transpiration does not take place. As a result, there is a reduced amount of water in the air for cloud formation. Fewer clouds may develop, and these clouds do not provide enough water in the area; therefore, the dry season becomes longer, and in turn some animal populations may suffer (for example, amphibians such as frogs). In short, if people remove part of a forest, the region may develop a drier climate and possibly move toward desertification (eventually becoming a desert).

Deforestation is a serious problem facing the world today, and it has already had negative effects on the Earth's environment. Loss of biodiversity, increasing erosion of the land, and changes in the water cycle are only three of its many effects. If we want to keep these and other effects to a minimum in the future, we must find a way to slow the rate of deforestation as soon as possible.

Essay Discussion

1. How many paragraphs are in this essay about deforestation?

2. Does this essay have the organization pattern discussed in Unit Two? Does it have all of the following?
   ____ an introduction
   ____ a thesis statement
   ____ two or three body paragraphs
   ____ a topic sentence for each body paragraph
   ____ supporting sentences that relate to the topic sentences
   ____ a concluding paragraph

3. What is the purpose of this essay? What kind of information is the writer trying to give to the reader?

4. What three results are discussed in this essay?

Results

┌─────────────────────┐
│   │
│   │
└─────────────────────┘

Deforestation ─────────⟶ ┌─────────────────────┐
                          │   │
                          │   │
                          └─────────────────────┘

┌─────────────────────┐
│   │
│   │
└─────────────────────┘

Practice: Essay Organization

Answer the following questions about the organization of the effect essay about deforestation.

1. What is the thesis statement of this essay? Write that sentence below.

   _____

   _____

   Does this thesis statement name the situation and its effects (results)?

   _____

2. What is the topic sentence of the first body paragraph? Write that sentence below.

   _____

   _____

   Does this sentence tell you one result or effect of deforestation? ____

   Is everything in this body paragraph about that effect? _____

3. What is the topic sentence of the second body paragraph? Write that sentence below.

   _____

   _____

   Does this sentence tell you one result or effect of deforestation? ____

   Is everything in this body paragraph about that effect? _____

4. What is the topic sentence of the third body paragraph? Write that sentence below.

   _____

   _____

   Does this sentence tell you one result or effect of deforestation? ____

   Is everything in this body paragraph about that effect? _____

Practice: Recognizing Causes and Effects

*Read each statement about the Earth's resources and environment and decide if it describes a cause or an effect. Write **C** for "cause" or **E** for "effect" on the line next to each one.*

1. ___ a. The Earth's resources are becoming depleted.

   ___ b. People use many of the Earth's natural resources.

2. ___ a. We are using large amounts of nonrenewable energy resources such as fossil fuels.

   ___ b. Governments are looking for new sources of energy.

   ___ c. The environment has been damaged by the emissions coming from the use of fossil fuels.

3. ___ a. Many countries became more aware of today's environmental problems caused by people.

   ___ b. The first Earth Summit was held in Rio de Janeiro in 1992.

4. ___ a. Cars that run on gas send harmful emissions into the atmosphere.

   ___ b. Some people have been buying hybrid cars.

   ___ c. Emissions that are harmful have been decreasing.

Discussion/Writing

Answer these questions in writing or through discussion. Try to use words and expressions showing reason, result, or condition in your sentences.

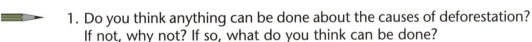

1. Do you think anything can be done about the causes of deforestation? If not, why not? If so, what do you think can be done?

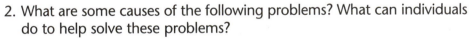

2. What are some causes of the following problems? What can individuals do to help solve these problems?

   • water pollution   • air pollution   • noise pollution

3. What are some effects of the following problems? Do you now live (or have you ever lived) in an area that has any of these problems? How do they affect the area?

   • water pollution   • air pollution   • overpopulation

Summary Writing

For an explanation of summary writing and practice of this skill, read pages 212–217 in the Appendix. Follow the instructions. Be sure to use words and expressions showing reason, result, or condition in your sentences.

1. Summarize each of the renewable alternative energy resources (geo-thermal, hydroelectric, tidal, solar, wind, and biomass) discussed in the reading on pages 105–108. Each summary should give three pieces of information about each alternative:
   - Define what it is.
   - State its good points or advantages.
   - State its bad points or disadvantages.

   Do not write more than two or three sentences for each of these summaries.

2. Summarize the result of each environmental setback discussed in the reading on page 119. Write only one or two sentences for each setback.

3. Summarize the entire essay about the effects of deforestation on pages 123–124. Do this by summarizing each paragraph in the essay in one to three sentences.

212 – 217

Writing Assignment

A. Picking the Topic

You are going to write a cause or effect essay of four or five paragraphs. Choose one of the following topics:

1. How do you personally affect the environment? Write an essay about what effects your lifestyle might have on the environment. You should have two or three effects to write about (two or three body paragraphs in your essay). Think about the following aspects of your lifestyle:
   - What kind of transportation do you usually use? Do you drive a car, take a bus or train, or ride a bicycle? If you use a car as your main kind of transportation, what kind of car do you drive?
   - Do you care about the kind of packaging on the products you buy? Do you try to use environmentally friendly products (without styrofoam, with recyclable plastics, etc.)? Do you try to recycle as much as you can?
   - How much energy do you use? Do you try to limit how much electricity you use? What kind of heating do you use?
   - What kind of food do you buy? Do you try to buy organic food? Are you careful about buying certain kinds of food products, such as endangered fish?

2. Think about the place you are living now or a place you have lived previously and know well. Which of these problems does this place have?
   - air pollution
   - water pollution
   - overpopulation
   - use of fossil fuels or nuclear energy
   - overfishing
   - loss of natural areas through deforestation or loss of coral reefs

   Write either a cause essay or an effect essay about one of these problems. You should have two or three causes or two or three effects in your essay. Do not write about both causes and effects.

3. Which two or three of the following environmental problems do you think are the most serious worldwide now or will be in the future?
   - air pollution
   - water pollution
   - noise pollution
   - overpopulation
   - deforestation
   - overfishing
   - damage to the Ozone layer
   - depletion of nonrenewable energy sources (oil and coal)

   Be sure to talk about the effects these problems are having or will have on people and the Earth. Be sure to include details and examples in your supporting sentences.

B. Understanding the Assignment/Answering the Question

Before you start to write, make sure that you understand the assignment. Your essay must answer the question and should not discuss other things. You should also make sure that your essay presents either causes or effects. Look at the following ideas for essays on the three possible topics and decide which ones fit the assignment and which ones do not. Cross out the ideas that you think will not work.

Topic 1: an essay that
- discusses why you live the lifestyle you do
- explains how you try to affect the environment as little as possible with examples in two areas listed above
- explains how you plan to change your lifestyle to be more aware of the environment
- discusses how you use environmentally friendly transportation and buy organic and recyclable products

Topic 2: an essay that
- explains why you won't live in a place that has air or water pollution
- discusses why people should make sure that deforestation slows down
- discusses causes of air pollution in the city you live in now
- explains the results of the bad air pollution in the city you live in now

Topic 3: an essay that
- discusses the causes and the effects of one environmental problem all over the world
- discusses the effects of two or three environmental problems on your city
- discusses how air pollution, noise pollution, and water pollution affect places in many parts of the world

Following the Steps in the Writing Process

Before You Write

■ **_Step One: Generating Ideas and Brainstorming_**
a. _Think about the three topics for the writing assignment._

1. In what ways does your lifestyle affect the environment?

   _____

   _____

2. What environmental problems on the list have you noticed in the
   place you are living now or in a place you used to live?

   _____

   What are the causes of these problems?

   _____

   What are the effects of these problems?

   _____

3. What two or three environmental problems on the list do you think are
   having (or will have) the most serious effects on the Earth worldwide?

   _____

   _____

   What are these effects?

   _____

   _____

b. _What kind of support (details or examples) can you provide for these topics?_
   Using lists or clustering diagrams, write your ideas in the spaces below.
   Don't worry about organization at this time.

My Personal Effects on the Environment

Causes or Effects of Environmental Problems in My Area

Environmental Problems with Serious Worldwide Effects

c. *Choose <u>one</u> of the lists or clustering diagrams you created for your essay. Then check the details to make sure that there are enough and they are all relevant.*

■ **Step Two: Organizing Ideas and Planning**
To begin organizing your ideas, think about the three parts of an essay.

INTRODUCTION WITH THESIS STATEMENT
a. Write a thesis statement for your cause or effect essay. Be sure to state the situation and either the causes or the effects you will discuss in your body paragraphs.

_____

_____

b. Write your thesis statement on the organizational chart for a cause or effect essay on page 134 at the end of this unit.

BODY PARAGRAPHS
Are you going to write about causes or effects? Write the causes or effects you will include in your essay on one of the charts below.

Causes

```
┌──────────────────────┐
│                      │
│                      │
└──────────────────────┘

┌──────────────────────┐
│                      │
│                      │
└──────────────────────┘
                              ─────────────────
                         ───────→ (problem or situation)
┌──────────────────────┐
│                      │
│                      │
└──────────────────────┘
```

Effects

```
                              ┌──────────────────────┐
                              │                      │
                              │                      │
                              └──────────────────────┘

─────────────────
(problem or situation)───→     ┌──────────────────────┐
                              │                      │
                              │                      │
                              └──────────────────────┘

                              ┌──────────────────────┐
                              │                      │
                              │                      │
                              └──────────────────────┘
```

Topic Sentences

a. What is the main idea of your first body paragraph (first cause or effect)? Write a topic sentence for this paragraph.

_____

_____

b. What is the main idea of your second body paragraph (second cause or effect)? Write a topic sentence for this paragraph.

_____

_____

c. What is the main idea of your third body paragraph (third cause or effect)? Write a topic sentence for this paragraph.

_____

_____

Write your topic sentences on the chart on page 134.

Support

Look back at your lists or clustering diagrams on page 130. Which supporting details or examples will you include in the essay?

Write notes about your support on the chart on page 134.

Be sure that all of your support relates to your topic sentences and thesis statement and that you have enough support for each body paragraph.

CONCLUDING PARAGRAPH

Write some ideas for a concluding paragraph on the chart on page 134. Will you summarize the main points of the essay, restate your thesis, or add final comments?

■ ***Step Three: Getting Feedback***

Your teacher may ask you to work with a partner and complete a peer review of your chart. Use the peer review sheet on page 234 of the Appendix.

When You Write

■ ***Step Four: Writing the First Draft (Rough Draft)***

Do the following when you write the first draft:

- Be sure to use connectors that show reasons, results, or conditions.
- Try to include as much sentence variety as possible. Include coordinating conjunctions, subordinating conjunctions, and transitions.
- Be careful to avoid fragments, run-ons, and comma splices.
- Include at least three or four vocabulary words from this unit in your essay.

After You Write

Check Your Work

After you finish writing the first draft and before you show it to anyone for feedback or revisions, check it for the following:

☐ This essay discusses effects of my lifestyle on the environment, causes or effects of environmental problems where I live or have lived, or environmental problems that have serious worldwide effects.

☐ This essay has three main parts: introduction, body, and conclusion.

☐ The introductory paragraph has several sentences. It starts out general and ends with a thesis statement.

☐ The thesis statement clearly states the problem or situation and either the causes or the effects.

☐ This essay has two or three body paragraphs that discuss causes or effects.

☐ Each body paragraph has a topic sentence. The topic sentence is about a cause or an effect.

☐ The supporting sentences in each body paragraph are related to the topic sentence of that paragraph.

☐ This essay has a variety of connectors that show reasons, results, or conditions.

☐ The sentences in this essay include a variety of coordinating and subordinating conjunctions and transitions.

☐ I looked for run-ons, comma splices, and fragments and corrected them.

☐ I used some of the vocabulary from this unit in the essay.

Getting Feedback

Your teacher will decide the type of feedback you will receive for the first draft. It may be peer review, teacher review, or both. For peer review, use the sheet on page 235 of the Appendix.

- ### *Step Five: Revising*
  After you receive feedback, revise the organization of your essay or any sentences in it, if necessary. You may want to change your thesis statement, your topic sentences, or parts of your introductory or concluding paragraph. You may want to add, take out, or change the order of some supporting sentences. Your teacher may want you to get feedback again after you revise.

- ### *Step Six: Editing*
  Make any necessary changes in grammar, spelling, punctuation, and capitalization. Your teacher may want you to have feedback after editing as well.

- ### *Step Seven: Preparing the Final Draft*
  Prepare your final draft to be handed in to the teacher.

Organizing Your Ideas for Writing a Cause or Effect Essay

TITLE: _____

INTRODUCTION

Thesis statement: _____

_____

BODY PARAGRAPH 1 (first cause or effect)

Topic sentence: _____

_____

Details/Support

_____

_____

_____

BODY PARAGRAPH 2 (second cause or effect)

Topic sentence: _____

_____

Details/Support

_____

_____

_____

BODY PARAGRAPH 3 (third cause or effect)

Topic sentence: _____

_____

Details/Support

_____

_____

_____

CONCLUSION

_____

_____

_____

Different People, Different Ways

Content Area: Cross-Cultural Studies
Native American Culture

Readings: Native Americans and Their Sacred Ways
Navajo Sandpaintings
Following the Old Ways or the New

Short Readings: Memorial Poles
Social Status in the Pacific Northwest

Sentence-Combining Focus: Relative/Adjective Clauses

Editing Focus: Fragments
Relative Clauses/Pronouns
Punctuation
Commas

Writing Focus: Organization of an Essay (Opinion)
Expressing Differences Between Facts and Opinions

PART 1   UNIT PREVIEW

Preview Activity: Learning about Native Americans

A. *What do you know about the Native Americans of North America? How did you learn about these people? Write **T** for "True" or **F** for "False" before each of these statements:*

F ___ 1. There were only about 10 or 15 tribes in North America when the first Europeans came there.

T ___ 2. Today more than 200 native tribal languages are spoken in North America.

T ___ 3. Today there are fewer than 2 million Native Americans living in the United States.

T ___ 4. Native Americans did not become United States citizens until 1924.

F ___ 5. All Native Americans live on reservations today.

F ___ 6. *Indian* is a name that people who lived in North America called themselves for hundreds of years.

B. *Look at the map showing where some tribes lived in North America before Europeans came to that area. Do you recognize the names of any of these tribes? Do you know anything about any of them?*

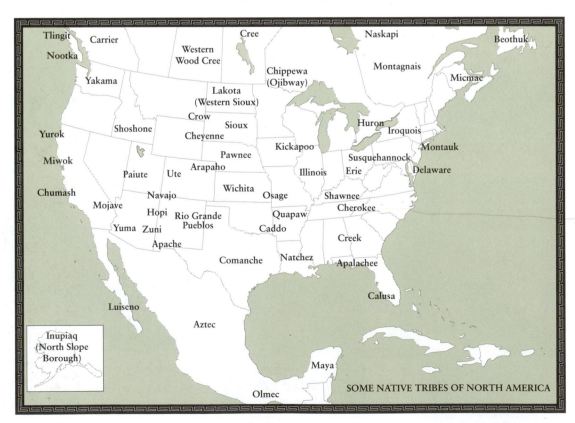

SOME NATIVE TRIBES OF NORTH AMERICA

Quickwrite

Write for five minutes about the following topic. Do not worry about grammar, spelling, or punctuation. Just write whatever comes into your mind about the topic.

- What kind of structure does your family have? Do you live with or spend time with many different family members or mostly your immediate family? How often do you see or speak to relatives who are not in your immediate family?

PART 2   READING AND VOCABULARY

Read the following about the native people of North America. Then answer the questions that follow.

Reading

Native Americans and Their Sacred Ways

What do you know about the traditional way of life, beliefs, and observances of the Native American people in North America? Does your knowledge of these people come from movies or television programs that you have seen? If your information is limited to these **sources,** you may be misinformed as to the true way of life of these people.

Like all societies throughout the world, Native Americans, who are also known as *The People,* **seek** their own way to explain people's origins and destinies in order to face the unknown and learn the power and meaning of natural laws and forces. Unlike the beliefs of many other societies, the Native American beliefs limit the amount of explaining that a person can do about the world we live in and its mysteries. Many Native American sacred teachings suggest that if people try to explain everything, they will bring **disaster** on themselves, for then they are trying to be more like gods than human beings.

When you explore the lives and classic **tribal** ways of Native Americans, you will find that originally their sacred ways and practices were at the heart of living and survival. Every part of their lives was touched by these traditions. However, these classic sacred ways do not try to explain or control all **phenomena** in the universe. In addition, one idea that the elders hold as very important is respect. Great respect is held for those people who protect sacred ways and help them grow. Thus, a human being's spiritual life is his or her most important expression of his or her humanity.

Learning the Way: Traditional Education

Basic education among Native Americans did not separate the search for knowledge from sacred learning or religious training. Learning the sacred ways of the tribe differed from community to community throughout North America. In order that the knowledge did not get separated from experience, the elders **stressed** listening and waiting, not asking why. In addition, religion and the sacred include the range of experiences that

some people might call "nonordinary." Learning that there is more to life than just what we can see is a large part of Native American learning.

Luther Standing Bear recalls the education of Lakota children as he explains: "Training began with children, who were taught to sit still and enjoy it. They were taught to use their organs of smell, to look when there was apparently nothing to see, and to listen intently when all seemingly was quiet. A child that cannot sit still is a half-developed child."

Larry Bird, a Keres man, explains: "You don't ask questions when you grow up. You watch and listen and wait, and the answer will come to you. It's yours then, not like learning in school."

Soge Track, a young woman from Taos Pueblo, says about her learning: "All through this time I never asked of them (grandmother and grandfather) or anyone, 'Why?' It would have meant I was learning nothing—that I was stupid. And in Western society if you don't ask why, they think you are stupid. So having been raised to not ask why but to listen, become aware, I take for granted that people have some knowledge of themselves and myself— that is religion. Then, when we know ourselves, we can put our feelings together and share this knowledge."

Some Ways of Learning Sacred Knowledge

There are both general and specific types of learning sacred ways and practices. In one way, training in sacred ways begins at the moment of birth because the sacred way is a part of everyday life. The way people act toward one another within the family and among kin is religious training. The way a person acts in different situations is also part of sacred learning. People in the community agree that at a certain age an individual is ready to learn about more complex and sacred parts of life. Before this, the individual may not have been able to understand completely.

There are often specific people who are made responsible for the sacred training of children. In most cases the uncles, the aunts and the grandfathers establish this kind of relationship with the children. Relatives, like uncles, often take the responsibility for disciplining the children of their sisters. This leaves the parents free to provide a warm, loving relationship with their children.

In other cases the **extended family** of kin and relatives are all "teachers," each member of the family giving something of his or her knowledge to the growing child. Since each kin member has different skills and different experiences, this allows a child to come in contact with many ideas and skills without ever having to leave the community.

For example, Mayor Hobson of the North Slope Borough in Alaska described traditional education of the Inupiaq people: "We Inupiaq people are a nation of people occupying the circumpolar Arctic from Siberia through Alaska and Canada to Greenland. We share common values, language, culture, and economic system. Our culture has enabled us to survive and flourish for thousands of years in the Arctic, where no other man or culture could. For thousands of years, our traditional method of socializing our youth was the responsibility of the family and community.

From the first, visitors to the Arctic have universally commented on the warm disposition of our children. Corporal punishment was absolutely unknown. Boys and girls began their education with the parents, and by the time they reached their teenage years, they had mastered the skills necessary to survive on the land here. From that time forward, the youth with his family and within his community devoted his attention to his intellectual and social growth."

Oral Tradition and Storytelling

Traditionally among Native Americans the oral tradition of a tribe was its most important way of teaching and passing on sacred knowledge and practices. There were no books, libraries, movies, filmstrips, tape recorders, radios, and televisions; therefore, the human voice, hand movements, and facial expressions had to serve as "mass media." This system worked very well because the elders knew that human memory can be a great storehouse. They tested and trained the memory along with the senses, so that the history and traditions of *The People* could be preserved and passed on. Oral tradition was one of the principal ways *The People* had to keep stability over the years in the tribal community.

One of the most important of the oral traditions was storytelling and the preservation of the origin histories. In these histories, *The People* were told where they came from, how the stars were created, where they discovered fire, how light became divided from darkness, and how death originated. It is through these stories too that they were given the basic tools and ways of knowledge with which to survive the world: healing ceremonies, prayers, dances, games, and models of behavior.

The Lakota man, Luther Standing Bear, told of the importance of stories to his people when he said: "These stories were the libraries of our people. In each story there was recorded some event of interest or importance, some happening that affected the lives of the people. There were calamities, discoveries, achievements, and victories to be kept. The seasons and the years were named for principal events that took place. But not all our stories were historical. Some taught the virtues—kindness, obedience, thrift, and the rewards of right living."

Comprehension Check

Circle the letter next to the best answer for each of the following:

1. In general, this reading is about
    a. how two or three specific Native American tribes lived.
    b. some of the common beliefs and traditions of Native American tribes.
    c. how young children learned in various Native American tribes.

2. The first paragraph states that movies and television shows about the lives of Native Americans

    a. are a good source of information about these people.

    b. may not show true information about these people.

    c. may have surprising but true information about these people.

3. The names *Native Americans* and *The People* refer to

    a. groups of people who no longer live in North America.

    b. two different groups of people who live in North America.

    c. all the original people who lived or are now living in North America.

4. Native Americans

    a. do not try to explain everything in the universe or all of life's mysteries.

    b. have always tried to explain everything in our universe.

    c. tried to explain life's mysteries in the past but have stopped recently.

5. The different communities of Native Americans

    a. had somewhat different ways of teaching about sacred ways but had some things in common.

    b. all had exactly the same way of teaching the sacred ways.

    c. all had completely different ways of teaching about sacred ways.

6. One important part of training Native American children and young people included their

    a. asking many questions and listening carefully to the answers.

    b. being very active while asking questions.

    c. watching, listening, and waiting when learning but not asking questions.

7. Traditional Native American societies believed that if a child did not ask questions, she or he

    a. would not be able to learn very much.

    b. could experience learning in a more direct way.

    c. should be in trouble and might be punished.

8. In traditional Native American societies, learning began

    a. at birth.

    b. when the community was ready to teach the child.

    c. when a child began to ask questions.

9. Who teaches the children in traditional Native American societies?

    a. parents only

    b. many different relatives

    c. special teachers from certain families

10. The most important method of teaching and passing on sacred knowledge was

    a. through telling stories orally.

    b. by writing history books.

    c. through special schools.

11. Which one of the following is *not* true about Native American storytelling?

    a. It included many different kinds of stories.

    b. It included only stories about history.

    c. It helped to preserve important history and traditions.

Inference

Answer the following questions based on what you learned in the reading. Do not try to find the answers directly in the reading. Use your ability to infer.

1. The second and third paragraphs of the reading state that traditionally Native Americans have been very spiritual and that religion played an important part in their daily lives. What can you infer about the relationship between these people and natural forces?
2. In the reading a Keres man named Larry Bird says that the Native American way of learning and getting answers is not like learning in school. What can you infer from this statement about how people usually learn in school? How is this different from the traditional Native American way of learning?
3. What can you infer from the reading about the importance of family in traditional Native American societies? What parts of the reading indicate this?
4. The reading says that the oral tradition or storytelling has always been important to tribal communities for several reasons, including stability for the community. How do you think this tradition could provide stability for a tribal community?

Vocabulary Study

A. Vocabulary in Context

Using your knowledge of vocabulary in context, try to guess the meanings of the words in bold in these sentences from the reading.

1. Does your knowledge of these people come from movies or television programs that you have seen? If your information is limited to these **sources,** you may be misinformed as to the true way of life of these people.
2. In order that knowledge did not get separated from experience, the elders **stressed** listening and waiting, not asking why.
3. They were taught to use their organs of smell, to look when there was apparently nothing to see, and to listen **intently** when all seemingly was quiet.
4. Relatives, like uncles, often take the responsibility for **disciplining** the children of their sisters. This leaves the parents free to provide a warm, loving relationship with their children.
5. In other cases the **extended family** of kin and relatives are all "teachers," each member of the family giving something of his or her knowledge to the growing child.
6. Oral tradition was one of the **principal** ways *The People* had to keep stability over the years in the tribal community.

B. Meanings

Choose a synonym from the following list for each of the underlined vocabulary words in the sentences. Write the letter of the synonym on the line next to the number of the sentence. One sentence has two different underlined words, but these have the same synonym.

a. holy, religiously important
b. family, relatives
c. ceremonies, customary practices
d. willingness to follow rules
e. grow, achieve success
f. constancy, no change
g. search for, look for
h. tragedy, great misfortunes

i. beginnings, sources
j. fate, future
k. character, temperament
l. goodness, morality
m. groups, societies
n. events, occurrences
o. keep, protect, maintain

___C___ 1. Some religious <u>observances</u> take place in a church, temple, or mosque, but other <u>observances</u> might take place in a person's home.

___g___ 2. Many societies <u>seek</u> answers to difficult questions about life through specific philosophies or religions.

___i___ 3. Sometimes the <u>origins</u> of a custom or practice are so old that nobody can remember how it started.

____ 4. Some people feel that <u>destiny</u> decides what will happen in life, but other people feel that they can control their lives through their own decisions and actions.

__a__ 5. Most religions consider certain places or areas <u>sacred</u> because they have special meaning.

__h__ 6/7. There could be many kinds of natural <u>disasters</u> in Native
__h__ American stories; these <u>calamities</u> include earthquakes, floods, hurricanes, and volcanic eruptions.

__n__ 8. <u>Phenomena</u> such as thunder and lightning storms or comets in the sky used to scare many people, but today we understand them more scientifically.

__m__ 9. In many areas of the world, people live in <u>tribes</u> and follow the ways of the community.

__b__ 10. In some societies people do not move away from their native land, and they stay near their <u>kin</u> their whole lives.

__e__ 11. If you take good care of living things (plants, animals, and people), they will <u>flourish</u>.

__k__ 12. Some people have a very quiet <u>disposition</u> and never get angry.

__o__ 13. When people move to another culture or society, they may want to <u>preserve</u> their own culture and not change to the new one.

__f__ 14. Some people like to move around and live in different places, but others want <u>stability</u> in their lives and choose to live in one place for many years.

__L__ 15. People who have a lot of <u>virtue</u> try to follow the Golden Rule and treat other people in a nice way.

__d__ 16. When you are in the military, you must show <u>obedience</u> to your superiors because following the rules is important in that environment.

Discussion/Writing

Answer these questions in writing or through discussion.

1. When you were growing up, how did you learn in school, just from listening to the teacher or also by asking questions? Was this a "typical" way to learn at that time and place? Which way do you prefer to learn?

2. Where you grew up, do parents usually raise their children by themselves or do other family members help? How important is the extended family in your culture?

3. Do you know any old or traditional stories that you were told during your childhood (perhaps by parents or grandparents)? How old are these stories? What are they about?

PART 3   WRITING SENTENCES WITH RELATIVE (ADJECTIVE) CLAUSES

Reading
Navajo Sandpaintings

Read the following about Navajo beliefs and sandpaintings. Then answer the questions that follow.

[1]The Navajos, whose homeland today is in northeastern Arizona, have developed sandpainting as part of their healing ritual probably more than any other Native American group. [2]In Navajo religion the universe is a very delicately balanced place which is full of powerful forces. [3]If these forces become upset, this can cause disaster or illness. [4]When someone becomes ill, it becomes necessary to perform one of the Navajo "songs" or "chants" in order to bring the patient back to harmony. [5]These ceremonies, which may last one to nine days, include prayers, medicinal herbs, songs, and sandpaintings. [6]All of these are performed under the direction of a "singer," or priest practitioner, who is known in Navajo as *hatathli*.

[7]The sandpaintings that are used in these ceremonies are created between sunrise and sunset of the same day. [8]These paintings, which people also sometimes call drypaintings, use crushed minerals and charcoal to make patterns. [9]Vegetable material, which may also be used in these paintings, usually comes from pollen or cornmeal. [10]The colors that the sandpainters use are symbolic. [11]Colors indicate directions: for example, white is east, yellow is west, black is north, and blue is south. [12]In addition, red represents sunshine. [13]The paintings range in size from 1 to 20 feet in diameter and may require a dozen or more people working most of the day to complete.

[14]After a singer completes a sandpainting, there is another step. [15]The person whom the painting is trying to help will sit on it. [16]The parts of the painting that relate to the illness are placed on the patient's body. [17]Through this ceremony the patient identifies with the hero of the song to gain the hero's strength. [18]In this way health returns, and harmony is restored. [19]Later that day the sandpainting is destroyed and buried in order to get rid of the evil that it absorbed during the ceremony.

Questions

1. Look at sentence 6 in the reading. How many clauses can you find? What word is joining these clauses together?
2. Look at sentences 2 and 5. How many clauses are in each of these sentences? What word is connecting these clauses?
3. Look at sentence 7. How many clauses are in this sentence? What word is joining these clauses together?

Explanation: Relative Pronouns as Subjects

1. Previously you learned about different ways of putting clauses together, using three kinds of connectors or signals: coordinating conjunctions, subordinating conjunctions, and transitions. You have used these words or expressions to write sentences by putting two clauses one after the other (next to each other) and adding the connector to the beginning or middle of the new sentence.

   EXAMPLES: In this way health returns, **and** harmony is restored.
   coordinating conjunction

   When someone becomes ill, it becomes necessary to
   subordinating conjunction
   perform one of the Navajo "songs" or "chants."

   Colors indicate directions; **for example,** white is east.
   transition

2. In this unit you will learn to combine clauses using another kind of connector. The name of this new group of connectors/signals is *relative pronouns.* When we use relative pronouns, we create dependent (subordinate) clauses that are called *relative clauses* or *adjective clauses.*

3. A relative clause can be used if the two simple sentences you want to combine have a noun or pronoun that is the same (a repeated noun or pronoun). A relative clause describes or gives more information about a noun or pronoun in the other clause.

   Follow this step-by-step process to combine sentences by making one of them a relative clause.

All of the ceremonies are performed under the direction of a priest practitioner who is known in Navajo as hatathli.

Step One
Start with the two sentences to be combined and find the repeated noun or pronoun.

All of the ceremonies are performed under the direction of a **priest practitioner.**
The **priest practitioner** (or **He**) is known in Navajo as *hatathli.*
   repeated noun   (or pronoun)

Step Two
Replace the repeated noun (in the second sentence) with a relative pronoun. In this case, use *who,* the subject pronoun for a person.

~~The priest practitioner~~ (or ~~He~~) is known in Navajo as *hatathli.*
   subject = who

Step Three
Place the relative clause next to the noun it is describing in the first sentence (in this case *priest practitioner*).

All of the ceremonies are performed under the direction of a priest practitioner **who is known in Navajo as** *hatathli.*
                                          relative clause

   NOTE: In modern usage, you may find the word *that* used as a relative pronoun to refer to a person. This is common in conversational English, but you may also see it in writing. Some people consider this informal, especially for academic writing.

4. When the repeated noun or pronoun is not a person, we use a different relative pronoun: *which* or *that*. Follow the same step-by-step process to combine two sentences using *that*.

In Navajo religion the universe is a very delicately balanced place which is full of very powerful forces.

Step One
Start with the two sentences to be combined and find the repeated noun or pronoun.

In Navajo religion the universe is a very delicately balanced **place. This place** (or **It**) is full of very powerful forces.
repeated noun (or pronoun)

Step Two
Replace the repeated noun (in the second sentence) with a relative pronoun. In this case, use the pronoun *which* or *that*.

~~This place (or It)~~ is full of very powerful forces.
   subject = which

Step Three
Place the relative clause next to the noun it is describing in the first sentence (in this case the word *place*).

In Navajo religion the universe is a delicately balanced place **which is full of very powerful forces.**
   relative clause

5. In some cases the relative clause does not follow the other clause but is placed inside it. This is because the relative clause must be next to the noun or pronoun it describes. Follow the step-by-step process again.

The sandpaintings that are used in these ceremonies are created between sunrise and sunset of the same day.

Step One
Start with the two sentences to be combined and find the repeated noun or pronoun.

The sandpaintings are created between sunrise and sunset of the same day.
The sandpaintings (or **They**) are used in these ceremonies.
    repeated noun   (or pronoun)

Step Two
Replace the repeated noun or pronoun (in the second sentence) with a relative pronoun.

~~The sandpaintings (They)~~ are used in these ceremonies.
    that

Step Three
Place the relative clause next to the noun it is describing in the first sentence (in this case the word *sandpaintings*).

The sandpaintings **that are used in these ceremonies** are created
            relative clause
between sunrise and sunset of the same day.

  NOTE: In this case the relative clause goes in the middle of the first sentence because the noun *sandpaintings* appears at the beginning of that sentence. The relative clause *must* go next to this word and cannot go at the end of the sentence.

---

6. The word *whose* is another relative pronoun that combines sentences a little differently. It replaces a possessive noun or pronoun. Follow this step-by-step process to use *whose*.

The Navajos, whose homeland today is in northeastern Arizona, have developed sandpainting as part of their healing ritual.

Step One
Start with the two sentences to be combined. In this case there is no repeated noun or pronoun but a possessive in the second sentence.

The Navajos have developed sandpainting as part of their healing ritual.
Their homeland today is in northeastern Arizona.
(Possessive pronoun *their* refers to Navajos in the first sentence.)

Step Two
Replace the possessive pronoun (but not the noun that follows it) with the relative pronoun *whose.*

whose
~~Their~~ homeland today is in northeastern Arizona.
possessive   noun

Step Three
Place the relative clause next to the noun in the first sentence that the possessive refers to (in this case *Navajos*).

The Navajos, **whose homeland today is in northeastern Arizona,**
                                    relative clause
have developed sandpainting as part of their healing ritual.

7. Important Errors to Avoid

a. A relative clause is a dependent (subordinate) clause; therefore, never write a relative clause all by itself. A relative clause without an independent clause is a fragment.

INCORRECT: According to Navajo religion, the universe is a very delicately balanced place.

Which is full of very powerful forces.
fragment (relative clause only)

CORRECT: According to Navajo religion, the universe is a very delicately balanced place *which* is full of very powerful forces.

NOTE: If a sentence begins with a question word, such as *who* or *which,* it should be a question, not a relative clause.

b. Remember to put the relative clause in the correct place in the combined sentence. The relative pronoun must go next to the word it describes. If you put it in a different place in the sentence, it may confuse the reader.

INCORRECT: The sandpaintings are created between sunrise and sunset of the same day **that are used in these ceremonies.**

CORRECT: The sandpaintings **that are used in these ceremonies** are created between sunrise and sunset of the same day.

In some cases, if you put the relative clause in the wrong place, the meaning of the sentence is affected.

INCORRECT: The Navajos have developed sandpainting as part of their healing ritual probably more than any other Native American group **whose homeland today is in northeastern Arizona.**

In this example it seems the writer is talking about the homeland of other Native American groups and not the homeland of one specific group (the Navajos).

CORRECT: The Navajos, **whose homeland today is in northeastern Arizona,** have developed sandpainting as part of their healing ritual probably more than any other Native American group.

c. Remember to remove (take out) the word you are replacing with the relative pronoun. Do not keep this word in the relative clause.

EXAMPLE: All of the ceremonies are performed under the direction of a priest practitioner **who ~~he~~** is known in Navajo as *hatathli.*

Practice: Relative Clauses

A. Identifying Clauses

Do two things with each of the sentences below:

a. Find the relative clause and put a line under it.
b. Find the word (or words) that the relative pronoun is referring to or explaining in the other clause of the sentence. Put a circle around the word or words.

EXAMPLE: All of the sentences in this activity are about (Native Americans) who lived in the Pacific Northwest.

1. The native people who lived in the Pacific Northwest used giant trees from local forests to make beautiful totem poles.
2. Cedar wood, which is durable but easily carved, is used for making totem poles.
3. You can recognize the animals that are carved on the totem poles from some specific characteristics.
4. The carvers, who were considered specialists, emphasized certain body features of the animals on their carvings.
5. For example, a beaver, which is often carved with two big front teeth, is easy to identify on a totem pole.

B. **Working with Clauses**   *To each of the numbered sentences below, add one of the relative clauses that follow the sentences. Write the whole sentence on the lines provided, and be sure to put the relative clause in the correct place for each sentence. Use each relative clause only one time. The first one has been done as an example.*

1. In the Pacific Northwest a kind of art is a totem pole. c

   In the Pacific Northwest a kind of art that is very well known is a totem pole.

2. People created totem poles from red cedar trees in the Pacific Northwest. *(who)* *(that)*

   _____

   _____

3. These Native American totem poles are made for storytelling. a

   _____

   _____

4. Each carved design represented a different clan or family group. f

   _____

   _____

5. On each totem pole you can see designs.   e

   _____

   _____

6. These animals are recognizable. b

   _____

   _____

    a.   which are found in many places in the Pacific Northwest
    b.   whose physical characteristics are carved into the poles
    c.   ~~that is very well known~~
    d.   who were skilled carvers
    e.   that are animals or supernatural creatures
    f.   which was called a *crest* or *totem*

C. **Sentence Writing**   *Combine each of the following pairs of sentences using a relative clause. For the pairs numbered 2, 3, and 4, use the relative pronoun given in parentheses. For the others, use any relative pronoun you think is correct. The first one has been done as an example. Do not worry about placement of commas for now. This will be explained later in this unit.*

1. Totem poles were not carved for religious reasons.

   They were a typical feature of northwest coastal art.

   (which) *Totem poles, which were a typical feature of northwest coastal art, were not carved for religious reasons.*

2. Beautifully carved totem poles told the story of the heritage of a family.

   ~~These poles~~ which could be found in every village in the Pacific Northwest.

   (which) _____

   _____

3. Carvers *whose* could become important in their society.

   Their work was particularly artistic.

   (whose) _____

   _____

4. Some of the carved images *that* were supernatural beings.

   The images were carved on the totem poles.

   (that) _____

   _____

5. These supernatural beings represented ancestors. *who*

   The ancestors started a *clan,* or related group of people.

   _____

   _____ *which/that* _____

6. The paints came from natural sources, such as charcoal, animal oil, berries, and pieces of rock.

   ~~The~~ paints were used to color the poles.

   _____

   _____

D. **Finding Sentence Problems**   *The following paragraph about a specific kind of totem pole has some problems with relative pronouns and clauses. Find the four mistakes in the paragraph and show how to fix them.*

Editing Focus
Relative pronouns,
Relative clauses,
Fragments

Memorial Poles

   Only wealthy and respected men were allowed to own a totem pole. The pole who was the most common was the memorial pole. A memorial pole was built when a chief died, and a new person took his place. Thus, this kind of pole was built to honor a chief who he had recently died. In addition, it would also announce a chief his position was new in the community. These poles had many kinds of symbols, such as family crest symbols. Some of the highest poles of all were memorial poles. Which could be 50 feet tall or more. Memorial poles were usually put up at huge celebrations.

Explanation: Relative Pronouns as Objects

1. Sometimes when we use a relative pronoun, the word we are replacing in the second sentence is an object, rather than the subject. Follow this step-by-step process to use a relative pronoun to replace an object.

These paintings, which people also sometimes call drypaintings, use crushed minerals and charcoal to make patterns.

Step One
Start with the two sentences to be combined and find the repeated noun or pronoun.

These paintings use crushed minerals and charcoal to make patterns.
People also sometimes call **the paintings** (or **them**) drypaintings.
                                          repeated noun (or pronoun)

Step Two
Replace the repeated noun or pronoun (in the second sentence) with a relative pronoun.

People also sometimes call **the paintings** (or **them**) drypaintings
                                which

Step Three
Put the relative pronoun at the beginning of the relative clause and place the whole clause next to the noun it is describing in the first sentence (in this case, the word *paintings*).

These paintings, **which people also sometimes call drypaintings,**
                                relative clause
use crushed minerals and charcoal to make patterns.

2. In formal English, when the repeated word refers to a person and is an object in the second sentence, we use the relative pronoun *whom.*

The person whom the painting is trying to help will sit on it.

Here is how to write such a sentence:

Step One
Start with the two sentences to be combined and find the repeated noun or pronoun.

The person will sit on it.
The painting is trying to help **the person** (or **him or her**).
                                repeated noun   (or pronoun)

Step Two
Replace the repeated noun (in the second sentence) with a relative pronoun.

The painting is trying to help **the person** (or **him or her**).
                                        whom

Step Three
Put the relative pronoun at the beginning of the relative clause and place the whole clause next to the noun it is describing in the first sentence (in this case, the word *person*).

The *person* **whom the painting is trying to help** will sit on it.
              relative clause

   NOTE: Native English speakers often use *who* instead of *whom*, especially in conversation.

Practice: Relative Clauses

A. **Identifying Clauses**   *On the blank lines after each sentence, write the two simple sentences that were combined to make it.*

EXAMPLE: These paintings, which people also sometimes call drypaintings, use crushed minerals and charcoal to make patterns.
   a. <u>These paintings use crushed minerals and charcoal to make patterns.</u>
   b. <u>People also sometimes call these paintings drypaintings.</u>

1. One idea that the elders hold as very important is respect.
   a. _____
   b. _____

2. Religion and the sacred include the range of experiences that some people might call "nonordinary."
   a. _____
   b. _____

3. Training and education began with children, whom the elders taught to sit still and enjoy it.
   a. _____
   b. _____

4. The colors that the sandpainters use are symbolic.
   a. _____
   b. _____

5. A sandpainting is buried to get rid of the evil that it absorbed during the ceremony.

a. _____

b. _____

B. Working with Clauses   *To each of the numbered sentences below, add one of the relative clauses that follow the sentences. Use each relative clause only one time. The first one has been done as an example.*

1. The totem poles tell stories of people's lives and clans.

   The totem poles that you find in the Pacific Northwest tell stories of people's lives and clans.

2. The images are of different kinds of animals.

   _____

   _____

3. Cedar trees were also used for other things, such as houses and tools.

   _____

   _____

4. A special kind of pole was a memorial pole.

   _____

   _____

5. A carver could become an important person in his society.

   _____

   _____

   a. that you see on the totem poles
   b. whom the chief considered very skilled
   c. that you find in the Pacific Northwest
   d. which carvers used for totem poles
   e. which a carver made to honor a dead chief

C. Sentence Writing   *Combine each pair of sentences below using a relative pronoun. For the first two pairs, use the pronoun given in parentheses. For the others, use any pronoun you think is correct for the sentence. Do not worry about placement of commas for now. This will be explained later in this unit.*

EXAMPLE: Another kind of carving is called a talking stick. Carvers make talking sticks in addition to totem poles.

(which) Another kind of carving is called a talking stick which carvers make in addition to totem poles.

1. A talking stick was often used by a chief.

   Carvers made a talking stick from cedar.

   (which) _____

   _____

2. The talking sticks were used by chiefs at community gatherings.

   Carvers designed the talking sticks with different kinds of figures.

   (that) _____

   _____

3. A chief had a talking stick.

   He tapped a talking stick on the floor to get people's attention before he spoke.

   _____

   _____

4. A chief would also use the talking stick to emphasize his point.

   The people followed the chief as their leader.

   _____

   _____

5. A talking stick resembles a miniature totem pole.

   Some important speakers still use a talking stick today.

   _____

   _____

Explanation: Relative Clauses and Commas

Some relative clauses require commas, but other relative clauses do not.

1. EXAMPLES OF RELATIVE CLAUSES WITH COMMAS
   a. Mayor Hobson, **who is from the North Slope Borough of Alaska**, described the traditional education of his people.
   b. The Navajos, **whose homeland today is in northeastern Arizona**, have developed sandpainting as part of their healing ritual.
   c. Cedar wood, **which is durable but easily carved**, is used for making totem poles.

In these examples, each relative clause gives extra information about the subject of the sentence. The subject is something specific, so we can understand who or what the sentence is about without the information given in the relative clause.

Example a Subject: Mayor Hobson = the name of a specific person
Example b Subject: Navajos = the name of a particular Native
                                American tribe

Example C Subject: cedar wood = a specific kind of wood

This kind of relative clause is called a *nonessential clause* because the reader doesn't need the information in the clause in order to know what the subject is. Some people call this kind of relative clause a *nonrestrictive clause* because the information in the clause does not limit (or restrict) the subject. The subject is already clear and does not need more explanation or description. Nonrestrictive clauses are often used with names or proper nouns.

2. EXAMPLES OF RELATIVE CLAUSES WITHOUT COMMAS
   a. People **who were skilled carvers** created totem poles.

   The subject of this example sentence is *people.* There are many kinds of people, but this relative clause limits this subject to skilled carvers and not any other kind of people. This information is *essential* or *restrictive.* That is, the information in this relative clause is necessary for the reader to understand exactly which people are included in the subject.

   b. The paints **which were used to color the poles** came from natural sources.

   The subject of this example sentence is *paints,* but there are many kinds of paints. The relative clause is essential (restrictive) because it tells the reader that the subject is only the paints used to color the poles and not other kinds of paint.

   c. A memorial pole was built to honor a chief **who had recently died.**

   In this example, the relative clause refers to the word *chief.* This relative clause is limiting (restricting) the kind of chief to only the one who had recently died. Other chiefs who were still living did not have a memorial pole built for them. The relative clause is necessary for the reader to understand that only the chiefs who were dead had memorial poles and other chiefs did not.

   These relative clauses are called *essential clauses* or *restrictive clauses,* and they do not require commas.

3. The following chart reviews relative clauses (adjective clauses).

Sentence Combining with Relative Pronouns

Position in Sentence

After independent clause

_____	_____	_____
independent clause	relative pronoun	relative clause

EXAMPLE: The art used some interesting paints which came from minerals.

Middle of independent clause

_____	_____	_____
noun or pronoun	relative clause	rest of independent clause

EXAMPLE: The paints which were used to color the poles came from natural sources.

Punctuation

_____	_____	____ _____

restrictive (essential) = no commas

EXAMPLE: A person who is a skilled carver can make a totem pole.

_____,	_____	____, _____
nonrestrictive	(nonessential)	= commas

EXAMPLE: Cedar wood, which is durable, is used for totem poles.

SUBJECT:	*who*
	which or *that*
OBJECT:	*whom*
	which or *that*
POSSESSIVE:	*whose*

4. Notice that a nonessential (nonrestrictive) clause in the middle of a sentence requires two commas: one comma just before the relative pronoun and the other comma at the end of the clause. If the relative clause is at the end of a sentence, we place a comma just before the relative pronoun and a period at the end of the sentence.

EXAMPLES: My friend's talking stick, which he keeps on his wall, is beautiful.

My friend has a beautiful talking stick, which he keeps on his wall.

5. When we use the relative pronoun *that,* we do not use commas. You will not find this pronoun in nonessential (nonrestrictive) clauses.

Practice: Relative Clauses

A. **Identifying Types of Relative Clauses**

1. Look at sentences a and b below.
   - In which sentence are all the students studying English? _____
   - In which sentence are only some of the students studying English? _____
   - In which sentence can you find a restrictive (essential) relative clause? _____

   a. The students who are studying English are learning about totem poles.

   b. The students, who are studying English, are learning about totem poles.

2. Look at sentences a and b below.
   - Which sentence tells you that there is only one example sentence? How do you know this? _____
   - Which sentence contains a nonrestrictive (nonessential) relative clause? _____

   a. The example sentence which is about totem poles is not difficult to understand.

   b. The example sentence, which is about totem poles, is not difficult to understand.

B. **Commas and Meanings of Relative Clauses**
Each of the following sentences contains a relative clause. Answer the questions about the meaning of these sentences. Circle the correct letter.

1. Native Americans, who are also known as *The People,* seek their own way to explain people's origins and destinies.

   This sentence says

   a. all Native Americans are known as *The People.*

   b. only some Native Americans are known as *The People.*

2. Great respect is held for those people who protect sacred ways and help them grow.

   This sentence says respect is held

   a. only for people who protect sacred ways.

   b. for all people.

3. Training began with children, who were taught to sit still and enjoy it.

   This sentence says the training was for

   a. only the children who could sit still and enjoy it.

   b. all the children.

4. A child who cannot sit still is a half-developed child.
   This sentence says

   a. all children from that tribe are half-developed.

   (b.) some children can sit still and some cannot.

5. The Navajos, whose homeland today is in northeastern Arizona, have developed sandpainting as part of their healing ritual.

   This sentence says

   a. the homeland of all Navajos today is in northeastern Arizona.

   b. only some Navajos have a homeland in northeastern Arizona today.

6. The paintings which are used in these ceremonies are created between sunrise and sunset of the same day.

   This sentence says

   a. all paintings in this tribe are created between sunrise and sunset of the same day.

   (b.) only the paintings used in this particular ceremony are created between sunrise and sunset of the same day.

7. These ceremonies, which may last one to nine days, include prayers, songs, and sandpaintings.

   This sentence says

   a. all of these ceremonies may last one to nine days.

   b. only some ceremonies last one to nine days.

C. Using Commas in Relative Clauses

Decide if each sentence below should have commas before and after the relative clause. Some sentences are followed by more information about the meaning given in parentheses. Use this information to help you decide about adding commas.

1. Carvers who trained from youth to create totem poles were deeply religious people. (All carvers trained from youth.)
2. A carver whose payment came in the form of blankets, food, and other valuable items received food and lodging from the pole owner while he worked. (All carvers received this payment.)
3. Thus, a carver who was very skilled could become very wealthy. (Some carvers were more skilled than others.)
4. The carvers who were the best trained had a special name and received the most pay for their work.
5. These special carvers whose work was expected to be without mistakes needed complete privacy when they carved.

Editing Focus
Fragments,
Relative Pronouns,
Punctuation

D. **Finding Sentence Problems**

The following short reading about social status in Native American societies of the Pacific Northwest has some problems related to the use of relative clauses. There are 14 mistakes: 3 fragments, 7 problems with commas, and 4 problems with relative pronouns or other pronouns. Find these mistakes and show how to fix them.

Social Status in the Pacific Northwest

Under the system of social ranking found in tribes on the Northwest coast, each villager was born to a specific status and clearly knew his or her social rank. There were several groups, that were ranked as follows:

- At the top of the system were the chiefs, who they were few in number. Their status, which gave them great influence over their people, made them function as heads of lineages. Each village was economically independent with a head chief who his inherited position made him the highest-ranking member of the group.

- The next group, which included younger brothers of chiefs, was the nobles. Some of the nobles were not brothers of chiefs but were born into high-ranking families. This still gave them a special status. Which they received at birth.

- The shamans were doctors. When the people became ill, they went to the shamans, whom could cure them with rituals, medicines, and special powers.

- The commoners whose numbers made up the largest part of the society were another group. A commoner could be a social nobody. Who fished and hunted for the chief in return for part of the profits. Other commoners which were excellent warriors and skilled woodcarvers could be important people in their society.

- The group, which was considered at the bottom of the social ranking, was the slaves. Slaves were usually women and children. Who were taken captive in wars. In some groups, slaves numbered as high as 20% of the population. These slaves, whose work included labor such as carrying water and firewood received protection from their masters. However, slaves were considered pieces of property, that a master could sell or give away.

Discussion/Writing

Answer these questions in writing or through discussion. Try to use relative clauses in your sentences.

1. Is any traditional artwork produced in the place you grew up or in the place you are living now? Is this artwork used only for enjoyment or also for more serious purposes? How is this artwork related to the culture?

2. In your opinion how important is knowledge of traditional culture in modern life? Explain your answer.

3. What kind of traditional social structure does your native culture have? Are there some people who have more status than others? What is the place of the elderly in your culture? Do older people hold an important place in society, and do younger people take care of them in certain ways?

PART 4   WRITING ESSAYS (OPINION)

Read this essay about customs. Then answer the questions that follow it.

Following the Old Ways or the New

When people move to a new country, they often find themselves surrounded by a whole new world which has a completely different environment from the one to which they are accustomed. They may not know the language, and this can cause trouble with communication. In addition, there are many customs and traditions that are new and perhaps seem strange. Newcomers may feel confused and uncomfortable because of all of this, but they may also enjoy and adapt to other parts of their new experiences. I believe that it is best for people to follow the customs of their new environment for two reasons: they will gain personal enrichment, and they will adapt better to their new environment.

When people try to follow the customs of their new environment, they gain an opportunity for personal enrichment. Through these new experiences, they learn about other people and places and new ways of doing things. For example, when I started school in this country, I found a very different way of learning in my classes. Students here do not have to remain silent and listen to the teacher's explanations as we do in my country. In fact, teachers, who often tell us to work in pairs or groups and have discussions with each other, expect us to ask and answer questions as part of the learning process. At first, this was

strange and difficult for me, but slowly I have started to be able to participate more, and I can appreciate this new way of learning. I am getting to know my classmates and new culture better; moreover, I am improving my language skills through this kind of participation. I now know that adapting to and following the culture of the new environment can be both enjoyable and enlightening.

Following the customs and traditions of a new place may also help newcomers adapt and acclimate to their new life. People who try to follow the ways of their new environment will gain an understanding of both their new neighbors and their surroundings, and with this understanding comes a feeling of comfort and belonging. For instance, when I first came here, I was confused about how to greet people and say hello or start a conversation. I watched people on the street and saw many different ways people did this, such as shaking hands, hugging, and even kissing one another. I learned from my friends at school how to greet people my age as well as my elders. I also learned it is important in this country to try to look people in the eye when I talk to them. As a result, since I started to follow some of the local customs when meeting and greeting people, I have not felt like such a stranger or outsider.

Living in a new country can be overwhelming and confusing at times. Some people may feel lost and uncomfortable and may want to cling to the customs and traditions that they are used to from their own culture. In my opinion it is good to keep some of these; however, it is important to try to embrace and adopt some new ways as well. Keeping some old ways and at the same time keeping an open mind about following some of the new ones may be the best way to help people feel comfortable and fulfilled in a new country.

Essay Discussion

1. How many paragraphs are in this essay?
2. Does this essay follow the organization pattern described in Unit Two? Does it have all of the following?
   ____ an introduction
   ____ a thesis statement
   ____ two or three body paragraphs
   ____ a topic sentence for each body paragraph
   ____ supporting sentences that relate to the topic sentences
   ____ a concluding paragraph

3. What is the purpose of this essay? What kind of information is the writer trying to give to the reader?

Expressing Opinions

In college writing students sometimes need to give their opinions about issues discussed in their classes. For example, students may be asked to agree or disagree with a statement or to give an opinion about a controversial topic. When they do this, they should be able to give reasons to support their opinion. The reasons given as support should be based on facts. Thus, it is important to know the difference between facts and opinions for this support.

Writing Focus

Organization of an Essay (Opinion), Words to Express Opinion, Facts versus Opinions

What opinion does the writer express in the essay titled "Following the Old Ways or the New"? _____

What words does the writer use to tell the reader this is an opinion?

_____

What two reasons does the writer give to support that opinion?

_____

_____

Words for Expressing Opinions

A writer can use certain words or expressions to signal that she or he is expressing an opinion. These include the following:

I think   I believe   in my opinion   I feel   I support (or *I do not support*)

Difference Between Facts and Opinions

A *fact* is something that can be proven. It is something that is always true and can be referred to as *objective.* For example, we know there are many different languages and cultures in the world. This is a fact.

Opinions are what people believe. An opinion expresses a particular way of thinking or a point of view. For example, saying that one culture or language is better or easier to understand than another is an opinion. People may have different ideas about what is better or what is easy or difficult. Those ideas depend on the people who are expressing them, and we can refer to them as *subjective.*

Look at the following examples of facts and opinions from the reading about Navajo sandpaintings (on page 144).

FACTS	OPINIONS
1. The homeland of the Navajos is in northeastern Arizona.	1. Navajos believe the universe is delicately balanced and has powerful forces.
2. Navajos make a sandpainting for a sick person.	2. Navajos think upsetting the forces of the universe can cause sickness in people.
3. A sandpainting has patterns in various colors.	3. Navajos feel a sick person can gain strength and harmony from a sandpainting.

Practice: Facts and Opinions

Decide whether each piece of information from the reading "Native Americans and Their Sacred Ways" (on pages 137–139) is a fact or opinion. Write F for "Fact" or O for "Opinion" on the line before each statement.

____ 1. Elders in Native American communities stressed listening and waiting but not asking why as a way to educate children.

____ 2. They taught children to sit still and enjoy it.

____ 3. If a child could not sit still, she or he was a half-developed child.

____ 4. If a child asked questions, he or she was stupid.

____ 5. At a certain age, a child is ready to learn more complex things.

____ 6. Native American education began at birth.

____ 7. It is better for parents to discipline their children less than other relatives do.

____ 8. Members of the extended family helped teach and discipline Native American children.

Discussion/Writing

Answer these questions in writing or through discussion. Try to use relative clauses in your sentences.

1. Do you agree or disagree with the opinion expressed in the essay about following the customs of a new environment (on pages 161–162)? Why?

2. Imagine you are going to write an essay that says people should *not* change their customs when they move to a new environment. What reasons can you give for this opinion?

3. What do you think are the most difficult parts of living in a new culture or country? What are the easiest parts for you?

Summary Writing

For an explanation of summary writing and practice of this skill, read pages 212–217 in the Appendix. Then follow the instructions. Be sure to use relative clauses in your sentences in these summaries.

1. Summarize the last three paragraphs of the reading "Native Americans and Their Sacred Ways" (pages 137–139). Summarize each of these paragraphs in two or three sentences.

2. Summarize each paragraph in the reading about Navajo sandpaintings on page 145. Do not write more than two or three sentences to summarize each paragraph.

3. Summarize the entire essay "Following the Old Ways or the New" (on pages 161–162) in one paragraph of four or five sentences.

Writing Assignment

A. Picking the Topic

You are going to write an opinion essay of four or five paragraphs. Choose <u>one</u> of the following topics to write about. Be sure to support your opinion with reasons. Add facts to your support.

1. What do you think is the best way for children to learn: actively (such as through asking questions) or passively (such as through listening and watching)?

2. Who do you think should have the most responsibility and influence in bringing up children, the parents or the extended family?

3. Do you think it is important for people to keep the traditional beliefs and ways of their culture and pass them on to their children?

B. Understanding the Assignment/Answering the Question

Before you start to write, make sure that you understand the assignment. Your essay must answer the question and should not discuss other things. You should also make sure that your essay gives an opinion. Look at the following ideas for essays on the three possible topics and decide which ones fit the assignment and which ones do not. Cross out the ideas that you think will not work.

Topic 1: an essay about
• why learning actively is better for children than learning passively
• why learning actively and learning passively are both good ways to learn
• why education is better in your native culture than it is where you are living now
• how learning passively can be very good for children

Topic 2: an essay about
- why your culture stresses the extended family's importance in life
- why you enjoy having an extended family
- why parents should be mostly responsible for bringing up their children
- why members of an extended family should have no responsibility for bringing up their relatives' children

Topic 3: an essay about
- how important it is to learn the ways of your culture and teach them to your children
- how you learned the traditional ways of your culture
- why traditional ways should not be carried on in modern life
- why you enjoy and feel most comfortable with your own culture

Following the Steps in the Writing Process

Before You Write

■ **Step One: Generating Ideas and Brainstorming**
A. Think about these three topics.

1. Will you talk about children learning actively or passively? _____

   What two or three reasons do you have for preferring one way of learning over the other?

   _____

   _____

   _____

2. Will you talk about whether parents or extended family should have more responsibility for bringing up children? _____

   What two or three reasons do you have for preferring one of these practices?

   _____

   _____

3. Will you talk about following traditional ways or forgetting about them? _____

   What two or three reasons do you have for preferring one of these choices?

   _____

   _____

B. What kind of support (facts, details, or examples) can you provide for the reasons you wrote above? Using lists or clustering diagrams, write your ideas in the spaces below. Don't worry about organization at this time.

Active or Passive Learning

Parents or Extended Family

Keeping or Not Keeping Traditions/Customs

C. *Choose one of your lists or clustering diagrams for your essay. Then check the details to make sure there are enough, and they are all relevant.*

■ **Step Two: Organizing Ideas and Planning**
To start organizing your ideas, think about the three parts of an essay.

INTRODUCTION WITH THESIS STATEMENT
Write a thesis statement for your essay. Be sure that this sentence answers the question with your opinion.

_____

_____

Write your thesis statement on the chart on page 171.

BODY PARAGRAPHS
Topic Sentences
How many body paragraphs will you have in your essay (two or three)?

_____

a. What is your first reason? What are the topic and controlling idea of the first paragraph?

   Topic: _____

   Controlling idea: _____
   Write your topic sentence on the organization chart on page 171.

b. What is your second reason? What are the topic and controlling idea of the second paragraph?

   Topic: _____

   Controlling idea: _____
   Write your topic sentence on the chart on page 171.

c. If you will have a third body paragraph, what is your third reason? What are the topic and controlling idea of the paragraph?

   Topic: _____

   Controlling idea: _____
   Write your topic sentence on the chart on page 171.

Support
Think about your support for the reasons presented in your body paragraphs. What facts, details, and examples can you give? Write notes about your support on the chart on page 171. Be sure all of your support relates to your topic sentences and thesis statement and that you have enough support for each body paragraph.

CONCLUDING PARAGRAPH
Write some ideas for a concluding paragraph on the chart on page 171. Will you summarize the main points of the essay, restate your thesis, or add final comments?

- **Step Three: Getting Feedback**
  Your teacher may ask you to work with a partner and complete a peer review of your chart. Use the peer review sheet on page 236 of the Appendix.

When You Write

- **Step Four: Writing the First Draft (Rough Draft)**
  When you write the first draft of your opinion essay, do the following:

  - Be sure to state an opinion and give reasons to support it.
  - Include relative clauses in some of your sentences.
  - Try to include as much sentence variety in your essay as possible. Use coordinating conjunctions, subordinating conjunctions, and transitions.
  - Be careful to avoid fragments, run-ons, and comma splices.
  - Try to include at least three or four vocabulary words from this unit.

After You Write

Check Your Work
After you finish writing the first draft, check it with the following checklist.

- [ ] This essay discusses one of the following: educating children actively or passively, bringing up children mostly by parents or extended family, keeping or forgetting about traditional ways and customs.
- [ ] This essay has three main parts: introduction, body, and conclusion.
- [ ] The introductory paragraph has several sentences. It starts out general and ends with a thesis statement.
- [ ] The thesis statement clearly states my opinion about the topic I chose.
- [ ] This essay has two or three body paragraphs that give reasons to support my opinion.
- [ ] Each body paragraph has a topic sentence.
- [ ] The body paragraphs are related to the thesis statement.
- [ ] Some of my sentences have relative clauses.
- [ ] The sentences in this essay include a variety of coordinating and subordinating conjunctions and transitions.
- [ ] I looked for run-ons, comma splices, and fragments and corrected them.
- [ ] I used some of the vocabulary words from this lesson in the essay.

Getting Feedback
Your teacher will decide the type of feedback you will receive for the first draft. It may be peer review, teacher review, or both. For peer review, use the sheet on page 237 of the Appendix.

■ ***Step Five: Revising***
After you receive feedback revise the organization of your essay or any sentences in it, if necessary. You may want to change your thesis statement, your topic sentences, or parts of your introductory or concluding paragraph. You may want to add, take out, or change the order of some supporting sentences. Your teacher may ask you to get feedback again after you have revised your essay.

■ ***Step Six: Editing***
Make any necessary changes in grammar, spelling, punctuation, and capitalization. Your teacher may want you to have feedback after editing as well.

■ ***Step Seven: Preparing the Final Draft***
Prepare your final draft to be handed in to the teacher.

Organizing Your Ideas for Writing an Opinion Essay

TITLE: _____

INTRODUCTION

Thesis statement: _____

_____

BODY PARAGRAPH 1

Topic sentence: _____

_____

Details/Support

_____

_____

_____

BODY PARAGRAPH 2

Topic sentence: _____

_____

Details/Support

_____

_____

_____

BODY PARAGRAPH 3

Topic sentence: _____

_____

Details/Support

_____

_____

_____

CONCLUSION

_____

_____

_____

The Changing Face of Business

Content Area: Business

Readings: The Value of the Customer
A Successful Neighborhood Restaurant
The Changing Music Industry
Obtaining Music from the Internet

Short Reading: Starting an Internet Business

Sentence-Combining Focus: Connectors of Contrast and Similarity

Editing Focus: Fragments, Run-ons,
Comma Splices,
Punctuation

Writing Focus: Compare/Contrast Essay Organization

PART 1 UNIT PREVIEW

Preview Activity: Consumer Questionnaire

What kind of consumer are you? Answer the following questions. Then discuss your answers with a partner.

1. When I shop for clothes, I like to buy:

   a. from a large department store.

   b. from small shops only.

   c. name-brand items only.

   d. from mail-order catalogs.

2. When I shop for electronic equipment (stereo components/CD players/ DVD players/televisions, etc.), I like to buy:

   a. from a large discount store.

   b. from a small shop.

   c. on the Internet.

   d. only the highest-quality, most expensive items.

3. When I shop for computer equipment or office supplies, I prefer to:

   a. buy on the Internet.

   b. buy from a large discount store.

   c. buy from a small dealer or store.

   d. look on the Internet for prices and then go to a store.

4. In general, how important is customer service to you? (Customer service includes having people at a store help you before you buy something, having a positive experience with a problem like a return or exchange, etc.)

Quickwrite

Write for five minutes about one of the following topics. Do not worry about grammar, spelling, or punctuation. Just write whatever comes into your mind about the topic.

- Do you enjoy shopping, or do you feel it is just a necessity? Why do you feel this way?
- What makes you want to do business with a particular store or company again?

PART 2   READING AND VOCABULARY

Read the following on providing service to customers. Then answer the questions that follow.

Over the past 10 years, **consumers** have been presented with many new avenues for buying products and services. For instance, customers all over the United States can find **competitive,** large chains of stores in industries from office supplies to health food to books. These chains have been able to gain control over many industries by offering self-service and lower prices than smaller stores selling the same products. In addition, these companies also can cover large areas with mass-market advertising and may have very large catalog and Web-based supply systems. Furthermore, thanks to the Internet and mobile wireless devices, customers are now armed with new tools with which they can find and contact a business as well as its competitors around the clock and around the globe. Using the power of the Internet, customers are inventing and improving new business models, including peer-to-peer file sharing (such as Kazaa) and auction-based marketplaces (such as eBay).

In this new business climate, smaller business **entrepreneurs** have worked hard to survive. Nonetheless, the number of independent bookstores has fallen by nearly half over the past decade, and this is a **trend** that has been repeated in a number of other industries. How do businesses, especially smaller companies, stay competitive? What is the best strategy to help them remain **profitable?** Although some small companies may want to reduce prices to keep up with the big chains, that can spell disaster for the average entrepreneur because small businesses don't have the **bulk** purchasing power of bigger companies. Some people think that the answer is to offer customers something known as **value-**added services.

This strategy means not competing on price but convincing customers that small businesses offer more value. Therefore, some companies focus on the quality and consistency of the customer experience they offer, and some have even reorganized themselves to manage by and for customer value. They measure what matters most to customers. They have learned that customers want great service, fair prices, and **innovative** offerings. These companies understand that if today's customers don't get these things, they can go to the competition with just a click of the mouse on their computer. In addition, they can easily tell many people all over the world about their experiences. The services that a small business offers can ensure customers' trust and encourage the belief that entrepreneurial businesses provide more homespun **authenticity.** In other words, when people feel that a company and its products are honest and real, they will often become **loyal** customers.

Services that make consumers believe they are receiving added value can take on several forms. For many companies service means traveling around the country to meet with customers and **gauge** their needs. For example, one owner of a small chain of home furnishing shops says she spends as much time as possible on the road visiting and talking to her clients. Another businesswoman, an owner of a chain of children's clothing stores in the suburbs of New York City, sends personal shoppers to some customers' homes with racks of clothes, so **clients** don't have to leave their houses to shop.

In other cases, offering value-added services simply means always having a knowledgeable employee available to handle customers' needs, which is something very few large corporations can do. For smaller businesses, this requires spending the money to have more employees on the floor than their giant competitors. For example, an owner of a health-food store in Connecticut provides this level of service by personally greeting every customer who comes through his door and asking each one what he or she is looking for. Even though this owner's competition is a larger health-food store (part of a chain) nearby, his store has benefited from that situation. This is because people come to the smaller store to ask questions about things they don't understand in the larger store. Then they stay in the smaller store and buy things.

This strategy can work even when there is no actual contact in a store setting. Even though a business may be Web-based, customers can still receive specialized service as shown by the owners of a Web-based **vintage** record company based in their home in California. These owners decided to pay others to help them with parts of their business that they don't know how to do (such as Web design) so that they can spend most of their time on the product they sell. They have educated themselves so completely about old records that they can provide more information about each LP than nearly any record store owner in the country. In addition, they write commentaries about each LP and communicate personally with customers through e-mail.

Some customers want capabilities that **retailers** haven't been able to offer in the past, but now some manufacturers are responding to such customers' needs and wishes. For example, customers of one company that manufactures backpacks and messenger bags have started to do this. Customers of this company have shown a preference for custom-**designing** their backpacks, but retailers do not want to take custom orders in their stores. Therefore, the manufacturer decided to go directly to the customers by having them design their own backpacks on the Internet and then shipping out the products within a day or two.

The value-added strategy can also be beneficial to employees of a business. Although larger companies can afford to pay slightly higher salaries, smaller companies are better able to offer employees a variety of roles and greater involvement in the business. This allows the owners to more easily empower their employees, so the workers have more knowledge, can make some decisions on their own when they are working, and can feel more **commitment** toward the company.

Many successful entrepreneurs also back up their promise of value-added services with a guarantee. The owners of the Web-based vintage record business promise that customers can return anything for any reason, and despite that risky strategy, they have **prospered** and established a strong base of regular customers. Other entrepreneurs take even larger risks to show customers the value of their services. For example, one owner of a software company received a contract from a local police department. When one of the other **firms** that was working for the police department went out of business, the owner of the software company decided her firm would take on the failed company's workload for free. By doing this, she gave up hundreds of thousands of dollars in **potential** fees. Nonetheless, the gamble worked. Her dedication to providing service favorably impressed the police department, which later gave her a new, larger contract.

Experts in the area of marketing believe that small business owners should move away from accepted methods of advertising to promote their value-added services. For example, entrepreneurs have traditionally stayed away from comparing their services to the services of the large chains. However, now the experts are saying they should not be afraid to emphasize their value-added services, in order to show the lack of service in the larger chain stores. Marketing consultants also suggest that entrepreneurs generally avoid radio and television advertisements. A small business owner wants to show his or her business is different because of its emphasis on value. Therefore, it's a good idea to show that the business will provide more personal service through other means of advertising such as a newsletter or face-to-face contact with the customers.

In this economy loyal customers have become a very important **commodity.** Sometimes the hardest thing for a company to obtain is not investment **capital,** products, or employees, or even a brand name, but customer loyalty. Customer capital can be at least as important as investment capital.

Comprehension Check

Circle the letter next to the choice that best completes each statement or answers each question.

1. Another good title for this reading might be
   a. "Problems in Small Businesses."
   b. "Small Businesses versus Large Corporations."
   c. "Customer-Oriented Business."

2. According to this reading
   a. large chain stores are not much competition for smaller businesses.
   b. small businesses have to work hard to compete with large chain stores.
   c. small businesses cannot possibly compete with large chain stores.

3. Large chain stores often

    a. offer better customer service than small businesses.

    b. can advertise over a wider area (to more people) than small businesses.

    c. have higher-quality products than small businesses.

4. According to this reading the Internet has changed the following for customers *except* that

    a. customers can establish their own prices for goods.

    b. customers can change the design of a product they buy.

    c. customers can bargain for products with many small businesses.

5. According to this reading, value-added services

    a. can be effective in any type of business, including one based in the Internet.

    b. can only be done in person and not by a Web-based business.

    c. should only be done in a store that is part of a large chain.

6. The main goal of value-added services in a small business is to

    a. ensure a base of loyal, satisfied customers.

    b. get as many one-time customers as possible.

    c. have the customers buy the most expensive products the business offers.

7. A small business owner might offer value-added services by

    a. providing more employees to help while the customer is shopping.

    b. visiting the customers personally, even if they live in different parts of the country.

    c. doing both a and b.

8. What did the owners of the Web-based vintage record company do in order to have an advantage over other companies in the same business?

    a. They had more records available to sell.

    b. They learned details about their records and shared that information with their customers.

    c. They e-mailed each customer with information about special sales.

9. What did the manufacturer of backpacks and messenger bags do that was unusual?

    a. It made new styles of its products to sell to stores.

    b. It asked stores that sell its products to supply custom-made products.

    c. It dealt with its customers directly to give them their specific requests.

10. Which of the following might *not* be a benefit to an employee working in a small company offering value-based strategy?

    a. She or he will earn a higher salary in the smaller company.

    b. She or he will learn more about the product in the smaller company.

    c. She or he will feel like an important part of the company.

11. The ninth paragraph of the reading talks about risks that some business owners have taken. One of the results of taking the risks was

    a. the creation of happy customers and a related increase in business.

    b. a loss of money because the customers were not happy.

    c. the learning of an important lesson about not taking risks in the future.

12. Marketing experts believe that small business owners should

    a. use only old-fashioned, accepted ways of advertising.

    b. never compare themselves to the large chain stores in their advertisements.

    c. try some new ways to advertise their value-added services.

Inference

Answer the following questions based on what you learned in the reading. Do not try to find the answers directly in the reading. Use your ability to infer.

1. At the end of the first paragraph, the reading mentions several ways customers can use the Internet. Why are these new practices important to businesses? What does this say about the power of the customer?
2. The reading discusses one manufacturer's decision to allow customers to design their own backpacks. Why do you think retailers do not want to take custom orders?
3. In the eighth paragraph the reading tells how a value-based strategy can be beneficial to employees. How can this strategy be beneficial to the employer as well?
4. The ninth paragraph gives examples of risks taken by the owners of two small businesses. Why are these examples considered risky?

Vocabulary Study

A. Meanings

Choose a synonym from the following list for each of the underlined vocabulary words in the sentences. Write the letter of the synonym on the line next to the sentence.

a. dedication
b. products, goods for sale
c. measure, evaluate
d. large quantity
e. creating, planning
f. one who organizes or manages a new business
g. direction, tendency
h. lucrative, money-making
i. genuine, real

j. vendors, sellers
k. significance, worth
l. possible, capable of developing into
m. faithful, devoted
n. new, creative
o. trying to perform better or to win something
p. funds or resources
q. succeed economically, flourish

_____ 1. Many people like to buy grains such as cereal and rice in <u>bulk</u> at health food stores because it is cheaper than buying them in small quantities.

_____ 2. John received a raise from his boss because he thought of an <u>innovative</u> way to bring more customers to the business.

_____ 3. Some <u>commodities</u> such as gold and silver are very expensive, but others are not.

_____ 4. Some small companies do not <u>prosper</u> because larger companies take away too much business.

_____ 5. Sometimes people change the way they spend their money, so it's important for a businessperson to watch each <u>trend</u> in buying.

_____ 6. My friend wanted to start a new business, but he did not have enough <u>capital</u>, so he had to go to the bank for a loan.

_____ 7. Many businesses like to advertise on the Internet because they know <u>potential</u> customers will read their advertisements.

_____ 8. Employers look for good workers who have a strong <u>commitment</u> to the company because they don't want to continually hire new employees.

_____ 9. A loyal customer has <u>value</u> to a business owner because the owner knows he can count on this customer to support his business.

_____10. In order to remain <u>competitive</u> with other businesses, one woman sends people to customers' homes with samples of her product to look at.

_____11. Some small business owners are <u>designing</u> new ways to give customers value-added services.

____ 12. Jean did not want to work for someone else, so she became an <u>entrepreneur</u> by starting her own business.

____ 13. Some customers look for <u>authentic</u> products because they want to know they are spending their money on quality products.

____ 14. When an employer treats his or her employees well and offers fair salaries and benefits, workers will probably be <u>loyal</u> and stay with the company.

____ 15. A good businessperson can <u>gauge</u> sales of products in order to know which items are selling well and which ones are not.

____ 16. Many big companies sell their products to <u>retailers</u>, and these businesses sell to the customers.

____ 17. If a business is not <u>profitable</u>, the owner may have to close it.

B. Vocabulary in Context

Using your knowledge of vocabulary in context, try to guess the meanings of the words in bold in these sentences.

1. Over the past 10 years, **consumers** have been presented with many new avenues for buying products and services. For instance, customers all over the United States can find competitive, large chains of stores.
2. An owner of a chain of children's clothing stores in the suburbs of New York City sends personal shoppers to some customers' homes with racks of clothes, so **clients** don't have to leave their houses to shop.
3. Even though a business may be Web-based, customers can still receive specialized service, as shown by the owners of a Web-based **vintage** record company. These owners educated themselves so completely about old records that they can provide more information about each LP than nearly any record store owner in the country.
4. When one of the other **firms** that was working for the police department went out of business, the owner of the software company decided her firm would take on the failed company's workload for free.

Discussion/Writing

Answer these questions in writing or through discussion.

1. Think about the stores in the neighborhood where you are living now or where you lived in the past. What kinds of stores are they (smaller and family-owned or larger chain stores)? Which ones do (did) you shop at the most? Why do (did) you prefer those places?

2. Have you ever shopped for something on the Internet? If so, what did you think about this way of shopping?

3. What is your favorite way to shop? How important are the following things to you when you shop?
- having many workers in a store to help me
- having the ability to customize a product to be exactly the way I like it
- having the owner of a company talk to me and/or help me personally
- knowing the product has a guarantee and I can return it if I am not happy with it

PART 3   WRITING SENTENCES WITH CONNECTORS OF CONTRAST

Reading
A Successful Neighborhood Restaurant

Read the story about a successful restaurant and then answer the questions that follow it.

[1]In downtown San Diego there is a small restaurant called Pokez, which serves Mexican food and is owned and run by Rafael (Rafa) Reyes. [2]Reyes never completed high school and was only 18 years old when he opened Pokez. [3]Although he was young and inexperienced in running a business, he created a popular restaurant. [4]In fact, his eatery has become more than just another taco shop among the many found in the area.

[5]Reyes decided to start his own business after working at a larger restaurant in downtown San Diego. [6]He was faced with the problem of not having much money, yet that did not stop him. [7]His restaurant immediately became a family business, with his brothers and sisters working in the kitchen and at the cash register. [8]His waiters and waitresses were friends who agreed to work there even though they received only tips with no regular salary. [9]In addition, Reyes has also been able to barter and trade for things, including equipment necessary to run his kitchen.

[10]Reyes also had to find a location for his business that fit his budget. [11]He found an affordable place to rent; however, it was not in the best part of town. [12]While the area was run-down at the time, it has changed quite a bit since then. [13]These days, the neighborhood has become full of hair salons, trendy bars, and boutiques, and many of the buildings have become expensive condominiums.

[14]Some people attribute much of this change to the presence of Pokez in the area. [15]Perhaps this is because the restaurant

has created its own unique atmosphere both inside and out. [16]On an outside wall a local artist has painted a mural with cultural imagery; inside artwork of loyal customers covers the walls, and fliers announce upcoming shows and performances. [17]Many of the customers are part of the local community, including artists, musicians, and skateboarders. [18]However, people from all walks of life form a diverse crowd at this restaurant.

[19]The food at Pokez has also become known for several reasons. [20]Every day Reyes buys fresh produce, and organic ingredients are used as much as possible. [21]The menu at Pokez offers traditional Mexican dishes with meat, but customers can also choose from more than 30 vegetarian selections. [22]In addition to high-quality food, this restaurant offers dining value because of its low prices, even on combination meals.

[23]Pokez has become known for many things, including tasty, healthy food and a sense of community. [24]Reyes has built a successful business; nevertheless, he has shown that his establishment is not only about profit.

Questions

1. In sentence 6, underline the clauses and circle the conjunction.
2. a. How many clauses are in sentence 3? Underline the clauses.
   b. What word is putting those clauses together? Circle it.
   c. Do you think this word is a coordinating conjunction or subordinating conjunction? Explain your answer.
3. a. Look at sentences 11 and 18. How many clauses are in each of these sentences?
   b. What transition do you find in these sentences?
4. a. Look at sentence 16. How many clauses are in this sentence?
   b. How many words or signals are linking the clauses together? What are they?

Explanation: Connectors of Contrast

1. You have already learned about using different kinds of conjunctions (coordinating and subordinating) and transitions as connectors (signals) that join clauses together. In this unit you will practice using conjunctions and transitions that show contrast.
2. As a review of how to use conjunctions and transitions, look at the following sentences in which some of these words and expressions show contrast.

> EXAMPLES: He was faced with the problem of not having much money, **yet** that did not stop him.
> coordinating conjunction

Sentence-Combining Focus

Connectors Showing Contrast

Although he was young and inexperienced in running a
subordinating conjunction
business, he created a popular restaurant.

He created a popular restaurant **although** he was young
subordinating conjunction
and inexperienced in running a business.

He found an affordable place to rent; **however,** it was not
transition
in the best part of town.

3. The following sentence-combining chart reviews connectors that show contrast.

Sentence Combining to Show Contrast

Coordinating Conjunctions	Subordinating Conjunctions	Transitions
Position in Sentence	**Position in Sentence**	**Position in Sentence**
Middle _____ ▭ _____ clause conjunction clause	Middle clause ▭ subordinator clause OR Beginning ▭ subordinator clause clause	Middle clause ▭ transition clause
Punctuation Comma _____ , ▭ _____ clause conjunction clause EXAMPLE: He rented a place, **but** it was not in the best part of town.	**Punctuation** No comma _____ ▭ _____ clause subordinator clause EXAMPLE: The area was run-down **although** it has changed since then. NOTE: Sometimes you will find a comma with subordinating conjunctions of contrast in the middle. Comma between clauses ▭ _____ , _____ subordinator clause clause EXAMPLE: **Although** the area was run-down, it has changed since then.	**Punctuation** Semicolon and comma _____ ; ▭ , _____ clause transition clause EXAMPLE: He has built a successful business; **nevertheless,** he is not only interested in profit.

CONTRAST: *but*
     yet
	CONTRAST: *although*
	     even though
	     though
	     whereas
	     while
		CONTRAST: *however*
		     nevertheless
		     nonetheless
		     on the contrary
		     on the other hand
		     in contrast

4. As you have learned, each time you want to put clauses together, you must add a connector as a signal. The connectors discussed so far have all been words or expressions (conjunctions, transitions, and relative pronouns). In the reading about Pokez, there is an example of a punctuation mark that can act as a connector. This is the semicolon (;). Two closely related clauses can sometimes be joined with just a semicolon. However, be careful about doing this.

   a. Do not use the semicolon too often. Do not have more than one or two sentences in your essay that use a semicolon alone (with no other signal) between clauses.

   b. The two clauses (simple sentences) you are combining must be closely related. Do not put just a semicolon between two clauses if they are very different in meaning.

      INCORRECT: Many people like to eat at Pokez; there are many other restaurants in the downtown area.

      CORRECT: Many people like to eat at Pokez; they enjoy the varied menu and interesting atmosphere there.

   c. When using a semicolon alone to combine sentences, be sure to have two complete clauses.

      INCORRECT: At Pokez you can choose from 30 vegetarian items;
                    clause
                    several kinds of vegetable burritos and tacos.
                    not a clause (no verb)

      CORRECT: At Pokez you can choose from 30 vegetarian items;
                  clause
                  the menu offers several kinds of vegetable burritos
                  clause
                  and tacos.

5. Important Errors to Avoid

   a. Do not use a coordinating conjunction at the beginning of a sentence.

      INCORRECT: He was faced with the problem of not having much money. **Yet** that did not stop him.

      CORRECT: He was faced with the problem of not having much money, **yet** that did not stop him.

b. **Fragments** Do not write a dependent (subordinate) clause as a sentence. Remember, when you use a subordinating conjunction, you must have both a dependent (subordinate) clause and an independent (main) clause.

INCORRECT: **Although** he was young and inexperienced in running
               dependent/subordinate clause only
               a business. **fragment**

CORRECT: **Although** he was young and inexperienced in running
               dependent/subordinate clause
               a business, he created a popular restaurant.
               independent/main clause

c. **Run-ons and comma splices**

- Do not connect clauses without a signal, such as a coordinating conjunction, a subordinating conjunction, a transition, or a semicolon. If you connect clauses without one of these, you will make a run-on sentence.

- Do not connect clauses with just a comma and no other signal. If you connect clauses with just a comma, you will make a comma splice.

INCORRECT: He was faced with the problem of not having much
               money that did not stop him.
               run-on
               He was faced with the problem of not having much
               money, that did not stop him.
               comma splice

CORRECT: He was faced with the problem of not having much
               money, **yet** that did not stop him.

               He was faced with the problem of not having much
               money, **though** that did not stop him.

               He was faced with the problem of not having much
               money; **however,** that did not stop him.

               He was faced with the problem of not having much
               money; that did not stop him.

               NOTE: There are usually several ways of correcting a
               run-on or comma splice.

Practice: Connectors of Contrast

A. Identifying Clauses and Connectors
For each of the following sentences, find the conjunction or transition of contrast that is putting clauses together. Then do two things:

a. Circle that word or expression.
b. Underline the clause that follows it.

EXAMPLE: He was faced with the problem of not having much
               money, (yet) that did not stop him.

1. His waiters and waitresses were friends who agreed to work there even though they received only tips with no regular salary.

2. While the area was run-down at the time, it has changed quite a bit since then.

3. The menu at Pokez offers traditional Mexican dishes with meat, but customers can also choose from more than 30 vegetarian selections.

4. Reyes has built a successful business; nevertheless, he has shown that his establishment is not only about profit.

B. Choosing the Correct Connector

Circle the word or expression in parentheses that best fits each sentence below. Be sure to check the punctuation carefully to help you make your choice. In some cases, there is more than one possible answer.

EXAMPLE: Many people want to start their own business, (however / (but) / in contrast) it is not always easy to do so.

1. Some people may want to open a new business; (nevertheless / although / yet), they are nervous about actually doing it.

2. Most people know they should start with the paperwork; (but / even though / however), they aren't aware of all the steps involved.

3. A home-based business may seem easier to establish, (in contrast / nevertheless / yet) that is not always the case.

4. (Even though / However / Although) many new business owners are very hopeful they will succeed, about 50% of all small businesses fail within the first 18 months of operation.

5. People who work for a company get paid for their time; (in contrast / while / however), a small business owner may work many more hours and not get paid for those extra hours.

6. Some people quit their jobs to start their own businesses, (nevertheless / but / yet) they don't realize how much more work they might have to do to earn the same amount of money.

7. (While / Nevertheless / Yet) owning your own business can be very rewarding, new owners should be patient about becoming successful.

C. Sentence Writing

Combine each pair of sentences below into one sentence, using the conjunction or transition given in parentheses and correct punctuation. Follow any other instructions that appear in the parentheses.

EXAMPLE: He was young and inexperienced in running a business.

He created a popular restaurant.

(but) He was young and inexperienced, but he created a popular restaurant.

(although—in middle of sentence) He created a popular restaurant although he was young and inexperienced.

(although—at beginning of sentence) <u>Although he was young and inexperienced, he created a popular restaurant.</u>

(nevertheless) <u>He was young and inexperienced; nevertheless, he created a popular restaurant.</u>

1. You may want to open your own business. You may be nervous about how to start it.

   (even though—in middle of sentence) _____

   _____

   (even though—at beginning of sentence) _____

   _____

   (however) _____

   _____

   (yet) _____

   _____

2. Some people prefer to shop in large chain stores. Other people like to shop in small, family-operated businesses.

   (whereas—in middle of sentence) _____

   _____

   (whereas—at beginning of sentence) _____

   _____

   (on the other hand) _____

   _____

   (but) _____

   _____

3. Large chain stores may have low prices and few salespeople. Family-owned businesses often offer more personalized service but have higher prices.

   (while—in middle of sentence) _____

   _____

   (while—at beginning of sentence) _____

   _____

   (in contrast) _____

   _____

   (yet) _____

   _____

4. Shopping on the Internet does not allow you to see the product in person. Many people prefer to shop online.

(though—in middle of sentence) _____

_____

(though—at beginning of sentence) _____

_____

(nonetheless) _____

_____

(but) _____

_____

D. Finding Sentence Problems

1. All of the following sentences have problems. Find the mistakes and correct them.

> INCORRECT: He rented a place it was not in the best part of town.
> run-on
>
> CORRECT: He rented a place, **but** it was not in the best part of town.
>
> He rented a place **although** it was not in the best part of town.
>
> He rented a place; **however,** it was not in the best part of town.

a. Family businesses may be smaller than their competitors. But they often offer better service to their customers.
b. Thirty-eight percent of family-owned firms have been in business for more than eighteen years, only twelve percent of non–family-owned firms have been in business for that long.
c. Family-owned businesses can be found in many areas, however, most are not in professions such as law and accounting.
d. Some people may want to start a family business in those areas. Yet they often do not have the money required to do that.
e. Some customers feel they can trust family-owned businesses; whereas they don't feel that they can trust the larger businesses as much.
f. Family businesses can be quite successful they may have some disadvantages.
g. In a family-owned business there is the possibility of family disputes in contrast those kinds of problems usually do not occur in larger non–family-owned stores.
h. Starting a family-owned business may be risky in some ways some of those businesses are successful and profitable for many years.

2. The following short reading offers some suggestions about establishing a business on the Internet. Each paragraph, including the introductory one, contains a mistake; one paragraph contains two mistakes. There are several kinds of mistakes, including fragments, run-ons, comma splices, and incorrect or missing punctuation. Find the mistakes and show how to correct them.

Starting an Internet Business

Are you thinking of starting a business on the Internet? The Internet has become a popular place for many people to conduct business, not all Internet businesses are successful. Here are some suggestions about how to try to make sure your Internet business succeeds.

1. Everyone likes to visit colorful, flashy Web sites; but, you must make sure you have good content on your site as well. In other words, make sure your business Web site does not simply catch people's attention. You must also explain your product or service well enough to make sure people want to do business with your company.

2. Although you may want to explain many things about your business on your Web site be careful about writing too much. People do not want to read long articles or too much information. You want to give enough information to inform your customers but, you do not want to ask them to read too much.

3. When customers use the Web to find a product or do business, they expect to find the most up-to-date information however many businesses do not update their Internet sites very often. Therefore, some customers may be upset to find old, outdated information. Be sure to continually monitor the information on your Web site.

4. Some customers may be nervous about using the Web to do business because they feel better about doing business in person. Even though your business may be on the Web. Make sure you provide good customer service and easy and secure payment methods.

5. Make it easy for your customers to find you by registering with some established search engines on the Web (such as Google) don't stop with registration. You should always check how many people are using these search engines to find you.

Discussion/Writing

Answer these questions in writing or through discussion. Try to use a variety of words and expressions of contrast in your sentences.

1. Some people prefer to work for others, while other people prefer to work for themselves or own their own business. Which do you prefer and why?

2. The reading about Pokez (page 182) described a small Mexican restaurant that became popular and helped change a neighborhood. Which of the value-added services discussed in the reading on pages 175–177 do you think the owner of Pokez uses in his business?

3. Have you ever thought about starting your own business? If so, what kind of business have you thought about? If you haven't thought about this before, try to imagine that you are going to open a new business. What kind do you think you might start?

PART 4   WRITING ESSAYS (COMPARE/CONTRAST)

Read this essay about the music industry and how artists record their music. Then answer the questions that follow it.

The Changing Music Industry

A sound revolution began with Thomas Edison's first phonograph in the late 19th century, and it is a revolution that continues to this day. Through the years consumers have been able to buy cylinders, records, tapes, and CDs; more recently, the Internet has made music even more available. This increased availability of music to consumers combined with an artist's ability to record on a personal computer has created a new kind of sound revolution. In the past musical artists had little hope of succeeding without the help of the music industry, but now these artists can work to create their own success. Musical artists trying to choose between working with recording companies or on their own will find both similarities and differences in recording, promoting, and distributing their work to the public.

There are several ways that recording companies and artists themselves can create successful music careers. Both recording companies and individual artists can make high-quality recordings available to consumers, usually in the form of tapes and CDs. In addition, recording companies provide promotion of these works; likewise, an individual artist wants to promote his or her own work as much as possible. Just as a recording company will advertise an artist's recordings to as large an audience as possible and sometimes provide promotional tours, an artist will also try to do the same when working on his or her own. In addition, a recording company will sell the music it records for a profit and give a percentage of that money to the artist in payments known as *royalties;* similarly, an artist will try to sell his or her own work for profit. Thus, there are several things that both recording companies and individual artists will do in order to try to establish their work in the industry.

While both the recording companies and the individual artists have some of the same basic goals in mind, there are several differences in the way these things are accomplished. Recording companies maintain state-of-the-art sound studios to ensure that the recordings they make will be of high quality. Individual artists also try to make excellent recordings, but they often do not have comparable studios. Instead, they now have the capability of making low-cost recordings of high quality on their personal computers. Although both recording companies and individual artists will try to promote their work as much as possible, they will not do this in the same way. Large companies have the financial resources to launch large advertising campaigns and promotional tours, while individual artists use their own Web sites or concerts to advertise and sell their work worldwide. Finally, the goal of both the recording company and the artist is to earn money, yet there is a difference in the way this is done. Recording companies sell their products at a profit and give the artist only part of that profit as royalties. In contrast, the individual artist can determine the amount of profit she or he will earn from the recordings through direct sales to consumers.

The music industry has been able to provide its products to consumers for many years. Nonetheless, computers and the Internet seem to have provided a kind of crossroad for this industry because they offer artists more choices as to how to record and promote their work to make money. As a result, consumers also now have more choices and can buy music in their own preferred way.

Essay Discussion

1. How many paragraphs are in this essay?

2. Does this essay have the organization pattern discussed in Unit Two? Does it have all of the following parts?

    _____ an introduction

    _____ a thesis statement

    _____ two or three body paragraphs

    _____ a topic sentence for each body paragraph

    _____ supporting sentences that relate to the topic sentences

    _____ a concluding paragraph

3. What is the purpose of this essay? What kind of information is the writer trying to give to the reader?

Organization of a Compare/Contrast Essay

The essay about the music industry discusses similarities and differences between artists working with recording companies and those who work independently. This kind of writing is called a *compare/contrast essay.* You may be asked to write comparisons and contrasts in essays and exams in many of your college courses, not just your English classes.

Comparing things involves discussing their similarities, and contrasting them involves discussing their differences. Therefore, in order to write a compare/contrast essay, you need to find a topic that shows similarities and differences. This means that you should not try to compare and contrast things that are so completely different that you will not have any basis of comparison. For example, you would not try to write a compare/contrast essay about the music industry and the public school system.

> **Writing Focus**
>
> Compare/Contrast
> Essay Organization,
> Connectors of
> Contrast, Expressing
> Similarity

Block Method

There are several ways you can organize a compare/contrast essay. One method is called the *block method,* and the essay on the music industry is an example of this type. In the block method the writer presents all the similarities between two things in one paragraph and all the differences between those things in another paragraph. Look back at the essay about the changing music industry on pages 191–192.

- What two things does the writer compare in this essay? _____
- Which paragraph discusses the similarities? _____
- Which paragraph discusses the differences? _____

Practice: Block Method

Fill in the chart below by taking information directly from the reading on pages 191–192. Two details (one from each body paragraph) have been provided as examples.

THE CHANGING MUSIC INDUSTRY

INTRODUCTION

Thesis statement: _____

_____

_____

_____

(continued)

BODY PARAGRAPH 1
(similarities between recording companies and independent artists)

Topic sentence: _____

_____

_____

Details/Support

Both make high-quality recordings—tapes and CDs._____

_____

_____

_____

BODY PARAGRAPH 2
(differences between recording companies and independent artists)

Topic sentence: _____

_____

_____

Details/Support

Companies make recordings in sound studios; individual artists

make recordings on personal computers._____

_____

_____

CONCLUSION (summarizes the essay)

_____

_____

_____

Words and Expressions for Comparing and Contrasting

Sentence Combining Focus

Review of Contrast Connectors, Connectors of Similarity

A. Contrast (differences)
In Part 3 of this unit, you learned about conjunctions and transitions that show contrast. Find some of those words or expressions in the reading about the music industry (pages 191–192). Write them on the lines below.

Coordinating conjunctions: _____

Subordinating conjunctions: _____

Transitions: _____

B. Comparison (similarities)
    1. Now find some words or expressions that show similarities in the reading. Write them on the line below.

       _____

       Do you think any of these words or expressions are conjunctions or transitions? How do you know this? _____

    2. Some conjunctions and transitions indicate similarity as shown in the following sentence-combining chart.

Sentence Combining to Show Similarity

Subordinating Conjunctions	Transitions
Position in Sentence Middle _____ subordinator _____ clause subordinator clause Beginning subordinator clause clause	**Position in Sentence** Middle _____ transition _____ clause transition clause
Punctuation No comma _____ subordinator _____ clause subordinator clause EXAMPLE: An artist may try to promote her work **just as** a recording company would. Comma between clauses subordinator clause , clause EXAMPLE: Just as a recording company will advertise an artist's recordings, an independent artist will try to do the same.	**Punctuation** Semicolon and comma clause ; transition , clause EXAMPLE: Recording companies provide promotion of artists' works; **likewise**, an individual artist wants to promote his or her own work.
SIMILARITY: *just as* *as*	SIMILARITY: *similarly* *likewise* *also*

In addition, there are other words and expressions that show similarity but do not combine sentences: *both/and, the same* (or *the same as*), *similar to.*

EXAMPLES: **Both** recording companies **and** individual artists can make high-quality recordings available to consumers in the form of tapes and CDs.

Just as a recording company will advertise an artist's recordings, an independent artist will try to do **the same.**

A recording company's goal to promote an artist's name worldwide may be **similar to** the artist's own desire to do this.

Practice: Showing Similarity

In each sentence several words or expressions that show similarity appear in parentheses, along with punctuation in some cases. Circle the one that best fits each sentence.

EXAMPLE: Recording companies provide promotion of these works; (likewise, / similar to, / just as) an individual artist wants to promote his or her own work.

1. Today musical artists may choose to work with recording companies (; just as, / just as / , just as) many of them did in the past.

2. Recording companies produce high-quality recordings in their studios (similarly / ; similarly, / similarly;) individual artists can produce high-quality music with their personal computers.

3. (Just / The same / Both) recording companies and individual artists will sell their products to consumers.

4. Individual artists try to promote their work to a large audience and recording companies try to do (similarly / the same / both).

5. Individual artists might sell their work through a Web site on the Internet; (both / just as / also), they will sell their work at concerts.

Now read this essay about how consumers can legally obtain music through the Internet. Then answer the questions that follow it.

Obtaining Music from the Internet

Through the years consumers have been able to buy cylinders, records, tapes, and CDs in order to listen to music. More recently, the Internet has made music more available than ever through downloading or participating in "peer-to-peer" (P2P) sharing of music files. This change in the availability of music has caused conflicting opinions about the legality of obtaining music over the Internet due to issues with copyright restrictions. However, now there are several services that provide legal means of obtaining music on the Internet. Although all of these companies provide consumers access to music, customers will find that not all of these Web sites operate in the same way.

All of the Web sites that provide music to consumers charge money for their services, but they don't all charge in the same way. For example, one company may charge a standard $0.99 per song, while another company may charge a variety of prices, often ranging from $0.79 to $1.14. A company may advertise on its Web site that a customer can buy songs at one low price. However, once consumers start to pay for services, they may find that most songs are not available at the lower price, and a more complicated price structure exists. Another company's Web site may charge a monthly subscription fee and then another fee for each song once the customer starts requesting specific music.

When using online music services, a consumer may find restrictions regarding transferring files to computers or making CDs; however, these limitations may be quite different from service to service. That is, one service may have few or no restrictions regarding how the digital files can be used, yet a different service may have several restrictions. For example, when a customer uses one particular service, she or he may be allowed to make many CDs with the downloaded files; in contrast, another service may allow its customers to make only a small number of CDs containing the downloaded music file. In addition, one service may allow the consumer to play the music file on one computer only, but another service may allow the customer to transfer the file to several computers.

In addition, some online music services may provide better service and quality than others. One service may be very reliable and provide exactly what the consumer asks for every time. In contrast, another service may not be reliable in this regard. For example, a customer may order a particular song performed by a particular artist or group, yet she or he may receive a completely different song when the order is filled. Furthermore, one company may provide high-quality music files with excellent sound while another company may deliver files of poor quality. Some customers will find that they receive files that crackle or have lower-quality sound overall.

Consumers have been able to buy and listen to their favorite music in many ways through the years. The Internet has provided some new and different ways for consumers to obtain music, but it has also caused some controversy regarding how this can be done legally. While several online services do provide legal means of getting music files, consumers should shop carefully and understand exactly how these services work before using them.

Essay Discussion

1. How many paragraphs are in the essay about obtaining music legally from the Internet?

2. Does this essay have the organization pattern discussed in Unit Two? Does it have all of the following parts?

_____ an introduction

_____ a thesis statement

_____ two or three body paragraphs

_____ topic sentence for each body paragraph

_____ supporting sentences that relate to the topic sentences

_____ a concluding paragraph

3. What is the purpose of this essay? What kind of information is the writer presenting?

Organization of a Compare/Contrast Essay: Point-by-Point Method

The reading about obtaining music from the Internet is a compare/contrast essay with a different kind of organization. In this essay the writer presents different points to compare and contrast. Each point is a paragraph. When you use the point-by-point method for writing a compare/contrast essay, you will have as many body paragraphs as points you are discussing. The essay about obtaining music from the Internet has three body paragraphs.

- What is the first body paragraph about? That is, what is the first point? _____

- What is the second body paragraph about? That is, what is the second point? _____

- What is the third body paragraph about? That is, what is the third point? _____

Practice: Point-By-Point Method

Fill in the following chart by taking information directly from the reading on pages 196–197. Three supporting details (one from each body paragraph) have been provided as examples.

OBTAINING MUSIC FROM THE INTERNET

INTRODUCTION

Thesis statement: _____

_____

_____

BODY PARAGRAPH 1
(cost)

Topic sentence: _____

_____

_____

Details/Support

standard price vs. variety of prices

_____

_____

_____

BODY PARAGRAPH 2
(restrictions regarding file use)

Topic sentence: _____

_____

_____

Details/Support

no restrictions regarding how files can be used vs. several

restrictions

_____

_____

BODY PARAGRAPH 3
(service and quality)

Topic sentence: _____

_____

_____

Details/Support

variation in reliability of receiving the song you order

_____

_____

_____

CONCLUSION (summarizes the essay)

_____

_____

_____

_____

Practice: Block and Point-by-Point Methods

Look back at the essay about the changing music industry on pages 196–197. It discusses several points about the similarities and differences between making recordings with companies and making them independently. Find three of these points and put them on the chart below. Then write some notes from the reading about details for each point.

	RECORDING STUDIOS	INDIVIDUAL ARTISTS
Point 1:		
Point 2:		
Point 3:		

Discussion/Writing

Answer these questions in writing or through discussion. Try to use words and expressions of similarity and contrast in your sentences.

1. How do you prefer to buy music? Do you buy tapes, CDs, or both?

2. What do you think about buying music on the Internet? Have you ever done this?

3. Imagine that you are a musician and you want to record some of your music and sell the recordings. Which way do you think you would choose to do this—through a recording company or by yourself? Why?

Summary Writing

For an explanation of summary writing and practice of this skill, read pages 212–217 in the Appendix. Follow the instructions. Be sure to use words and expressions that show contrast and similarity in your sentences.

1. Summarize the first two paragraphs of "The Value of the Customer" on page 175. Summarize each paragraph in no more than three sentences.

2. Summarize the entire reading "A Successful Neighborhood Restaurant" (pages 182–183). You should summarize each paragraph in one or two sentences.

3. Summarize each body paragraph in the essay about the changing music industry on pages 191–192. Each paragraph summary should have no more than three sentences.

Writing Assignment

A. Picking the Topic

You are going to write a compare/contrast essay of four or five paragraphs. Choose one of the following topics:

1. What are some similarities and differences between owning your own business and working for another person or a company?

2. How is shopping on the Internet different from and similar to shopping in stores?

3. How do people shop in your native culture (or in a place where you lived before) and where you are living now? Think about the following when you answer this question:
   - shopping in small businesses owned by individuals versus large chain stores
   - shopping in small stores versus shopping malls
   - shopping in stores or through catalogs or the Internet

B. Understanding the Assignment/Answering the Question

Before you start to write, make sure you understand the assignment. Your essay must answer the question and should not discuss other things. You should also make sure that your essay makes comparisons and/or contrasts. Look at the following ideas for essays on the three possible topics and decide which ones fit the assignment and which ones do not. Cross out the ideas that you think will not answer the question.

Topic 1: an essay that
- compares and contrasts two jobs you had working for two different companies

- discusses similarities and differences between working for a family-owned business and working in a large company
- discusses how your last two jobs were very different
- compares and contrasts working in a store you own and working in a chain store

Topic 2: an essay that
- discusses similarities and differences between buying things from different Web sites
- compares and contrasts several ways of shopping, such as using catalogs, the Internet, and the telephone
- compares and contrasts buying from a Web site and buying from a store in a shopping mall
- discusses why some people prefer to shop on the Internet

Topic 3: an essay that
- compares the different malls and shopping centers in the area where you now live
- discusses how people in your native culture shop very differently than the people where you live now
- discusses how some people in your native culture shop in traditional ways and others in your native culture use more modern ways
- shows similarities and differences between shopping where you live now and shopping where you lived in the past

Following the Steps in the Writing Process

Before You Write

■ **Step One: Generating Ideas and Brainstorming**
A. Think about the three topics for the writing assignment.

1. What aspects of owning a business and working for another person or company will you discuss?

_____

_____

Which of these aspects are the same for both situations, and which are different?

_____

_____

2. What aspects of shopping on the Internet and shopping in stores will you discuss?

_____

_____

Which of these aspects are the same for both situations and which are different?

_____

_____

3. What shopping habits of people in your native culture (or a place where you lived before) and people where you live now will you discuss?

_____

_____

Which shopping habits are the same, and which are different?

_____

_____

B. What kind of support (details or examples) can you provide for these topics? Using lists or clustering diagrams, write your ideas in the spaces below. Don't worry about organization at this time.

Working for Myself versus Working for Someone Else

Shopping on the Internet versus Shopping in Stores

(continued)

Shopping in My Culture versus Where I Live Now

C. Choose <u>one</u> of your lists or clustering diagrams for your essay. Then check the details to make sure there are enough, and they are all relevant.

■ *Step Two: Organizing Ideas and Planning*
First, decide which method of organization you will use for your essay: block or point-by-point. Then, organize your ideas from Step One according to the method you choose.

BLOCK METHOD
(ONE PARAGRAPH FOR SIMILARITIES AND ONE PARAGRAPH FOR DIFFERENCES)
In the spaces below the topic you are going to write about, fill in the information about similarities and differences from your list or clustering diagram.

1. Owning a business versus working for another person or company

SIMILARITIES	DIFFERENCES

2. Shopping on the Internet versus shopping in stores

SIMILARITIES	DIFFERENCES

3. Shopping habits in my native culture versus shopping habits where I live now

SIMILARITIES | DIFFERENCES

**POINT-BY-POINT METHOD
(TWO OR THREE PARAGRAPHS THAT COMPARE AND CONTRAST
THE TOPIC)**

First, circle one topic you want to write about:

- working for myself versus working for someone else
- shopping on the Internet versus shopping in person
- shopping habits of people in my native culture versus shopping habits of people where I live now

Then, write your topic on the line provided. Next, on the lines provided, write two or three points you will discuss. Finally, fill in the spaces with the details/support about similarities and differences for each point.

Topic: _____

SIMILARITIES | DIFFERENCES

Point 1: _____

Point 2: _____

Point 3: _____

Now think about the three parts of an essay.

INTRODUCTION WITH THESIS STATEMENT
Write a thesis statement for your essay. Be sure to state clearly what two things you are going to compare and contrast. Make sure your thesis also includes the general idea of your comparison/contrast.

_____

_____

Write your thesis statement on the chart for a compare/contrast essay on page 209.

BODY PARAGRAPHS
Topic Sentences
BLOCK METHOD (TWO BODY PARAGRAPHS)
a. What is the main idea of your first body paragraph? Write a topic sentence.

_____

_____

b. What is the main idea of your second body paragraph? Write a topic sentence.

_____

_____

Write your topic sentences on the chart on page 209.

POINT-BY-POINT METHOD (TWO OR THREE BODY PARAGRAPHS)
a. What is the main idea of your first paragraph (your first point)? Write a topic sentence.

_____

_____

b. What is the main idea of your second paragraph (your second point)? Write a topic sentence.

_____

_____

c. What is the main idea of your third paragraph (your third point, if you have one)? Write a topic sentence.

_____

_____

Write your topic sentences on the chart on page 209.

Support
Look back at your notes in the chart you completed for Step Two. Which similarities and differences will you include in the essay? Write those in the support sections of the chart. Be sure that all of your support relates to your topic sentences and thesis statement. Be sure you have enough support/details for each body paragraph.

CONCLUDING PARAGRAPH
Write some ideas for a concluding paragraph on the chart on page 209. Will you summarize the main points of the essay, restate your thesis, or add final comments?

■ *Step Three: Getting Feedback*
Your teacher may ask you to work with a partner and complete a peer review of your chart. Use the peer review sheet on page 238 of the Appendix.

When You Write

■ *Step Four: Writing the First Draft (Rough Draft)*
Do the following when you write the first draft:

- Be sure to use words that show contrast and similarity.
- Try to include as much sentence variety as possible. Include coordinating conjunctions, subordinating conjunctions, transitions, and relative clauses.
- Be careful to avoid fragments, run-ons, and comma splices.
- Try to include at least three vocabulary words from this unit.

After You Write

Check Your Work
After you finish writing the first draft, read it again and check it for the following:

☐ This essay discusses similarities and differences between owning a business and working for another person, between shopping on the Internet and shopping in stores, or between shopping in my native culture and shopping where I live now.

☐ This essay has three main parts: introduction, body, and conclusion.

☐ The introductory paragraph has several sentences. It starts out general and ends with a thesis statement.

☐ The thesis statement clearly states what I am comparing and/or contrasting.

☐ This essay has two or three body paragraphs that discuss similarities and differences.

☐ I used either the block method or the point-by-point method to organize my body paragraphs.

☐ Each body paragraph has a topic sentence.

☐ The supporting sentences in each body paragraph are related to the topic sentence of that paragraph.

☐ I included a variety of compare/contrast words and expressions.

☐ The sentences in this essay include a variety of coordinating and subordinating conjunctions, transitions, and relative clauses.

☐ I looked for run-ons, comma splices, and fragments and corrected them.

☐ I used some of the vocabulary from this unit in the essay.

Getting Feedback

Your teacher will decide the type of feedback you will receive for the first draft. It may be peer review, teacher review, or both. For peer review, use the sheet on page 239 in the Appendix.

Step Five: Revising

After you receive feedback, revise the organization of your essay or any sentences in it, if necessary. You may want to change your thesis statement, your topic sentences, or parts of your introductory or concluding paragraph. You may want to add, take out, or change the order of some supporting sentences. Your teacher may want you to get feedback again after you revise.

Step Six: Editing

Make any necessary changes in grammar, spelling, punctuation, and capitalization. Your teacher may want you to have feedback after editing as well.

Step Seven: Preparing the Final Draft

Prepare your final draft to be handed in to the teacher.

Organizing Your Ideas for Writing a Compare/Contrast Essay

TITLE: _____

INTRODUCTION

Thesis statement: _____

_____

BODY PARAGRAPH 1

Topic sentence: _____

_____

Details/Support

_____

_____

_____

BODY PARAGRAPH 2

Topic sentence: _____

_____

Details/Support

_____

_____

_____

BODY PARAGRAPH 3

Topic sentence: _____

_____

Details/Support

_____

_____

_____

CONCLUSION

_____

_____

_____

Appendix

SUMMARY WRITING

Summary writing is an important skill for college students. Summaries can be long or short, depending on the original work you are summarizing. For example, if you are summarizing a paragraph, you may write only one to three sentences (depending on the length of the paragraph). If you are summarizing an essay, your summary will be longer, and if you are summarizing a book, your summary could be several pages.

Sometimes you may want or need to summarize a paragraph in its concluding sentence or an essay in its concluding paragraph. In addition, there may be other times you will need to write summaries in your English or ESL classes or in other classes. Each unit of this book has summary writing assignments.

Explanation: Summaries

1. What is a summary?
   A summary is a brief (short) review of a piece of written material. It should always be shorter than the original or larger work you are summarizing.
2. What kind of information should be in a summary?
   A summary should include only main ideas and important supporting information. It should not include details or any personal opinions.
3. How is a summary the same as the original work?
   A summary should have the same basic meaning as the original work. In other words, the summary should not have new or different information that is not in the original work.
4. How is a summary different from the original work?
   A summary should not include many of the exact words as the original work. The writer should use his or her own words in the summary to express the same general ideas found in the original work.

Steps for Writing Summaries

The following steps will help you when you summarize:

1. First, read the original work you are going to summarize and find the main idea(s).
   a. If you are summarizing a paragraph, find the topic sentence and then the main supporting ideas of that paragraph.
   b. If you are summarizing an essay, find the thesis statement and topic sentences of the body paragraphs. Then find the main supporting ideas.
   c. If you are summarizing a larger work, find the main ideas and main support. For example, in addition to looking for topic sentences in the paragraphs, you may want to look for chapter titles, headings, and/or subheadings in the longer work.

2. Write down a few key words or phrases to help you remember the main idea(s) as you write the summary. You may also want to write a brief outline of the main ideas in the same order as they appear in the original work. However, do not write too much or use full sentences. Be sure to write only words or short phrases in your outline. This way you can make sure the summary wording is not exactly the same as the original wording.

3. Since the summary should not use too many of the same words that appear in the original, try not to look at the original work while you are writing the summary. If you do that, it will be too easy to copy the original words or phrases.

4. After you write the summary, read both the original work and the summary again.
   a. Check to see that you have included only the main idea(s).
   b. Check the wording of the summary to see that you did not use too many of the same words used in the original.
   c. Check that you did not include your opinion in the summary.

NOTE: There is no one perfect way to write a particular summary. One person may choose to write a summary one way, and another person may write it in a slightly different way. As long as the summary highlights all the main ideas, is not too long (doesn't contain too many details), and does not have the same wording as the original work, it can be a good summary.

Examples of Summaries

A. One-Paragraph Summary

Below is the introductory paragraph of the first reading in Unit One (page 3). Read the paragraph and then read the two summaries that follow it.

Are you having trouble learning new information in a class? You may want to find out more about your unique learning style. Your learning style is the way you prefer to learn. It is not related to how intelligent you are or what skills you have, but it is related to how your brain works most efficiently to learn new information. Your learning style has been a part of you since you were born.

SUMMARY ONE:
Everyone is born with an individual learning style. A learning style is each person's own way of learning new things, and it is related to how his or her brain processes information.

SUMMARY TWO:

A learning style is each person's way of learning new information according to how his or her brain works. Each person's learning style may be unique because we are all born with our own individual way of learning.

B. Multi-Paragraph Summary

Below are three paragraphs from the first reading in Unit One. Each paragraph describes a type of learning style. Read these paragraphs and then read the two summaries that follow them.

Visual Learning. Visual learners learn best when they can see information either in written language or in a picture or design. These learners also may need to see a teacher's nonverbal communication (body language and facial expressions) to fully understand the content of a lesson. In a classroom visual learners benefit from instructors who use a blackboard (or whiteboard) or an overhead projector to list important points of a lecture or use visual aids such as films, videos, maps, and charts. In addition, visual learners may learn best from class notes and outlines or pictures and diagrams in textbooks. They may also like to study by themselves in a quiet room and may visualize a picture of something or see information in their mind when trying to remember it.

Auditory Learning. Auditory learners learn best when they can hear information or when they are learning in an oral language format. In a classroom these learners benefit most from listening to lectures or participating in group discussions. Auditory learners may also read text aloud or use audio tapes or CDs to obtain information. When trying to remember something, these learners can often "hear" the information the way someone told it to them or the way they previously repeated it out loud. In general, these people learn best when interacting with others in a listening/speaking exchange.

Tactile/Kinesthetic Learning. Tactile/kinesthetic learners like to be physically engaged in "hands-on" activities or to actively explore the physical world around them. In the classroom they benefit from a lab setting, where they can manipulate materials to learn new information. These people learn best when they can be physically active in their learning environment. They may find it difficult to sit in one place for long periods of time, and they may also become distracted by their need to be exploring and active. Tactile/kinesthetic learners benefit most from instructors who encourage in-class demonstrations, hands-on learning experiences, and field work outside the classroom.

SUMMARY ONE (shorter version):

The three learning styles are visual, auditory, and tactile/kinesthetic, and each one is related to a different sense. The visual style is related to what the learner can see and visualize in his or her head. The auditory style involves listening as well as verbal interaction with others. The tactile/kinesthetic style is related to the sense of touch or to body movement and involves the active participation of the learner.

SUMMARY TWO (longer version):
The three learning styles are visual, auditory, and tactile/kinesthetic, and they are each related to a different sense. The visual style is related to what the learner can see. Visual learners learn best from information in writing or on charts, pictures, and other visual aids. The auditory style involves listening and speaking. Auditory learners like to hear information, such as on tape or in lectures, and they learn best when they can interact verbally with others. The tactile/kinesthetic style is related to the sense of touch or to body movement. Learners strong in this style like to actively participate in their learning and enjoy hands-on experiences both inside and outside the classroom.

Practice: Summaries

A. Identifying Summary Problems

Each of the following summaries has one or two of these problems:

a. The summary uses too many of the same words as the original.
b. The summary is too short.
c. The summary is too long and contains too many details.
d. The summary does not contain all the main ideas.
e. The summary contains an opinion.

Read each of the summaries and decide which of the above problems it has. Write the letter(s) of the problem(s) on the line at the end of the summary. Summaries 1 and 2 are about the following paragraph.

Are you having trouble learning new information in a class? You may want to find out more about your unique learning style. Your learning style is the way you prefer to learn. It is not related to how intelligent you are or what skills you have, but it is related to how your brain works most efficiently to learn new information. Your learning style has been a part of you since you were born.

1. Everyone is born with an individual learning style. You may want to learn more about your unique learning style. A learning style is related to how your brain works most efficiently to learn new information.
   _____

2. A learning style is each person's way of learning new information. I think learning visually is easier than learning with the other styles.
   _____

Summaries 3 and 4 are about the three paragraphs describing the different learning styles that appear on page 214.

3. The three learning styles are visual, auditory, and tactile/kinesthetic, and each is related to a different sense. The visual style is related to what the learner can see and visualize in his or her head. The auditory style involves listening and speaking. _____

4. The three learning styles are visual, auditory, and tactile/kinesthetic, and each is related to a different sense. The visual style is related to what the learner can see. Visual learners learn best from information in writing and on charts, pictures, and other visual aids. These learners do well in a class where the teacher uses a lot of body language and facial expressions as well as a whiteboard or blackboard and visual technology such as overhead projectors and videos. The auditory style involves listening and speaking. Auditory learners like to hear information presented on tapes or in lectures, and they learn best when they can interact verbally with others. They like to participate in discussions either with a group or with a partner. The tactile/kinesthetic style is related to the sense of touch or to body movement. Learners strong in this style like to actively participate in their learning and enjoy hands-on experiences both inside and outside the classroom. Because they can get bored easily by sitting in one place, they need to take field trips, work in lab settings, and use their hands. _____

B. *Writing a Summary* Read this paragraph from the reading in Unit One and follow the steps to summarize it.

While there is no "good" or "bad" learning style, there can be a good or bad match between the way you learn best and the way a particular course is taught. Suppose you are a visual learner enrolled in a traditional lecture class. It seems that the instructor talks on for hours, and you can't pay attention or stay interested. There's a mismatch between your learning style and the instructional environment of the class. As soon as you understand this mismatch, you can find ways to adapt your style to help make sure you will be successful in the class. You might start tape-recording the lectures so that you don't have to worry about missing important information. You might decide to draw diagrams that illustrate the ideas presented in lectures. You might go to the media center and check out a video that provides some additional information on course material you're not sure about. What you're doing is developing learning **strategies** that work for you because they are based on your knowledge of your own learning style.

Step 1 What are the main ideas of this paragraph?

_____

_____

_____

_____

Step 2 List some important words or phrases from the original paragraph.

_____

_____

_____

_____

Step 3 Now write your summary.

_____

_____

_____

_____

_____

_____

_____

_____

_____

_____

Step 4 Read your summary and check for the following:

____ Does your summary include all the main ideas of the original paragraph?

____ Are there details in your summary that should not be there?

____ Is the summary in your own words?

Extra Summary Assignments

Unit One

1. Summarize the second paragraph of the introduction of the reading "Learning Styles." Your summary should be no longer than two sentences.
2. Summarize the entire reading "Learning Styles." You should have only one or two paragraphs in your summary.
3. Summarize the entire reading "Learning Styles" by writing a one-sentence summary for each paragraph in the reading. You should have a total of eight sentences in your summary.
4. Write a one-paragraph summary of the reading about intelligence at the beginning of Part 3.

Unit Two

1. Summarize the fourth paragraph of the reading about Frederick Douglass' first experience living in Baltimore (the paragraph that begins with the words "on the plantation"). Your summary should be no more than three or four sentences.
2. Summarize Frederick Douglass' escape from slavery by summarizing the last two paragraphs of the reading. Your summary should be one paragraph.
3. Summarize the background note that comes just before the reading about Rosa Parks. Your summary should be no longer than two sentences.
4. Summarize the two body paragraphs of the reading about Rosa Parks. Your summary should be one paragraph only.
5. Summarize the entire reading about Frederick Douglass. Do this by summarizing each paragraph in one or two sentences.
6. Summarize the reading at the beginning of Part 3 about Frederick Douglass' life after he escaped slavery. Summarize by writing one or two sentences for each paragraph in the reading.

Unit Three

1. Summarize the first body paragraph in the process essay about stress and stress management in Part 4. Your summary should be no more than four or five sentences.
2. Summarize the second body paragraph in the process essay about stress and stress management in Part 4. Your summary should be no more than four sentences.
3. Summarize the entire essay about stress and stress management in Part 4. Write no more than two to three sentences about each paragraph in this essay.
4. Summarize the four paragraphs in the reading under the subtitle of "areas of health and wellness." Write one or two sentences for each of the paragraphs you are summarizing.
5. Summarize the five paragraphs in the reading under the subtitle of "factors affecting health and wellness." Your summary should be one paragraph.
6. Summarize the first paragraph of the reading in Part 3. Your summary should be no more than three sentences.
7. Summarize the second paragraph of the reading in Part 3. Your summary should be three to five sentences.

Unit Four

1. Summarize the first two paragraphs (the introduction) of the reading in Part 2. Your summary should be one paragraph.
2. Summarize the information about reserves and resources in the reading in Part 2. Write one to three sentences to summarize each paragraph.
3. Summarize the first paragraph of the reading in Part 3. Your summary should be no more than two sentences.
4. Summarize the information in the exercise about pollution in London. Your summary should be one paragraph.
5. Summarize each body paragraph (each cause) in the essay about causes of deforestation. Your summary should be one paragraph.
6. Summarize each paragraph (each effect) in the essay about effects of deforestation. Your summary should be one paragraph.

Unit Five

1. Summarize the quotation from Mayor Hobson in the reading in Part 2. Your summary should be no more than three or four sentences.
2. Summarize the first three paragraphs in the section "Some Ways of Learning Sacred Knowledge." Your summary should be one paragraph.
3. Summarize the entire reading about sandpaintings. Your summary should be one paragraph.
4. Summarize the last exercise about the social status of Native American societies of the Pacific Northwest. You should summarize each paragraph in one sentence.
5. Summarize each body paragraph in the essay "Following the Old Ways or the New." Each summary should be no more than three sentences.

Unit Six

1. Summarize paragraphs 4, 5, 6, and 7 of the reading "The Value of the Customer." Summarize each paragraph in two–three sentences.
2. Summarize paragraph 10 in the reading "The Value of the Customer." Your summary should be one paragraph of no more than four sentences.
3. Summarize the fifth paragraph in the reading "A Successful Neighborhood Restaurant" about the food at Pokez. Your summary should be no more than three sentences.
4. Summarize the second body paragraph in the essay "The Changing Music Industry." Your summary should be no more than four–five sentences.
5. Summarize the entire essay about obtaining music from the Internet. Summarize each paragraph in the essay in one–three sentences.

JOURNAL WRITING

Journal writing is often a personal kind of writing and usually does not have a grade or corrections. Instead, journal writing gives students a chance to communicate ideas without thinking about organization, grammar, and details such as spelling and punctuation. Therefore, students often feel more comfortable writing in a journal than writing assignments that will be graded.

Your teacher may want you to do some journal writing as you study this book. When you write in your journal, feel free to include your thoughts and opinions about the topics your teacher assigns. In addition, sometimes your journal writing can help you with ideas for the more formal academic writing you need to complete for a grade.

 Discussion/Writing questions recommended for journal entries have this icon next to them.

TIMED WRITING

The writing you are learning about and practicing in this book follows the process of writing. This kind of writing takes place over a period of time, perhaps a week or two. However, sometimes you will have to finish a piece of writing in a more limited amount of time; this kind of writing is called *timed writing.* In timed writing the writer is given a specific amount of time to think about, plan, organize, write, and check his or her work. Sometimes the writer may see the question or topic to write about before the time of writing, but often she or he will not. For some people this type of writing can be very difficult and stressful. Timed writing is common in college level classes, and you may be asked to do this kind of writing in many different courses. These assignments often take the form of essay questions on in-class exams.

Although you might not be given much time in this kind of assignment, you can still follow some of the steps in the writing process as follows:

Step 1   **Understand the Question** Make sure you understand the question! You cannot answer the question properly if you do not understand what it is asking you to write about.

Step 2   **Brainstorm and Plan** Before you write, you should make a basic plan of your ideas. Depending on how much time you have to complete the assignment, you can spend the first 5 to 10 minutes thinking about your ideas and organizing them. If you make a general plan of your ideas, it will be easier to write in the time you are given. If the instructor allows it, you can brainstorm a list or clustering diagram or make an outline or chart of your ideas on a piece of paper. Do not worry about writing full sentences for your notes; some words and phrases should be enough. The purpose of this step is to help you decide which ideas you will write about and to organize them, and this should be done quickly.

NOTE: When you are working on a timed writing assignment, be careful not to write *too* much in this step or spend *too* much time planning and organizing your ideas.

Step 3   **Write** The actual writing will take most of your time. Use the notes you made in the first few minutes of planning and try to write quickly. Try to write correctly, but think about how you are answering the question and how you are organizing your ideas as you write.

Step 4   **Revise and Edit** You may not have too much time for revising or editing, but you should try to leave the last 5 to 10 minutes for checking your work. Look for fragments, comma splices, and run-ons, and check the grammar, spelling, and punctuation as best you can.

PUNCTUATION REVIEW

The different kinds of punctuation used in English are listed below. Units in this book that provide information about using some kinds of punctuation are identified.

period	.
comma	, (Units One through Six)
semicolon	; (Units Three, Four, and Six)
question mark	?
exclamation mark	!
quotation marks	" " or " " (Unit Two)
parentheses	( )
brackets	[ ] or { }
colon	:
apostrophe	' or '
asterisk	*
dash/hyphen	—/-
slash	/

Most of the punctuation in the list above should not be placed at the beginning of a line. However, you may use the following at the start of a new line.

quotation marks	" or "
parenthesis	(
bracket	[or {
asterisk	*

Punctuation

Apostrophe

- The apostrophe + *s* is used with singular and plural nouns to show possession.
    Jim**'s** computer   the children**'s** toys
    My boss**'** file   the Smiths**'** house [Only the apostrophe is needed when a word ends in *s*.]
- The apostrophe + *s* is used to show ownership.
    Pedro and Ana**'s** CDs [The *'s* on the second name shows they own the CDs together.]
    Pedro**'s** and Ana**'s** hats [The *'s* on both names shows they each own different hats.]
- The apostrophe is used in contractions.
    I**'**m (= I am)   they**'**ll (= they will)

Brackets

- Brackets are also used to add your own information in quoted material.
    Jason said, "This is a good time **[**meaning today**]** for us to start looking for a new apartment."
- Brackets with three dots are used when you omit words from a quotation.
    Jason said, "This is a good time **[**...**]** for a new apartment."

Colon

- The colon is used with clock time.
    11**:**30   9**:**45
- The colon is used to introduce a list.
    Jean enjoys all kinds of physical activity**:** hiking, playing tennis, and even cleaning house.
- The colon is used in the salutation of a business letter.
    Dear Ms. Mansfield**:**

Comma

- Commas are used with dates and addresses.
    Monday**,** December 1**,** 1964   16 Terhune Street**,** Teaneck**,** NJ 07666
- Commas are used to set off items in a series.
    They served pizza**,** pasta**,** lasagna**,** and salad at the party.
- Commas are used to set off added information in nonrestrictive phrases or clauses.
    Mr. Karas**,** my sister's teacher**,** comes from Greece.
    Rita**,** who almost never misses class**,** is absent today.
- Commas are used in the salutation in informal correspondence and at the close of a letter.
    Dear Grace**,**   Sincerely yours**,**

Dash

- Dashes are used instead of commas when the added information contains commas.
    The school offers several math courses**—**algebra, geometry, and trigonometry**—**as well as a wide variety of science classes.

Exclamation Point

- An exclamation point is used after a word or group of words to show strong feeling.
  Stop**!** Don't run over that cat**!**

Hyphen

- Hyphens appear in compound words or numbers.
  Mother-in-law   twenty-one
- Hyphens are used to divide words at the end of a line.
  After Mrs. Leander finished exploring all her options, she de-
  cided the best plan was to return home and start out tomorrow.

Parentheses

- Parentheses are used with nonessential information and with numbers and letters in lists.
  We left the party **(**which started at 7:00 P.M.**)** sometime after midnight.
  My requirements are **(1)** a room with a view and **(2)** a working air conditioner.

Period

- A period is used at the end of any sentence that is not a question or an exclamation.
  Rutgers University offers a wide variety of social science courses**.**
- A period is used after many abbreviations.
  Mr**.**   etc**.**   P.M**.**   Jr**.**   i.e**.**

Question Mark

- A question mark is used after a word or sentence that asks a question.
  What**?**   Did you say you don't have a ride home**?**

Quotation Marks

- Quotation marks are used to set off a direct quotation but not an indirect quotation.
  Smithers said, "Homer, you must go home now."
  Smithers said Homer must go home.
- Quotation marks are used with the titles of short written material such as poems, short stories, chapters in books, songs, and magazine articles.
  My favorite poem is "A spider Sewed at Night" by Emily Dickinson.

Semicolon

- The semicolon is used to link independent clauses when there is no coordinating conjunction (such as *and, but, or, nor,* or *for*) between them.
  Some people like country music**;** some people don't.
- The semicolon is also used to link independent clauses before a connector or conjunctive adverb (such as *however; furthermore*).
  Some people like country music**;** however, other people dislike it intensely.

Slash

- The slash separates alternatives.
  and/or
- The slash divides numbers in dates, and divides numerators and denominators in fractions.
  the memorable date 9/11/01   Ten and 50/100 dollars
- The slash is used when quoting lines of poetry to show where each line ends.
  My favorite lines from this poem are, "She slept beneath a tree / remembered but by me."

Capitalization

Capitalize proper nouns and proper adjectives.

- Main words in titles: **G**one with the **W**ind
- People: **J**ohn **L**ennon, **P**élé
- Cities, nations, states, nationalities, and languages: **I**stanbul, **T**urkey, **C**alifornia, **B**razil, **A**merican, **S**panish
- Geographical items: **M**ekong **R**iver, **M**ount **O**lympus, **C**entral **P**ark
- Companies and organizations: **F**ord **M**otor **C**ompany, **H**arvard **U**niversity, **N**ational **O**rganization of **W**omen
- Departments and government offices: **E**nglish **D**epartment, **I**nternal **R**evenue **S**ervice
- Buildings: the **E**mpire **S**tate **B**uilding
- Trademarked products: **K**leenex tissue, **S**cotch tape
- Days, months, and holidays: **T**uesday, **J**anuary, **R**amadan
- Some abbreviations without periods: **AT&T**, **UN**, **YMCA**
- Religions and related words: **H**indu, **B**ible, **M**uslim
- Historical periods, events, and documents: **C**ivil **W**ar, **D**eclaration of **I**ndependence
- Titles of people: **S**enator **C**linton, **P**resident **L**incoln, **M**s. **T**anaka, **D**r. **L**ee
- Titles of printed matter: *Heinle's Newbury House Dictionary of American English*

Proofreading Marks

Teachers often use the following correction abbreviations and symbols on students' papers.

Problem area	Symbol	Example
agreement	**agr**	He **go** to work at 8:00.
capital letters	**cap**	the United **s**tates
word division or hyphenation	**div** **hy**	disorienta**ti** **-on**
sentence fragment	**frag**	**Where she found the book.**
grammar	**gr**	It's the **bigger** house on the street.
need italics	**ital**	I read it in **The Daily News**.
need lower case	**lc**	I don't like **P**eanut **B**utter.
punctuation error	**p**	Where did you find that coat.
plural needed	**pl**	I bought the **grocery** on my way home.
spelling error	**sp**	Did you rec**ie**ve my letter yet?
wrong tense	**t**	I **see** her yesterday.
wrong word	**ww**	My family used to **rise** corn and wheat.
need an apostrophe	⌄	I **don⌄t** know her name.
need a comma	⌃	However⌃ we will probably arrive on time.
delete something	⨪	We had the ~~most~~ best meal of our lives.
start a new paragraph	¶	. . . since last Friday. ¶ Oh, by the way . . .
transpose words	⌒	They live on the floor first.

FEEDBACK: PEER REVIEW

Getting feedback about your planning and writing can help you during the writing process. You are probably used to receiving suggestions and corrections from your teacher, but other people can often provide helpful feedback as well. For example, other students in your class (your peers) might be able to help you with your ideas and organization and even sometimes with grammar and sentence structure.

Your teacher may ask you to participate in peer review from time to time, using the sheets provided on the following pages. When you participate in these peer reviews, you will answer the specific questions on the sheets, which apply to the writing assignments in each unit of this book. Your teacher will decide how many of these peer review sheets you will complete for each writing assignment. Try to be honest when you answer questions about your classmates' work. Be sure to discuss both the good points and any parts you think should be changed.

Important: Some students question whether other students can provide helpful feedback because they are learners themselves. Of course, your peers will not be able to give you as much feedback as your teacher can. However, it is always good to hear what other people think of your work and to see what other people write about a particular topic (when you review their papers).

Your peers may not be able to help you with everything or tell you all of your mistakes. However, they can probably help you think about how you answered the topic question, or they may be able to help you organize your thoughts. They might also be able to help you with some specific areas that you have studied together in this class, such as sentence writing.

UNIT ONE PEER REVIEW SHEET
Organization Chart for a Paragraph

Your Name: _____   Partner's Name: _____

1. Exchange charts with a partner. Read your partner's chart and answer these questions:
   - Does your partner's chart have a topic sentence about his or her learning style, his or her strongest type(s) of intelligences, or the types of intelligences necessary for success?

        _____ yes _____ no

   - Is the topic sentence general enough for all the information in the paragraph?

        _____ yes _____ no

   - Does your partner's chart have enough support (facts, details, or examples) about a learning style or types of intelligences?

        _____ yes _____ no

   - Does all of the support on the chart relate to the topic sentence?

        _____ yes _____ no

   - Is there a concluding sentence on the chart?

        _____ yes _____ no

2. Do you have any questions for your partner about this paragraph? Is there anything on his or her chart that you do not understand?

_____

_____

_____

_____

_____

_____

_____

_____

_____

_____

_____

_____

_____

_____

UNIT ONE PEER REVIEW SHEET
First Draft of a Paragraph

Your Name: _____   Partner's Name: _____

1. Exchange drafts with a partner. Read his or her draft and check it using the following checklist.

____ This paragraph discusses the writer's personal learning style, his or her strongest type(s) of intelligences, or necessary intelligences for success.

____ This paragraph has a topic sentence.

____ The topic sentence is general enough for the support in the paragraph.

____ This paragraph has several supporting sentences.

____ All of the supporting sentences relate to the topic sentence.

____ This paragraph has a concluding sentence.

____ Some sentences in this paragraph include coordinating conjunctions.

____ This paragraph does not have run-ons or comma splices.

____ The writer used some of the vocabulary words from this unit in the paragraph.

2. Tell your partner what you liked about his or her paragraph.

_____

_____

_____

_____

_____

3. Do you have any questions about this paragraph? Did the writer follow all the items on the checklist above? Is there anything you might change in this paragraph? Do *not* write any changes on your partner's paper. Just discuss your suggestions. Think about the items on the checklist above when you make your suggestions. Your partner will do the same for you.

_____

_____

_____

_____

_____

_____

_____

UNIT TWO PEER REVIEW SHEET
Organization Chart for a Narrative Essay

Your Name: _____   Partner's Name: _____

1. Exchange charts with a partner. Read your partner's chart and answer these questions:
   - Does your partner's chart have a thesis statement about his or her difficult decision, problem, or risk?

     _____ yes _____ no

     If you said yes, what was this problem, decision, or risk? Write your answer on the lines below.

     _____

     _____

   - Does your partner's chart show one or two body paragraphs?

     _____ one _____ two

   - Does each body paragraph on the chart have a topic sentence?

     _____ yes _____ no

     What do you think each paragraph will be about? Write your answers on the lines below.

     Paragraph 1: _____

     Paragraph 2: _____

   - Does the chart have enough support for each body paragraph?

     _____ yes _____ no

   - Is there any information in the conclusion part of this chart?

     _____ yes _____ no

2. Do you have any questions for your partner about this essay? Is there anything on the chart that you do not understand?

   _____

   _____

   _____

   _____

   _____

   _____

   _____

   _____

UNIT TWO PEER REVIEW SHEET
First Draft of a Narrative Essay

Your Name: _____   Partner's Name: _____

1. Exchange drafts with a partner. Read his or her draft and check it using the following checklist.

___ This essay discusses a time your partner overcame a problem, took a risk, or made an important decision.

___ This essay has three main parts: introduction, body, and conclusion.

___ The introduction has several sentences. It starts out general and ends with a thesis statement.

___ The thesis statement describes the problem, decision, or risk.

___ This essay has one or two body paragraphs that tell the story as it happened.

___ Each body paragraph has a topic sentence.

___ The body paragraphs are related to the thesis statement.

___ There are several supporting sentences with enough details or examples in the body paragraphs.

___ The supporting sentences in each paragraph relate to the topic sentence of that paragraph.

___ Some sentences in this essay include coordinating or subordinating conjunctions.

___ This essay does not have any run-ons, comma splices, or fragments.

___ The writer used correct punctuation for any quotations included in this essay.

___ The writer used some of the vocabulary from this unit in the essay.

2. Tell your partner what you liked about his or her essay or what he or she did well.

_____

_____

_____

3. Do you have any questions about this essay? Did the writer follow the items on the checklist above? Is there anything you might change in this essay? Do *not* write any changes on your partner's paper. Just discuss your suggestions. Think about the items on the checklist above when you make your suggestions. Your partner will do the same for you.

_____

_____

_____

UNIT THREE PEER REVIEW SHEET
Organization Chart for a Process Essay

Your Name: _____   Partner's Name: _____

1. Exchange charts with a partner. Read the thesis statement on your partner's chart.

   Is this thesis statement about a process for making or using a home remedy, relieving stress, or following an exercise or fitness routine?

   _____ yes _____ no

   If you said yes, what specific process will the essay be about? How many body paragraphs do you think will be in this essay? What will each paragraph be about?

   Process: _____

   Paragraph 1: _____

   Paragraph 2: _____

   Paragraph 3: _____

2. Now read the topic sentence for each body paragraph.

   Does each topic sentence name one step of the process?

   _____ yes _____ no

   Is each topic sentence general enough for the paragraph?

   _____ yes _____ no

3. Read the support for each body paragraph.

   Does the chart have enough support for each body paragraph?

   _____ yes _____ no

   Is all of the support listed for each paragraph related to the topic sentence?

   _____ yes _____ no

4. Read the ideas for the conclusion.

   Do you think the conclusion will be general enough?

   _____ yes _____ no

5. Do you have any questions for your partner about this essay? Is there anything on the chart that you do not understand?

   _____

   _____

   _____

UNIT THREE PEER REVIEW SHEET
First Draft of a Process Essay

Your Name: _____   Partner's Name: _____

1. Exchange drafts with a partner. Read his or her draft and check it using the following checklist.

___ This essay explains a process for making or using a home remedy, relieving stress, or following an exercise or fitness routine.

___ This essay has three main parts: introduction, body, and conclusion.

___ The introduction has several sentences. It starts out general and ends with a thesis statement.

___ The thesis statement gives a process and has two or three main steps.

___ This essay has two or three body paragraphs that describe the steps of the process in chronological order.

___ Each body paragraph has a topic sentence.

___ The body paragraphs are related to the thesis statement.

___ There is enough support in each body paragraph.

___ Some sentences in this essay include coordinating or subordinating conjunctions.

___ Some sentences in this essay include transitions (both introductory and linking).

___ This essay does not have any run-ons, comma splices, or fragments.

___ The writer used some of the vocabulary from this unit in the essay.

2. Tell your partner what you liked about his or her essay or what he or she did well.

_____

_____

_____

_____

3. Do you have any questions about this essay? Did the writer follow the items on the checklist above? Is there anything you might change in this essay? Do *not* write any changes on your partner's paper. Just discuss your suggestions. Think about the items on the checklist above when you make your suggestions. Your partner will do the same for you.

_____

_____

_____

_____

UNIT FOUR PEER REVIEW SHEET
Organization Chart for a Cause or Effect Essay

Your Name: _____   Partner's Name: _____

1. Exchange charts with a partner. Read the thesis statement on your partner's chart. Is this thesis statement about causes or effects of a problem or situation?

    _____ yes _____ no

    If you answered yes, what specific problem or situation and what causes or effects will the writer discuss? How many body paragraphs do you think will be in this essay? What will each paragraph be about?

    Problem or situation: _____

    Paragraph 1: _____

    Paragraph 2: _____

    Paragraph 3: _____

2. Now read the topic sentence for each body paragraph.

    Does each topic sentence name one cause or effect?

    _____ yes _____ no

    Is each topic sentence general enough for the paragraph?

    _____ yes _____ no

3. Read the support for each body paragraph.

    Does the chart have enough support for each body paragraph?

    _____ yes _____ no

    Is all the support listed for each paragraph related to the topic sentence?

    _____ yes _____ no

4. Read the ideas for the conclusion.

    Do you think the conclusion will be general enough?

    _____ yes _____ no

5. Do you have any questions for your partner about this essay? Is there anything on the chart that you do not understand?

    _____

    _____

    _____

    _____

UNIT FOUR PEER REVIEW SHEET
First Draft of a Cause or Effect Essay

Your Name: _____ Partner's Name: _____

1. Exchange drafts with a partner. Read his or her draft and check it using the following checklist.

___ This essay discusses effects of the writer's lifestyle on the environment, causes or effects of a place's environmental problems, or environmental problems that are having serious worldwide effects.

___ This essay has three main parts: introduction, body, and conclusion.

___ The introduction has several sentences. It starts out general and ends with a thesis statement.

___ The thesis statement clearly states the problem or situation and either the causes or the effects.

___ This essay has two or three body paragraphs that discuss causes or effects.

___ Each body paragraph has a topic sentence. The topic sentence is about a cause or an effect.

___ The supporting sentences in each body paragraph are related to the topic sentence of that paragraph.

___ The writer included a variety of cause-and-effect words and expressions.

___ The sentences in this essay include a variety of coordinating and subordinating conjunctions and transitions.

___ This essay does not have any run-ons, comma splices, or fragments.

___ The writer used some of the vocabulary from this unit in the essay.

2. Tell your partner what you liked about his or her essay or what he or she did well.

_____

_____

_____

3. Do you have any questions about this essay? Did the writer follow the items on the checklist above? Is there anything you might change in this essay? Do *not* write any changes on your partner's paper. Just discuss your suggestions. Think about the items on the checklist above when you make your suggestions. Your partner will do the same for you.

_____

_____

_____

UNIT FIVE PEER REVIEW SHEET
Organization Chart for an Opinion Essay

Your Name: _____   Partner's Name: _____

1. Exchange charts with a partner. Read the thesis statement on your partner's chart. Does this thesis statement give an opinion that answers one of the questions?

   _____ yes _____ no

   If you said yes, what is the specific opinion? How many body paragraphs do you think will be in this essay? What will each paragraph be about?

   Opinion: _____

   Paragraph 1: _____

   Paragraph 2: _____

   Paragraph 3: _____

2. Now read the topic sentence for each body paragraph.

   Does each topic sentence give one reason?

   _____ yes _____ no

   Is each topic sentence general enough for the paragraph?

   _____ yes _____ no

3. Read the support for each body paragraph.

   Does the chart have enough support for each body paragraph?

   _____ yes _____ no

   Is all of the support listed for each paragraph related to the topic sentence?

   _____ yes _____ no

4. Read the ideas for the conclusion.

   Do you think the conclusion will be general enough?

   _____ yes _____ no

5. Do you have any questions for your partner about this essay? Is there anything on the chart that you do not understand?

   _____

   _____

   _____

UNIT FIVE PEER REVIEW SHEET
First Draft of an Opinion Essay

Your Name: _____   Partner's Name: _____

1. Exchange drafts with a partner. Read his or her draft and check it using the following checklist.

___ This essay discusses one of the following: whether children learn best actively or passively, whether parents or the extended family should bring up children, or whether traditional ways should be followed or forgotten.

___ This essay has three main parts: introduction, body, and conclusion.

___ The introduction has several sentences. It starts out general and ends with a thesis statement.

___ The thesis statement clearly states the writer's opinion about the question.

___ This essay has two or three body paragraphs that give reasons to support the writer's opinion.

___ Each body paragraph has a topic sentence.

___ The body paragraphs are related to the thesis statement.

___ Some of the sentences in this essay have relative clauses.

___ The sentences in this essay include a variety of coordinating and subordinating conjunctions and transitions.

___ This essay does not have any run-ons, comma splices, or fragments.

___ The writer used some of the vocabulary from this unit in the essay.

2. Tell your partner what you liked about his or her essay or what he or she did well.

_____

_____

_____

_____

3. Do you have any questions about this essay? Did the writer follow the items on the checklist above? Is there anything you might change in this essay? Do *not* write any changes on your partner's paper. Just discuss your suggestions. Think about the items on the checklist above when you make your suggestions. Your partner will do the same for you.

_____

_____

_____

_____

UNIT SIX PEER REVIEW SHEET
Organization Chart for a Compare/Contrast Essay

Your Name: _____   Partner's Name: _____

1. Exchange charts with a partner. Read the thesis statement on your partner's chart. Does this thesis statement make a comparison and/or contrast about working or shopping? _____ yes _____ no

   If you said yes, what specific comparison and/or contrast will the essay make? How many body paragraphs do you think will be in this essay? What will each paragraph be about?

   Comparison and/or contrast: _____

   Paragraph 1: _____

   Paragraph 2: _____

   Paragraph 3: _____

2. Is the writer using the block method or the point-by-point method?

   If the writer is using the block method, answer these questions about the topic sentences for the body paragraphs:

   Is each topic sentence about
   either similarities or differences? _____ yes _____ no

   Is each topic sentence general
   enough for a paragraph? _____ yes _____ no

   If the writer is using the point-by-point method, answer these questions about the topic sentences:

   Does each topic sentence tell you about one point that is being made to compare and/or contrast two things? _____ yes _____ no

   Is each topic sentence general
   enough for a paragraph? _____ yes _____ no

3. Read the support for each body paragraph.

   Does the chart have enough support
   for each body paragraph? _____ yes _____ no

   Is all of the support listed for each paragraph
   related to the topic sentence? _____ yes _____ no

4. Read the ideas for the conclusion.

   Do you think the conclusion
   will be general enough? _____ yes _____ no

5. Do you have any questions for your partner about this essay? Is there anything on the chart that you do not understand?

   _____

   _____

UNIT SIX PEER REVIEW SHEET
First Draft of a Compare/Contrast Essay

Your Name: _____   Partner's Name: _____

1. Exchange drafts with a partner. Read his or her draft and check it using the following checklist.

    ____ This essay discusses similarities and differences about working situations or shopping habits.

    ____ This essay has three main parts: introduction, body, and conclusion.

    ____ The introduction has several sentences. It starts out general and ends with a thesis statement.

    ____ The thesis statement clearly states what the writer will compare and/or contrast.

    ____ This essay has two or three body paragraphs that discuss similarities and differences.

    ____ The writer has used either the block method or the point-by-point method for organizing the body paragraphs.

    ____ Each body paragraph has a topic sentence.

    ____ The supporting sentences in each body paragraph are related to the topic sentence of that paragraph.

    ____ The writer included a variety of words and expressions that show contrast and similarity.

    ____ The sentences in this essay include a variety of coordinating and subordinating conjunctions, transitions, and relative clauses.

    ____ This essay does not have any run-ons, comma splices, or fragments.

    ____ The writer used some of the vocabulary from this unit in the essay.

2. Tell your partner what you liked about his or her essay or what he or she did well.

    _____

    _____

    _____

3. Do you have any questions about this essay? Did the writer follow the items on the checklist above? Is there anything you might change in this essay? Do *not* write any changes on your partner's paper. Just discuss your suggestions. Think about the items on the checklist above when you make your suggestions. Your partner will do the same for you.

    _____

    _____

    _____

The following chart is provided to help you understand the sentence combining taught in this book. Fill in each part of the chart as you complete Part 3 of each unit.

Sentence-Combining Chart*

Coordinating Conjunctions	Transitions	Subordinating Conjunctions	Relative Pronouns
Position in Sentence	Position in Sentence	Position in Sentence	Position in Sentence
Punctuation	Punctuation	Punctuation	Punctuation
Addition	More Information		Subject
Contrast	Contrast	Contrast	Object
	Time	Time	Time
Result	Result		Possessive
Reason	Example	Reason	
Choice	Summary	Condition	
Negative	Similarity	Similarity	

VOCABULARY INDEX

SKILLS INDEX

Text Credits

Thomson ELT gratefully acknowledges the following publishers for permission to use materials from these publications.

Unit 1, pp. 3–5 Bogod, Liz. "Learning Styles/ Multiple Intelligence." [Available Online] WETA [cited October, 2004]; Available from www.ldpride.net/learningstyles.MI.htm.

Unit 2, p. 37–39, 42–43 Thomas, Sarah. "The Slave Years." [Available Online] University of Rochester [cited October, 2004]; Available from http://www.history.rochester.edu/class/douglass/part1.html.

Unit 3, p. 72–74 Boskin, Graf and Kreisworth. *Health Dynamics Attitudes and Behaviors.* Saint Paul: West House Publishing Co., 1990.

Unit 3, p. 77–78 Gatchell, Chip. "Folk Medicine." [Available On] Alternatives for Healthy Living [cited October, 2004];

Available from http://www.alt-med-ed.com/practices/folkmed.htm.

Unit 4, p. 105–108 Chernicoff, S. and Fox, H. and Tanner, L. *Earth: Geological Principles and History.* Boston: Houghton Mifflin Company, 2002.

Unit 5, p. 137–139 Beck, Peggy and Francisco, Nia and Walters, Anna. *The Sacred—Ways of Knowledge, Sources of Life.* Tsaile: Navajo Community College Press, 1996.

Every effort has been made to trace all sources of information in this book, but if any have been overlooked, we will be pleased to make the necessary arrangements at the first opportunity.

Recommended Further Reading

Unit 1

Gardner, H. "A Multiplicity of Intelligences." *Scientific American* Winter Volume 9, Number 4 (1998).

Ceci, S. "IQ Intelligence: The Surprising Truth." *Psychology Today* July/ August (2001). http://cms.psychologytoday.com/pto/feedback.php

Yam, Philip. "Intelligence Considered." *Scientific American* Winter Volume 9, Number 4 (1998). http://www.sciam.com/page.cfm?section=repub_quotation

Sternberg, R. "How Intelligent Is Intelligence Testing." *Scientific American* Winter Volume 9, Number 4 (1998). http://www.sciam.com/page.cfm?section=repub_quotation

Bogod, Liz. "Learning Styles/ Multiple Intelligence." [Available Online] WETA [accessed October, 2004]; Available from www.ldpride.net/learningstyles.MI.htm.

Miller, Suzanne. "DVC Online: Introduction to the DVC Learning Style Survey for College." [Available Online] Diablo Valley College [accessed October 2004]; Available from http://www.metamath.com/lsweb/dvclearn.htm.

Unit 2

Altman, Susan. *Extraordinary Black Americans from Colonial to Contemporary Times.* Chicago: Children's Press, 1989.

African American Master Student Profiles by Osborne Robinson Jr. Houghton Mifflin, Boston, MA. www.pr.usm.edu/oola1.htm

Chew, Robin. "Martin Luther King, Jr. Civil Rights Leader." [Available Online] Lucid Interactive Article [accessed October 2004]; Available from http://www.lucidcafe.com/library/96jan/king.html.

Dove, Rita. "Rosa Parks: Her Simple act of protest galvanized America's civil rights revolution." [Available Online] Time Inc. [accessed October 2004]; Available from http://www.time.com/time/time100/heroes/profile/parks01.html.

"Interview with Rosa Parks." Scholastic Press [accessed October 2004]; Available from http://teacher.scholastic.com/rosa/interview.htm.

Parker, Robert. "Meet Mrs. Bethune." [Available Online] Mary McLeod Bethune Council House [accessed October 2004]; Available from http://www.nps.gov/mamc/bethune/meet/frame.htm.

Robinson, Osborne Jr. *African American Master Student Profiles: Thurgood Marshall.* New York: Houghton Mifflin, 1998.

Esten, Hugh. "Biography: Oprah Winfrey." [Available Online] Academy of Achievement [accessed October 2004]; Available from http://www.achievement.org/autodoc/page/win0bio-1.

Wertz, Sharon. "Osceola McCarty Donates $150,000 to Southern Miss." [Available Online] The University of Southern Mississippi [accessed October 2004]; Available from http://www.pr.usm.edu/oola1.htm.

Unit 3

Gatchell, Chip. "Folk Medicine." [Available On] Alternatives for Healthy Living [accessed October, 2004]; Available from http://www.alt-med-ed.com/practices/folkmed.htm.

Aikman, Lonnelle. *Nature's Healing Arts: From Folk Medicine to Modern Drugs.* New York: National Geographic Society, 1977.

Bobroff, Linda B. *Healthstyle: A Self-Test,* U.S. Department of Health and Human Services Public Health Service, DHHS Publication Number (PHS) 81-50155. University of Florida, Institute of Food and Agricultural Sciences Document FCS 8553, 2002. Available from http://edis.ifas.ufl.edu.

Unit 4

Barber, Chris and Chromentowski, Walter and Skole, David and Urquhart, Gerard. "Tropical Deforestation." [Available Online] Earth Observatory [accessed October, 2004]; Available from http://earthobservatory.nasa.gov/Library/Deforestation/ .

"Rain Forest at Night." [Available Online] *NationalGeograhic.Com* [accessed October, 2004]; Available from http://www.nationalgeographic.com/earthpulse/rainforest/gallery2.html.

Klesius, Michael. "State of the Planet." *National Geographic* Vol. 202 No. 3, September (2002) .

Todd, Shipman, and Wilson. *An Introduction to Physical Science.* Boston: Houghton Mifflin Company, 2003.

Trucksess, Chris. "Deforestation and Biodiversity Presentation Essay." [Available Online] ENVS 02 [accessed October, 2004]; Available from http://fubini.swarthmore.edu/~ENVS2/ctrucks1/essay05.html.

Torres, Allison. "Save the Clouds, too—Spectrum—deforestation changes weather patterns." *The Futurist* March-April v. 44 (2002): (4).

Unit 5
Bahti, Mark and Bahti Tom. *Southwestern Indian Arts and Crafts.* Tucson: Bahti Indian Arts, 1975.

Bahti, Mark and Bahti Tom. *Southwestern Indian Ceremonials.* Las Vegas: KC Publications, 1982.

Liptak, Karen. *The First Americans the Indians of the Pacific Northwest.* Oxford: International Book Marketing Ltd., 1991.

Stewart, Hilary. *Totem Poles.* Seattle: University of Washington Press, 1993.

"The World of the American Indian." *The National Geographic Society* (1988) : 150-155.

Unit 6
Kurlantzick, Joshua. "Most Valuable Player." *Entrepreneur* June (2003).

Garin, Nina. "Building Block—Rafa Reyes' success provides a solid foundation for his family, friends and an emerging neighborhood." *SD Union Tribune* San Deigo, CA, May 9, 2002.

"Small Businesses Face Large Number of Obstacles on Path to Success." *Knight Rider Tribune* June 2, 2002.

"Survey finds family businesses offer customers a better service." *Financial Advisor* Oct. 2, 2002.

"The Seven Sins of the Web." [Available Online] BT Group [accessed October, 2004]; Available from http://www.btopenworld.com/create/webpage/stickysites.

Photo Credits